THE EMERGENCE OF MODERN INDIA

THE EMERGENCE OF
MODERN INDIA

Arthur Lall

♔ 1981
COLUMBIA UNIVERSITY PRESS/NEW YORK

Library of Congress Cataloging in Publication Data

Lall, Arthur Samuel, 1911–
The emergence of modern India.

Includes bibliographical references and index.
1. India—Politics and government—20th
century.   I. Title.
DS480.45.L33   954   80-25028
ISBN 0-231-03430-X

Columbia University Press
New York   Guildford, Surrey

Copyright © 1981 by Columbia University Press
All Rights Reserved
Printed in the United States of America

CONTENTS

PREFACE

I am extremely grateful to Columbia University Press, and particularly to Bernard Gronert, for their indulgence in allowing me all the time I have needed to complete this work, which has taken me on frequent visits to India for many discussions with those who were making the events, those who saw them from the inside as members of the various administrations in the country, and those who were astute observers, commentators, or scholars. This continuing process has in a measure maintained the flavor of my own involvement in Indian affairs, sometimes minor, sometimes not so minor, and my observation of them as an insider. For me this involvement started at the end of 1929, by which time I had already done some youthful speechmaking on India's problems and read exhaustively the works of Indian and British historians and political scientists, former governors, and other prominent persons. The present work is to a considerable extent a personal distillation of some fifty years of close attention to the subject.

For many years my involvement and observation were centered in India's foreign affairs. Beginning in 1947 and for the next seventeen years, I successively held the positions of Krishna Menon's closest aide at the London High Commission (India's embassy there), Consul General at New York, Permanent Representative and Ambassador of India to the United Nations, Ambassador to Austria and a governor of the International Atomic Energy Agency, India's representative at the Geneva Conference on the Question of Laos—one of the series of long (fourteen months) and delicate negotiations affecting Southeast Asia and the converging but competing interests of the United States, the USSR, and China, with the stake of India being to guide events toward the spread of nonalignment in the region.

Thereafter, ' was India's negotiator at the eighteen-nation Disarmament Committee (now grown to twice that membership), the highly frustrating so-called negotiation to reduce armaments which has been in more or less continuous session since March 14, 1962, and has yet to achieve the first reduction of armaments! Between these major assignments were briefer ones, sometimes of high importance and great delicacy and at other times largely formal, which took me to Latin America, Ireland, the USSR, Hungary, Germany, Yugoslavia, Pakistan, New Zealand, Samoa, and elsewhere.

Since then I have tried my hand at unofficial private diplomacy, at times acting in conjunction with Betty Goetz Lall, my wife. There have been some small successes and some lamentable failures. In general, private negotiators are highly expendable, frequently being repudiated by those who at one stage or another encouraged, approved, or invited their efforts. This could be the subject of another book, but I mention it here because my continuing activities have, from time to time, brought me in close touch with India's problems, attitudes, and diplomatic efforts.

Arthur Lall

January 1981

THE EMERGENCE OF MODERN INDIA

Chapter One

THE PURSUIT OF SYNTHESIS

During India's history, which extends over a period of some five thousand years, the central theme is the patient endeavor to integrate a variety of ethnic and cultural streams. Although knowledge of some of the earliest periods is scanty, evidence from many parts of India has shown that there was already a flourishing and sophisticated civilization in the third millennium before Christ. Archeological fragments were first discovered at Harappa and Mohenjo-Daro, now in Pakistan, where the remains of ancient cities were unearthed. Later, further evidence of the same or related civilizations was found in western India in the state of Gujarat, as well as in the hinterland in Rajasthan and the Punjab.

These ancient civilizations, with their well-planned cities, equipped with good drainage, granaries, and a considerable degree of civic planning, had to face the oncoming hordes of the Aryan peoples who set out from the region of the Caucasus and farther west and then moved into Iran and India. These people brought with them notions about life which were, in many respects, not unlike those of the ancient Greeks. Their early pantheon of deities was much like that of the first Hellenes. In India they came in contact with a civilization that was in many respects more highly developed than their own.[1] The interaction of the two sets of peoples seems to have given an impetus to the rise of the system of philosophy that ever since has been a major influence in India and, in one form or another, has penetrated large parts of Asia and is now beginning to attract some atten-

1. There are reputable scholars who hold that between the era of the ancient highly developed civilization and the coming of the Aryans there intervened a relatively brief dominance by another, less civilized group. See *A History of India* by Romila Thapar (London: Penguin Books, 1966), 1:24.

tion in the West, including the United States. This system of philosophy known as the Vedanta is, pared of its inessentials, the personal attestation, both intellectually and in realization through meditation, of an all-pervasive cosmic system which becomes the basis of a sense of unity for all forms of life, not just human life. This philosophical route excludes the espousal of one particular set of views, one dogma, or one set of principles and the consequent rejection of other views. Essentially it is a nondogmatic philosophical approach. It is animated by the conviction that there is a discernible interaction among all phenomena that makes it necessary to see oneself as part of the cosmic whole, rather than as a discrete fragment of the life manifestation.

There has been much speculation about why this philosophy took hold. Perhaps the Aryan hordes, worn out by their long anabasis, and somewhat overcome by the hotter climate of India, were seeking an answer to their situation other than that of having to conquer, subdue, or slaughter the peoples with whom they came in contact. In any event, the answer transformed the clash of civilizations and major ethnic groups into a social multilogue which greatly mitigated the initial confrontation, though it did not by any means totally resolve sociological problems.

The Aryans, who were dominant when it came to the martial arts, through their priests (the Brahmins) gave divine sanction to a hierarchical structure for Indian society that has come to be known as the caste system. In its earliest form this system was perceived in India as a compartmental one—into which the great racial and cultural oneness that had been achieved philosophically in the Vedanta was divided up for reasons of practical expediency and sociological compromise.

The Indian elite came to be the thinkers, scholars, teachers, and priests. It was this group, not the temporal leadership, that framed the rules of the system. Naturally, in time it gave itself a host of social and economic privileges while acknowledging that the Kshatriya caste (the rulers and the fighters) were the temporal lords just as they themselves were the spiritual lords. Thus Kshatriya honor was satisfied. Indeed, in some parts of India they have never fully admitted the dominance of the Brahmins, regarding them simply as the philosophic and spiritual bulwark of the system of Kshatriya authority. However, by and large, India is a country which is under the dominance of those to whom spiritual and intellectual leadership has been vouchsafed.

The third caste consisted of the merchants, traders, and farmers and was known as the Vaishya caste. Then came the lowest of the four castes, the Sudras—the menials and other workers at the bottom of the economy. This four-stage hierarchy spawned a fifth category, one too lowly to be counted within the system. To this category were sonsigned those who engaged in "unclean" activities such as tanning or scavenging, and those who handled night soil. In later times they came to be known as "untouchables."

So the philosophical victory of the Vedanta was not translated in practice into a completely homogeneous and internally mobile society, and this flaw has been the major weakness of the Indian system, largely accounting for the retarded growth of an overall national civic consciousness and the inflation of family and caste consciousness.

This restrictive system, and the uncomfortable dichotomy between the philosophical oneness and the practical fragmentation, could not go unchallenged. After dominating the scene for about a thousand years they were rejected in the sixth century B.C., by Gautama, the Buddha, who took his stand firmly against the caste system. By about 250 B.C. India had become a largely Buddhist country and was greatly influenced sociologically by the views of the founder of the religion. In this context we are referring to an India that also included the other modern states of the subcontinent, namely present-day Pakistan, Bangladesh, and Nepal, as well as Afghanistan. In this vast region a strongly Buddhist sentiment developed that pushed caste aside. The triumph of ethnic and group integration in a quarter of the world was emerging as full and complete.

But the Brahmins and the old traditions were still alive. Always noted for their intelligence and extreme subtlety, the Brahmins reacted with characteristic far-sightedness. Throughout the land they made it known that the Buddha was an avatar of Vishnu—a reincarnation of the Preserver in the Hindu Trinity, which consists of Brahma, Vishnu, and Siva. This meant that theologically there was no longer any place for Buddhism as a separate religion in India. So strong was the appeal of the old regime of worship and of the epistemology that went with it, that the people, with relief, reentered the door to a life under the aegis of the Brahmins. There was a basic rightness to this development: it represented another triumph of synthesis over divisiveness.

The second level at which the Brahmins, as the custodians of the "purity" of Aryavarta—the land of the Aryans—reacted to Buddhism was less laudable. This was to spread the word that although Buddhism was fit for export, it was not quite good enough for the people of India. This subtly pandered to the sense of superiority of the Indian people and enhanced their pride in the beauty of the Vedas and the Upanishads. By these moves India was again effectively Hinduized—indeed, the Brahmin theory was that it had never really changed—and, in time, the net effect was that caste again strongly asserted itself.

The process of integration that India evolved in resolving the potentially genocidal conflict between Aryan and non-Aryan was subsequently applied successively to other large incursions of peoples into the subcontinent. After the great Aryan demographic movements came waves of Greeks, Bactrians, Parthians, Scythian Goths, and others. These inroads were made by about the time of the commencement of the Christian era, and all the peoples concerned were integrated into the Indian Hindu system. They were welcomed, were not treated as outsiders and, in recognition of their acceptance of the accommodation the Indian system afforded them, they were not relegated to inferior castes. On the whole, the massive interactions between the many waves of Aryans and others and the pre-Aryans, which by A.D. 300 had gone on for nearly two thousand years, produced a highly diversified society subject to cultural and sociological norms that were widely accepted on the subcontinent though local practice could, and frequently did, vary somewhat from what the most orthodox would have deemed to be standard requirements.

The next great interaction on the subcontinent came when the Turkic and other groups of people of west-central Asia, who had been brought under the banner of Islam, came into the country. This interaction was quite different from previous experiences. As we have noted, the salient fact about previous interactions was that the Aryan people had wisely decided that the best way of dealing with ethnic confrontations was to contract alliances and relationships with the indigenous peoples in accordance with the Vedantic philosophical framework, which could contain all of them. The sociological integration was accompanied by the essential counterpart of intellectual and spiritual comingling that was stimulated and made possible by the rejection of religious dogma in favor of the acceptance of a large variety of styles, views, and practices. No one book had the prominence accorded to the Bible or the Koran by the religions developed in the Middle East. There were the four Vedas, the Vedantic Upanishads—full of philosophical speculations—the two great epics, the *Mahabharata*—which contains the *Bhagavad-Gita*—and the *Ramayana*. All these books were regarded as valuable encyclopedias of the great truths revealed or experienced by men, and to them were added, at a slightly lower level, a series of works called the Puranas, and other shastras. Together, all these have continued to be the great books of the Indian cosmogony.

This wide-based, flexible epistemology was, with the arrival on the scene of the Muslim invaders, confronted with the notion that there was but one Book, dictated by God himself to the final prophet, and that on this point there could be no compromise, no mingling of truths, no way of finding mutual accommodations. On the Indian subcontinent this was an entirely new approach to life, and it was backed by tremendous zeal and a claim that there was divine authority to destroy the *kafir*, the unbeliever. The remarks of E. B. Havell, a British historian, are pertinent:

Indo-Aryan polity, instructed by the Buddha and other great Aryan teachers of the military caste, was firmly based on the principle that right is might, or, as the Mahabharata puts it, that "the heavens are centered in the ethics of the State." But it reckoned without the Huns and the sword of Islam as wielded by Turkish warlords of the eleventh and twelfth centuries, Mahmud of Ghazni and Ala-ud-din.[2]

To the Indian people the new invaders brought a baffling experience, one they did not understand because it was totally unrelatable to their own experience of 2500 years or more in the art of trying to arrive at integration and synthesis. They would have been open to any suggestion that the Prophet Muhammed might be fitted into their own pantheon, but to the invaders such a suggestion would have been sacrilegious, preposterous, just as a parallel suggestion with regard to Jesus would have been to Western Christians when they arrived in India in the sixteenth and seventeenth centuries. Clearly, the finding of a relatively peaceable way of dealing with this new force was going to be extremely difficult.

2. E. B. Havell, *The History of Aryan Rule in India* (London: G. Harrap, 1918), p. xiv.

Indian society closed ranks; the caste system became more rigid as a defense against the stalwart people, Turks and Mongols, who came brandishing their iconoclastic weapons. Anyone opting out of the Indian system would become a *malaiche,* which is the name for those who are beneath contempt and total outcastes. The result was that those converted to Islam were, most frequently those who were already outcastes in Hindu society and who could improve their status in the more egalitarian Muslim society.

Determined to deny themselves to the invader, upper-caste Hindu women, on hearing of the defeat by the enemy of their men, would on occasion go so far as to throw themselves on huge pyres of burning wood and be consumed alive. Socially there was complete non-cooperation with the conqueror. This was not quite the same thing as mass civil disobedience, but it bore similarities to the latter phenomenon which, in the twentieth century, Gandhi developed into an effective weapon against the British. The eventual result of Indian non-cooperation was that the Muslim conquerors were drawn into a process of coming to terms with the Hindu people. This was not an easy step because India was the first country in Asia to which the Muslims had gone in which the vast majority of the people remained non-Muslim.

For several centuries the relationship between the people and the conquerors was uneasy, but the longer the invaders remained in the country the more they realized that the situation was unstable. The great Akbar, the Mogul emperor who was nearly an exact contemporary of Elizabeth I of Britain, did so in magnificent degree. He saw that it was impossible for Muslims to live on Indian soil without adopting many of the attitudes of the Hindu people, including the tempering influence of the outlook of the Vedanta. Akbar himself became a vegetarian, wore caste marks on his forehead, and married a Hindu princess, who was not inducted into the Muslim religion. Moreover, he adopted a form of administration which was an amalgam of his own ideas and existing Indian practices. His renowned land revenue administration (land revenue was the major source of governmental funds; it was the income tax and corporation tax of those days, all in one) was elaborated by a high Hindu functionary, Rajah Todar Mal. Moreover, as his military commander-in-chief Akbar appointed a Hindu Rajput prince, and he sent one of the same group of princes to be the Mogul governor of the turbulent province of Kabul or Afghanistan. Thus Akbar strove in many ways to create a movement for integration between the Turkic Islamic people from whom he had descended and the flexible people of India.

To all these steps in his chosen direction, he added another remarkably daring one. After much pondering and discussion with the wise men of his time, he decided that India needed a synthesized religion based on Hinduism, Islam, and Christianity. He called his new faith Din-i-Ilahi, the Divine Faith, and built a magnificent city at Fatehpur Sikri, near Agra, as the headquarters of the new religion and as his royal seat. However, Akbar was well ahead of his times; it was beyond the vision of his successors to emulate him. His son, Jahangir, was a full-time hedonist, much in his cups, but also a patron of the arts and a lover of good writing. The next emperor was the great builder Shah Jahan, who commissioned the Taj Mahal, and when it came to the next generation there was one prince among them who was a throwback to the era of the most iconoclastic and cruel of his early forebears. After killing off his brothers, this prince ascended the throne of Delhi as Aurangzeb. He dismissed all the high Hindu functionaries at the court and reimposed the *jiziya,* a poll tax on non-Muslims sanctioned by strict Islamic law, thereby guaranteeing widespread revolt in the subcontinent that had the empire in shambles by the time Aurangzeb died in 1707. Two generations later, even much of northern India, where demographically the Muslims were strongly entrenched, was wrested from the descendants of the Turks by the Sikhs, who created a powerful kingdom that endured until the British conquered it in 1849.

While the disintegration of the Mogul empire was proceeding, particularly through the later half of the eighteenth and the early part of the nineteenth centuries, there were growing signs that the Indian people and their erstwhile conquerors from central Asia were arriving at the long-awaited synthesis, of which there had been a foretaste under Akbar. For example, though the Mogul emperor had ceased to be a political and military force in the country, he was maintained on the throne of Delhi by the descendants of those very Hindus of western and central India who had led the revolt in the second half of the seventeenth century against Aurangzeb's tyrannical version of an Islamically directed polity. The emperor became a pensioner of these people, the Maharattas (who inhabit the suburbs of the modern city of Bombay), being retained as a symbol of the unity of India. This was a striking move, one which showed restraint (the Moguls could easily have been ousted) and a realization of the paramount value of a policy of synthesizing.

Similarly, lesser Muslim chiefs who were operating in principalities lying to the east of Delhi and further east in Bengal, and in the south in Hyderabad and Mysore, were not under great presure or attack from the resurgent Hindus, because they too were increasingly practicing synthesis with the larger Hindu populations. In Hyderabad, however, the ruling family were latecomers from Persia and were quite un-Indian. They sought to keep themselves in power by contracting military alliances successively with the French and the British, moves that only increased their own insularity in the Indian world that was forging a considerable degree of unity.

In the later half of the eighteenth century it looked very likely that a full-fledged synthesis would emerge between the old Indian India and the newly Indianized Muslim element. There was respect for each other's customs. Hindus attended religious ceremonies of the Muslims and vice versa. The elites of both communities shared cultural tastes in music, literature, and painting; and they enjoyed camaraderie in hunting and feasting. The course was well set for the achievement of a new hybrid India.

However, the fabled wealth of India had by now attracted the West. The British, at exactly the time when the new Indian phase of synthesizing was in progress, switched from being merely traders to the role of empire builders, and this entirely unexpected—but in terms of world developments almost inevitable—intrusion immensely complicated the process of synthesizing. Indeed, as we shall see, the British became a truly massive impediment to the process that would almost certainly have brought into being an Indian confederation embracing at least the entire subcontinent.

This confederation did not happen. Instead, India became the largest component by far in the British Empire. How and why this vast territory succumbed to the arms and blandishments of the British are questions about which much as been written. The reasons can be stated briefly as follows. First, as we have seen, India's attention was turned to the process of internal readjustment, of rediscovering its own synthesis. So engaged, it was not in a position simultaneously to face another major problem, that posed by the British intrusion. Second, because the internal synthesis was by no means completely accomplished, there were rulers who were willing to try another course: that of entering into alliances with the British. This became the prelude to the British taking power in various parts of the country. They did not consolidate their control until the middle of the nineteenth century, when the Sikh kingdom of "the Punjab, Kashmir, and Beyond," ridden with dissension over the question of succession, fell to them under the vigorously expansionist Governor General Lord Dalhousie. The "and Beyond" in the official title of the Sikh rulers, which was recognized by the British government, was interesting for its implication that the Indian system extended somewhat into the region of central Asia. This was by no means a new or recent development. As far back as the end of the fourth century, Fa Hien, a Chinese pilgrim who also carried official documents from the Chinese emperor, had made a journey to India by the overland route. In his diary he had noted that all the people west of Lok Nor, where the present Chinese government conducts its nuclear tests, practiced the rules of India and learned the Indian language.[3] Three centuries before Fa Hien's time there had been a battle between the Indian Kushan ruler of North India and the forces of the Chinese emperor in the same region of Sinkiang.

After subduing the Sikh kingdom it remained for the British to add a few bits and pieces of the subcontinent, namely Assam in the 1880s and later the North-West Frontier areas of the present Pakistan. In North-West Frontier, in 1894, the British staked their claim to the area up to the Durand Line. (In 1893 a boundary commission under Sir Mortimer Durand had demarcated the boundary, which came to be known as the Durand Line.) The Afghans were unhappy with this boundary and periodic wars ensued, particularly in 1919 and 1936–37.

A third reason for Britain's success in taking over India was the technological advantage it had acquired as a result of the Industrial Revolution. Its armaments and the mobility of its forces were superior to those of the Indians.

These three reasons do not complete the explanation of the successful advance of the British in India. There is a fourth reason, the most important of all: the Indian understanding of the nature of the British presence in their country was entirely different from what the

3. *A Record of Buddhistic Kingdoms. Being an account by the Chinese monk Fa-Hien of his travels to India and Ceylon*, A.D. 399–414 (New York: Paragon Book reprint, 1965), pp. 13–14. (This work, translated by James Legge, was first published by the Clarendon Press, Oxford, in 1886.)

new intruders intended in this regard. When the British made the transition from trade to political power, they chose to remain an outside incubus in occupation of India. The Indians, who for over four thousand years had accommodated a host of conquerors, had become accustomed to their visitors settling in, and eventually becoming parties to the continuing process of integration and synthesis with the indigenous peoples. When faced with the British conquest of India, the Indian mind said to itself: "Well, here is another group of people that wishes to find a home here. They will soon enough learn our ways; they will establish intimate relations with us, we will receive them as we have received so many other peoples over the ages, and our lives will probably be enriched by this new infusion." The Indians would have accepted Christ as an *avatar* of Vishnu, and they would have taken very kindly, particularly in north India, to the blond fair-skinned people of Britain. It is part of the cultural heritage of India, dating from the Aryan inroads, that young men, especially in the northern states of the country, aspire to contract marriages with fair-skinned women. The Indians therefore looked forward to a process of sociological and political integration with the British. But it is impossible to embark on such a process if the other party is unwilling. Thus no integration was possible, and the British became the first demographic injection into India that insisted on excluding itself from, though preying upon, the Indian scene.[4]

---

4. Any synoptic account of so large a scene as the Indian, covering several thousands of years in the compass of a short chapter, must inevitably exclude matters and views which other writers might have thought fit to include. However, in the judgment of the author, the accounts presented in this and the following chapter sketch many salient features of the developing Indian situation which deserve to be kept in mind.

Chapter Two

THE PEACEABLE INFLUENCE OF
THE INDIAN SYSTEM

The political framework of the India of which the British took full command before the end of the nineteenth century consisted of both a highly centralized system of government and a remarkable degree of decentralization and microcosmic autonomy. This is not a contradiction. It simply means that the Mogul emperors and the Hindu rulers in various parts of the Indian world thought of themselves, and acted, as the final repository of power rather than of day-to-day authority. They were the ultimate interpreters of the law of the land. In the time of the Hindu rulers, that law was the *dharma,* or the code of duties imposed upon the various categories of castes and peoples engaged in activities to maintain themselves as well as society as a whole. The king was to see to it that each person observed his *dharma,* i.e., the norms prescribed for him. As Kautilya, the renowned Indian political thinker of the fourth century B.C., put it: "The observance of one's own duty leads one to *Svarga* and infinite bliss. When it is violated, the world will come to an end. . . . Hence the king shall never allow people to swerve from their duties; for whoever upholds his own duty, ever adhering to the customs of the *Aryas* . . . will surely be happy both here and hereafter." [1] The emperor Asoka (third century B.C.) was also extremely concerned that the *dharma* of the citizenry and of the ruler should be scrupulously adhered to. He inscribed his views in a number of royal edicts ("rock edicts") that were carved into rock surfaces and on pillars studded across his vast empire which, in addition to most of present-day India, covered Afghanistan, Nepal, Pakistan, and Bangladesh. One of

1. Kautilya's *Arthasastra,* R. Shamasastry, tr. (Mysore, 1951), p. 7.

his edicts contains the following language: "This record relating to the Dharma has been caused to be written by me on stone for the following purpose: that people may act according to it and that it may endure for a long time." [2]

The king himself was not to overstep the law. Kautilya has the king addressing his army as follows: "I am a paid servant like yourselves." [3] In the case of the Moguls, there were no comparably clear guidelines, but as soon as they understood the Indian tradition they became interpreters of the law, and if they were wise and interpreted the law reasonably, they were held in great respect.

I have already mentioned that the system of revenue was based on a universal land tax paid to governors of the provinces of India who, for this purpose, operated through agents in the rural areas. This brings us to the other end of the Indian political spectrum, namely the village. The Indian village has long been a largely self-governing unit. Indeed, the tradition of democratic societies on the subcontinent goes back to the early Aryans. It had wider application than simply to the microcosmic village societies. Rhys Davids, the eminent Pali scholar, writing on the states in northeast India in the sixth century B.C., finds from the records of the time that they were democratic self-governing societies. The people elected elders or a council of rulers which, in the exercise of authority, remained responsible to the citizens. This finding prompted another British author, E. B. Havell, to comment, "It will be a surprise to many readers to discover that the Mother of the Western Parliaments [the British Parliament] had an Aryan relative in India, showing a strong family likeness, before the sixth century B.C." [4] This is a fair enough statement, for the electorate in Britain until well into the nineteenth century was probably smaller than the sixth century B.C. electorates in certain Indian states, even if one accepts the view of certain writers that only a section of the population was enfranchised. [5]

In the villages of India, the rule became that of a council of five persons (*panchayat*), elected by the village assembly. It attended to the affairs of the village, including criminal and civil offenses as well

2. *Inscriptions of Asoka,* D. C. Sircar, ed. (New Delhi: Government of India, Publication Division, March 1957), p. 68.

3. Kautilya's *Arthasastra,* p. 395.

4. E. B. Havell, *The History of Aryan Rule in India* (London: G. Harrap, 1918), p. xiii.

5. H. N. Sinha, *The Development of Indian Polity* (London: Asia Publishing House, 1963), pp. 74–75.

as social and economic matters. Irrespective of who was in power at Delhi or at the other capitals—Aryan, Maurya, Mogul, Chola, Sikh, or British—this system of panchayat rule endured to a considerable degree. A striking illustration of the accuracy of this statement is provided by E. B. Havell. He records the testimoney of a senior British administrator, also stating his own views. He writes:

Officially [i.e., by the British government in India] the Indo-Aryan political system has long been regarded as dead. But, says Mr. [Sidney] Webb, an able Collector of long service in Central India, who was totally unaware of any survival of that system in the villages over which he ruled, he was led to make enquiries into the matter. He then discovered "in village after village a distinctly effective, if somewhat shadowy, local organization, in one or other form of *panchayat*, which was, in fact, now and then giving decisions on matters of communal concern, adjudicating civil disputes, and even condemning offenders to reparation and fine."[6]

The long continuity of the panchayat system goes to the root of India's political structure. It creates a strongly autonomous and democratic base. As a result, Indian society may grumblingly put up with limited forms of more or less benevolent authoritarianism at the top, provided that the lives of the people are not subjected to tyrannical diktats. When Aurangzeb imposed poll taxes and other tyrannical regulations in the seventeenth century, his whole empire collapsed. When Mrs. Gandhi in June 1975 declared a national emergency, there was no great popular objection as long as the lives of the people in general were not subjected to arbitrary measures. However, as soon as the lower officials began irresponsibly to exercise their power in unjust acts—the effects of which were widely felt—the whole system instituted by the Emergency proclaimed by her broke down. This took place even though before the Emergency there was little doubt that Mrs. Gandhi's prestige in the country was high and that she was widely regarded by the people as a good leader. Indian political history indicates that the broad masses of the Indian people have a strong attachment to individual liberties, and that any system which negates those liberties will be rejected even if, for a time, the intellectuals, professionals, and businessmen might be intimidated, for they tend to be more pliable than the great rural population of India.

The foreign relations of the country, before the medieval conquests, which dealt a severe blow to the integrity of the Indian fabric,

6. Havell, *Aryan Rule*, pp. xi–xii.

were quite extraordinary. Asoka had such good relations with Antiochus II Theos, the Greek ruler of Asia Minor, Ptolemy II Philadelphus of Egypt, and with the kings of Macedonia, Cyrenaica and Epirus that in their territories he claimed to have "arranged for two kinds of medical treatment, viz., for men and for animals. . . . On the roads, wells have been caused to be dug and trees have been caused to be planted for the enjoyment of animals and men."[7] In another rock edict Asoka tells us that he has renounced the notion of an expanding empire in favor of "conquest through dharma," and that he has achieved this conquest not only in his own dominions but also in the kingdoms of the aforementioned Middle Eastern, North African, and eastern European rulers.[8] He claims that his envoys penetrated to all these territories with the result that "everywhere people are conforming to the instructions in Dharma imparted by the Beloved of the Gods [i.e., himself]."[9] This Asokan foreign policy well exemplifies the philosophical approach of India. It was no transient phenomenon: it continued in various ways, and was the direct ancestor of Gandhi's policies in his relations with the British in the struggle for India's independence as well as of Nehru's concept of nonalignment in international affairs—to use the current rubric by which his foreign policy has come to be known, even though it over-abbreviates and distorts that policy.

For a thousand years, commencing with the year A.D. 65, India's relations with China expressed the same unusual quality that characterized Asoka's foreign relations. The traditional interpretation is that in the year A.D. 65 Emperor Ming of the Han dynasty sent ambassadors to India to invite Buddhist missionaries to China. From then on, for many centuries, Indian scholars went to China, while Chinese scholars and monks—sometimes with credentials from the rulers of China—came to India. They came always in the entirely peaceable pursuit of exchanges in philosophy, religion and, indirect, in art and literature. By now India was politically fragmented, but this did not destroy or even diminish its cultural integrity, the facet of man's expression that has always been of far greater importance to the Indian than empire building, political unity, or the discipline of organized existence. Political organization is generally regarded to be a condition necessary for the maintenance of order

7. *Inscriptions of Asoka*, p. 40 (Rock Edict no. *II*).
8. *Ibid.*, p. 54 (Rock Edict no. *XI*).
9. *Ibid.*

and peace in a society. In Indian society the emphasis is primarily on
the individual and the poise he must cultivate, then on the family,
and then on the village. Larger structures have been regarded as the
playthings of the less worthy ambitions of certain men, to be tolerated and carefully neutralized by strong injunctions from the
dharma.

Over the centuries, a vigorous Indian cultural infusion spread peacefully throughout China, Japan, Southeast Asia, and Sri Lanka,
enriching the heritage of those vast areas. We should bear in mind
that foreign relations are a reflection of the ideas and norms peoples
develop and practice in their own lives. India's foreign relations were
of a piece with India's own civilization. The well-known British historian A. L. Basham has not overlooked this point:

Inequality of birth was given religious sanction, and the lot of the humble
was generally hard. Yet our overall impression is that in no other part of the
ancient world were the relations of man and man, and of man and the state,
so fair and so humane. In no other early civilization were slaves so few in
number, and in no other ancient law book are their rights so well protected
as in the *Arthashastra*. No other ancient lawgiver proclaimed such noble
ideals of fair play in battle as did Manu. In all her history of warfare Hindu
India has few tales to tell of cities put to the sword or of the massacre of
noncombatants. The ghastly sadism of the kings of Assyria, who flayed their
captives alive, is completely without parallel in ancient India. There was spo-
radic cruelty and oppression no doubt, but, in comparison with conditions in
other early cultures, it was mild. To us the most striking feature of ancient Indian civilization is its humanity.[10]

To return to foreign relations, it was the practice of scholars to
come from many countries to the great schools of learning at Tak-
shila, Nalanda, and elsewhere. Nalanda was the site of one of the
most renowned universities from the seventh to the fourteenth centuries. Unfortunately, at the end of the fourteenth century it was
completely destroyed, its libraries burned, and those of its scholars
who were unable to flee were killed by a misguided conqueror. It was
apparently intolerable to the rigid adherents to one book, the early
Muslims, to see such a diversity of literature of a religious and philosophical character being studied and revered. The destruction of Nalanda and other great schools in India was a profound misfortune in
Asian history.

10. A. L. Basham, *The Wonder That Was India* (New York: Evergreen Press,
1959), pp. 8–9.

Meanwhile, the long period of peaceful exchanges with India left a deep impression on China, which was invariably on the receiving end of art motifs, art forms, philosophy, religion, and literature. The well-known contemporary Chinese author and lexicographer, Lin Yutang, has pointed out that China has no systematic philosophy of its own and has drawn heavily on India: "For what is the Chinese philosophy, and does China have a philosophy, say, like that of Descartes or Kant, a logically built and cogently reasoned philosophy of knowledge or of reality or of the universe? The answer is proudly 'No.' That is the whole point. So far as any systematic epistemology or metaphysics is concerned, China had to import it from India." [11]

It was not only in the intellectual and religious spheres that China was influenced by India. That influence permeated the political texture at times, as is illustrated by the following episode of the sixth century, reported by René Grousset in his masterful work, *La Chine et son art*. He tells of the case of the Nanking emperor, Liang Wu-ti (502–49 A.D.):

This brilliant representative of a younger imperial branch, having reached the throne solely through his own merit, first showed himself to be a model sovereign according to the Confucianist ideal, a firm and generous statesman, energetic, humane and skilful, a successful captain and valiant soldier. But having subsequently been converted to Buddhism, he embraced its ideas with such zeal that he became a monk and, by dint of practising Indian "Nonviolence" [*ahimsa*], finally allowed his dynasty to crumble. [12]

A vivid instance, indeed, of the non-warlike nature of Indian thought.

In the period of the medieval conquests the old India was overtaken; its cultural vigor, which had given so much to the rest of the world, was weakened by internal struggle. As the Moguls became Indianized the situation tended to alter, but before any great degree of contact with the rest of the world could be reestablished the British commenced their march toward political dominance, and relatively quickly the vast Indian subcontinent became an occupied country cut off from direct contact with the rest of the world.

At the start of the twentieth century, the British Indian empire, comprising as much as a quarter of the world's people, became in ef-

11. Lin Yutang, ed., *The Wisdom of China and India* (New York: Random House, 1942), p. 568.
12. René Grousset, *Chinese Art and Culture* (Engish ed.) (New York: Grove Press, 1959), p. 145.

fect an economic reservation of the British, who used the great market of India for their own economic advantage. In addition, it was useful as a training ground for the British army, which was constantly vigilant and which was called upon to fight a series of actions, particularly on India's North-West Frontier. For good measure, India provided a fascinating playground, as well as remunerative careers, for a revolving population of some quarter of a million British personnel in the various governmental services and in business.

Chapter Three

THE CURTAIN RISES ON THE
TWENTIETH CENTURY

In the year 1900, an Englishman who chose to come to India might well find himself embarking on a life far more exciting, adventurous, ego-serving and, of course, lucrative than would have been available at home. All the high posts in the central and provincial administrations were held by the British. At the apex was the Indian Civil Service, at that time a group of about a thousand men who governed literally a quarter of the world's peoples. The name "Indian Civil Service" was simply an expression of the British preference for understatement. The men of the then awesome ICS were chosen on the basis of a stiff competitive examination that they took in London after completing their university work at Oxford or Cambridge. Formally they were in service for thirty-five years, but seven or so of these years were spent on "home leave" in England. Far from being civil servants, these men were much more accurately the equivalent of medieval barons and princelings who, at a very tender age (sometimes in their late twenties) were placed in authority over "districts" that were large tracts of territory, each containing, on an average, a million persons or more. As chief administrator of a district, the collector, or deputy commissioner, was at the head of all aspects of the administration, including the magistracy, the police, the health services, local government, agriculture, land taxation (the main source of revenue), and a miscellany of other agencies. In his person he represented the dignity, honor, and power of the King Emperor— in reality, of the British imperial machine in London and Calcutta. He alone was permitted to fly the Union Jack from the flagstaff in his garden and on his car; and wherever he went on tour in his district the flag was raised. He drew a salary that was, in those days, extremely high—the ICS was known as the best paid governmental career in the world—and that permitted him, if he so wished, to indulge in expensive sports such as polo, pig sticking, and hunting while, of course, tennis, soccer, field hockey, etc., were also all available to him.

These British satraps lived their lives completely insulated socially from India except for a ceremonial "garden party" sociability with a small selection of notables, such as big estate owners and a few loyalist city folk. Amazingly, these men who ruled the people of India rarely learned anything more than the poorest smattering of the Indian languages. At no time were there more than a dozen British administrators who had acquired real proficiency in any Indian tongue. This insulation was practiced because the British had chosen to be a purely occupying power. None of them intended to settle in India; it was in no sense their home. Home was ever Britain, where they sent their savings and their children for schooling. Later, when transport became swifter, their spouses went home for the summer.

There were, of course, more than a few who became deeply interested in the Indian people, particularly the peasantry, though they too retained a great deal of their social insularity. In any event, these few exceptions were not at the heart of the establishment; they did not rise to be the prestigious and powerful governors of provinces, or members of the viceroy's cabinet or the cabinets of the provincial governors. The more insular a British officer remained, the more he seemed to rise in the country's administrative hierarchy.

What of the Indians themselves at the opening of the twentieth century? A senior British princeling, the Commissioner of Fyzabad, wrote at about this time: "It has been calculated that about 60 percent of the entire native population are sunk in such abject poverty that, unless the small earnings of child labour are added to the small general stock by which the family is kept alive, some members of the family would starve."[1] Specifically this statement refers to a large section of the United Provinces—now Uttar Pradesh, the largest state in the Union of India—but, drawing on his vast experience of India as a whole, the same British satrap adds: "The impression is perfectly true as regards a varying, but always considerable part of the year, in the greater part of India."[2]

1. R. C. Dutt, *The Economic History of India* (reprinted by Government of India, Publications Division, 1960), 2:460.
2. *Ibid.*

Notwithstanding this parlous state, the British so conducted the affairs of India as to permit the large British-controlled trading houses to export great quantities of food grains and edible oils. In 1901–2, of a total export of merchandise valued at £88.6 million, food grains and seeds were by far the largest item, accounting for £22.5 million, or over 25 percent of India's total export trade.[3] Without this export, India's trade was balanced, so there was no need to denude the starving countryside of food. In that fiscal year there was a favorable trade balance of £21 million.

The whole system was a heavy drain on Indian resources. One item in the Indian budget was called Home Charges, under which was included the high cost of running the various government establishments in London and elsewhere in Britain that were connected with the administration of the British empire in India. It also included the annual remittances sent home by British personnel serving in India. Together, these costs and remittances, all incurred from the "wealth" of India and taken away from the country, amounted to nearly half of India's net revenues.[4] Such was the effect of the imperial system, in the heyday of British power, on the economy of India.

In summing up the period of British rule to 1905, R. C. Dutt, a contemporary, largely loyalist writer, himself a distinguished member of the ICS who resigned because he could not continue conscionably to be part of the British administrative system, wrote:

. . . these thirty years [1875–1905] were marked by three Acts restricting the liberty of the Press in India, three needless and wasteful wars beyond the frontiers of India, three famines, the most widespread and fatal of which history keeps any record; by a plague which has desolated towns and villages, by a surrender of Indian revenues and the imposition of an excise duty on Indian mills in the interests of Lancashire, by an increase of the Land Revenue by 50 percent, an increase in general taxation by raising the value of the rupee, and by a marked increase in the military expenditure, the cost of the European [i.e., British] services, the Home Charges, and the Public Debt. The period of Imperialism has not been a period of progress or of prosperity in India.[5]

This unfortunate state of affairs was bound to exist because the British had elected against any integration between themselves and India. Since there was no question of integration or a new synthesis

3. *Ibid.,* p. 458.
4. *Ibid.,* p. 462.
5. *Ibid.,* p. 343.

on the subcontinent that would have led the British to quiet social tensions in the country, or to resolve them, the occupying power acted instead to create as much division and tension as it could. This policy was consistent with the objectives of occupation which could be assured of continuity only as long as the Indians were at odds with each other. The pursuit of this policy also kept down expenditure. In any case, given Britain's limited natural and human resources and its far-flung world commitments, the strains of occupation would have been beyond endurance had it not been possible to call into play a vigorous policy of sowing discord and dissension.

The various groups and communities in India were progressing relatively well at their own synthesis in the eighteenth century. We have seen how the indigenous rulers, both Hindu and Muslim—as well as the Sikhs in the north—were gaining in mutual understanding and had decided to maintain the powerless Mogul emperor in Delhi as a symbol of the unity of India.

However, particularly after the uprising against the British in 1857–58, the imperial rulers decided that they must show far greater skill in devising policies to keep apart and divide the various groups in India, and especially the Hindus and the Muslims. In addition to potential conflicts among the main religious groups, there were also potential differences between agriculturalist and urbanite, prince and commoner, intellectual and non-intellectual, which could, and frequently were, stimulated by the imperial ruler.

The British administrative structure in India and its legal basis are both replete with instances of these divisive tactics. Take, for example, the policy the British government followed after 1857–58, regarding recruitment for the Indian army. Previously, the bulk of the recruits—enlisted men and noncommissioned officers (there were then no Indians with the rank of lieutenant or above)—were from Bengal, Bihar, the United Provinces of Agra and Avadh (now Uttar Pradesh), Madras, and virtually all areas over which the British had gained control. This army served the British well, even to the point of fighting for the expansion and consolidation of the British Raj in India. However, much of it rebelled in 1857–58, and the British decided that in the future recruitment would have to be on a highly selective basis so as to exclude elements of the population that could foment another rebellion in the armed services. They came up with a solution that was both highly divisive and highly insulting to most parts of the country. They determined that there were certain groups of people in the country who were "martial races," and they decided to restrict recruitment to them. The people so designated, were precisely those who inhabited the least politically aware regions; they were from the Northwest, the Punjab, the Terai area (including Nepal, for the recruitment of Gurkhas), to a lesser degree from Rajasthan and, merely for form's sake, there were a sprinkling from Maharashtra—the land of the Maharattas, whose prowess was known by bitter experience but who were now to be regarded nevertheless as rebellious but nonmartial. Most of the other people were declared nonmartial, including almost all those who had so far filled the ranks of the British Indian army! Even in a given region, such as the Punjab, one community—the bulk of the Hindus—was declared nonmartial, even though a fair proportion of the rank and file of the powerful Sikh army, and a considerable portion of its officers, had been drawn from these very Hindu groups of Khatris and Aroras.

The point is that, though certain regions were favored, even in those regions the Hindus tended to be excluded on the basis of a contrived formula—the real reason being the creation of a rift, beneficial to the imperial power, between the favored and the not favored. This policy led to a highly disproportionate recruitment of Muslims—as much as 40 percent against a population ratio of less than half this amount. The general effect was to create the impression that the Muslims were placed near to the ruling elite while the Hindus were relegated by and large to the position of subject peoples. This could hardly be conducive to good relations between the communities.

Another example of divisive policies was the Punjab Land Alienation Act of 1904. Much was made of the intention to protect the small landowners and peasant farmers against the avarice of the moneylender. This was a laudable objective that should have been pursued by prescribing low ceilings on interest rates and by requiring that only those loans attested by the revenue authorities would be actionable in a court of law. Furthermore, stays on dispossession could have been legislated for specified grace periods. Instead of this rational and equitable system, the British government, whose objectives were political rather than protective of the poor, decreed in the act of 1904 that no land owned by tribes and groups declared to be "agriculturist" could pass by sale or in collection of debts to groups declared to be "nonagriculturist." The bulk of Hindus, who themselves had been dispossessed of their lands by frequent conquests in the Punjab, were declared to be nonagriculturists and therefore not eligible for acquisition of land from the vast majority of landowners, even if those landowners wished to sell their land to such persons. The small peasants suffered doubly by this legislation. First, it meant that they were not able to get the market price when they wanted to sell because most of those who were in a position to offer good prices were "nonagriculturists." Second, they could, and frequently did, lose their lands to the bigger landowning "agriculturists" when they were unable to pay their debts to the latter.

It is difficult to avoid the conclusion that the act of 1904 was a deliberate piece of deception to bolster the feudal rich at the expense of the rural poor and at the same time screen off the bulk of the Hindus from landed property in the rural areas because they were generally both educated and politically conscious. In a country where land was the most respectable form of property, the Hindus were by and large relegated to an inferior landless position. From the point of view of the British, the act of 1904 succeeded in its real though covert objectives of dividing the communities and strengthening the position of the feudal landed class which came increasingly to look to the British, rather than to the old process of synthesis, for the continuance of its discriminatory well-being.

In their arrangements for assessing and collecting the land tax, or land revenue, as it was called, in the vast areas of Bengal, Bihar, and the United Provinces, the British ignored peasant rights to the land by dealing with descendants of the Mogul tax collectors, giving them—something they had not had previously—full ownership of the land and a special status as a baronial class. The purpose was to secure the loyalty of a feudal group and to deepen the division between it and the peasantry.

An unswerving advocate of these divisive policies of the British in India was the somewhat tricky and intellectually pretentious Lord Curzon of Kedleston, the British Viceroy from 1899 to 1905. As a student at Oxford Curzon had aspired for high honors—a First—but had to settle for a humdrum Second. However, wealth was an asset which he certainly had, and he soon became a rising figure in the Conservative party in Britain, and was able to secure appointment as Viceroy of India. He was determined to consolidate in every way the power of British rule, professing, as the "enlightened" dictator often will, a benign interest in the peoples of India. Because of his professed benignity, he sponsored the Punjab Land Alienation Act of 1904. Another strikingly important so-called reform was the partition of Bengal, consummated in 1905. This was imperial action at its best, for it laid the foundation of the later partition of that part of India when independence was gained in 1947.

True enough, Bengal had become an extremely difficult area to administer as a unit. But what contributed to its administrative cumbersomeness was the fact that three non-Bengali areas, the provinces of Bihar (a very large state), Assam, and Orissa (also large), were included in the presidency (as the British called it) of Bengal, the whole constituting one administrative unit. Some division was clearly desirable, but the sensible reform would have been to separate the three provinces into three administrative areas. But the fact is that Curzon was playing an imperial game and not thinking primarily of good sense. There was an outcry against the partition of Bengal. Why should people with the same language, eating habits, social customs, and even some religious observances at the popular level be divided simply because of religion? The answer was so as to encourage the politically more backward East Bengali groups to reject the influence of the very active Indian nationalism of the advanced Bengalis around Calcutta. Seven years later the partition was undone, but the bitter seed had seen sown and it was cultivated more subtly by the British, with the assistance of some of the feudal notables whom they protected in affluence and privilege.

Even more far-reachingly divisive policies were instituted by the British as the twentieth century waxed, but before we look at them the picture we have sketched in must be completed with additional facts about the political scene in the country which, in spite of the arrogant confidence of the upper echelons of the British satrapy in India and Viceroy Curzon and his immediate entourage, was becoming increasingly stormy.

Chapter Four

FIGHTING FOR THE POLITICAL INITIATIVE

Even before the armed revolt of 1857–58, peaceful organizations had been established to discuss the problems created by British rule in India. In Calcutta the British Indian Association was established in 1851 to promote discussion of the administration and to present polite memoranda to the British government on such matters as the need for increased participation by Indians in the administration of their own country. A similar body, the Bombay Association, was founded in 1852, to be followed by the Madras Native Association in 1853.

However, it was not until 1885 that Indian sentiment and opinion began to formulate themselves on a large, virtually country-wide, scale. In that year, with some encouragement from one or two retired maverick members of the British satrapy in India, notably Allan Octavian Hume, whose father was a well-known Liberal in England, the Indian National Congress was established. Within twenty years, the Congress, frustrated by the lack of response from the British authorities to its polite memos, as well as its plaudits for the administration, became a political party with its sights set on *swaraja*, or self-rule, for India. Increasingly it found itself locked in a battle of wits with the British government.

The transformation of the initially thoroughly loyalist and pro-British Indian National Congress into a mass-based freedom movement was in itself an eloquent demonstration of the logic of the relationship between an imperial ruler and a subject people. The speeches made during the first dozen years of the life of the Congress were full of expressions of loyalty to Britain. For example, Dadabhai Naoroji the great, Parsi statesman and leader of the end of the last century and the early years of the present one, in his presidential address at the opening of the second annual session of the Indian National Congress, said:

I put the question plainly. Is this Congress a nursery for sedition and rebellion against the British Government [cries of "No! No!"]; or is it another stone in the foundation of the stability of that Government? [cries of "Yes! Yes!"] There could be but one answer, and that you have already given, because we are thoroughly sensible of the numberless blessings conferred upon us, of which the very existence of this Congress is a proof in a nutshell [cheers].[1]

At that time the belief was that if only there could be well-organized meetings and discussions the British, themselves members of a democratic society, would embark on a series of administrative reforms leading eventually to the creation of parliamentary organs in India. As the years passed it became clear that this was a pipedream of the Anglicized Indian leaders.

However, the Indian National Congress persevered, building itself up as an association of all the various creeds, peoples, and regions of India. The first president of the Congress party was W. C. Bonarji, a Christian from Bengal. He was followed by Naoroji. Another early president was Badr Tyabji, a Muslim from Bombay. Though they and their followers were conciliatory, moderate, and loyal to Britain, their *raison d'être* as an association was to bring to the notice of their rulers the burdens and problems of their people; this involved criticism of the imperial satrapy in India. Even these moderate criticisms were, however, most unwelcome to the British and brought ugly reactions. This seems to be an inevitable response from imperial and other forms of tyrannical rule. The foreign ruler or tyrant constantly fears that any form of criticism reflects more widespread discontent, and foolishly, but inevitably suppresses it sternly.

Twelve years after the inauguration of the Indian National Congress there was an outbreak of plague accompanied by widespread famines in the land. It seemed that instead of improving, conditions were deteriorating under the British. This provoked a new leader of the Congress, B. G. Tilak, to express his criticisms of the administration more sharply and without the sugarcoating of adulation to which the British were accustomed. The British were furious

1. Wm. Theodore de Bary et al., eds., *Sources of Indian Tradition* (New York: Columbia University Press, 1958), p. 670.

and responded not by offering to parley with the national leaders but by throwing Tilak into jail for a term of seven years—and all because of a few critical sentences! "We'll teach the bastards" was the prevailing philosophy of the administration, with the full backing of London, and thus Tilak became the first in what was to be a great river of political prisoners—some of whom never were put on trial—in the remaining decades of British rule in India.

Tilak introduced a few new elements into the Indian political scene. First, he stated unequivocally that complete political freedom was the birthright of India. Second, he advocated the *swadeshi* movement, the exclusive buying of indigenously manufactured goods, as a form of economic boycott of Britain. A third point was his disdain of the position of such leaders as Naoroji, whom he referred to contemptuously as "moderates." Tilak was the first verbally militant leader of peaceful Indian nationalism. Fourth, there was an unfortunate negative aspect in his position: he tended to overlook a considerable part of India's history and its complex fabric. He ignored the thousands of years of integration that had gradually assimilated various cultures. In particular, Tilak ignored one of the most salient of those influences, the Islamic one. This was both a factual error and a serious political blunder, which his own Maharashtrian forebears had been too sagacious to commit. Those sturdy peoples of southwest and central India had deliberately maintained the Muslim, but thoroughly Indianized, Mogul emperor on the throne of Delhi as a symbol of the unity of India. They recognized that the originally foreign Muslims had settled in India, become part of it, intermarried, adopted many of the customs of their new homeland, and passed to other Indians some of their own customs. Tilak, by ignoring all this, did a disservice to the unity of the country and thus did not best serve the interests of a full-blown national movement.

In spite of Tilak, the Indian National Congress continued to be predominantly a party of loyalists and moderates. Even so, it was becoming increasingly less acceptable to the British authorities. Curzon, the zealous caesar previously mentioned, wrote in 1900: "My own belief is that the Congress is tottering to its fall, and one of my great ambitions while in India is to assist it to a peaceful demise." [2] This assessment by the British viceroy was typical of his arrogance and gross ignorance. The Congress did not weaken during Curzon's

2. A. K. Majumdar, *Advent of Independence* (Bombay: Bharatiya Vidya Bhavan, 1963), p. 360. (Text of letter from Lord Curzon to Lord Hamilton, Nov. 18, 1900.)

tenure; it g ,w ever stronger. Blunders of his, such as the partition of Bengal and the Punjab Land Alienation Act, provided further fuel for its "incendiary" activities. It was during the agitation against the partition that Tilak gave currency to the word that became the battle-cry for the next forty years: *swarajya!* (self-rule).

The British continued to think that they could handle Tilak in the classic ways of imperial rulers. In 1907 they again sentenced him, this time to six years in prison, and did so in the belief that they were giving a signal to the loyalist elements to come to the fore. They did their best. They engaged in secret talks with their special friends, such as the Aga Khan, to organize Muslim opposition to the Congress party. As if in revenge against the nationalists, whose strength in all sectors of the population was growing fast, they intensified their policies of divide and rule—reactions typical of an irresponsible ruler, who destroys or weakens as much as possible what he must yield sooner or later. It was at this time that the British authorities and their efficient satrapy embarked on the path that laid the foundations of division of the subcontinent into several sovereign states.

The year 1905 has frequently been referred to by British writers as marking the watershed in the era of British dominance in India. In that year Curzon stepped down from the viceroyalty, and it is contended that this concluded the era of British paternalism. From then on some sharing of the estate would be necessary.[3] In a sense this was to be the case, but the sharing was not to be that of a parent with his offspring, but rather that of a self-seeking stepfather with his stepchild.

From 1906 onward it was clear to the British that they would have to make some adjustments in their own attitudes so as to control and limit the mounting pressure in India for constitutional change. Though the Congress party was not talking of severing the relationship with Britain, it was certainly calling loudly for a sharing of power. However, the Congress was not in the least attracted to the course of armed rebellion, even of the guerrilla type, which could have been waged successfully in many parts of the large Indian land mass. This striking fact about India and the attitudes of its people greatly facilitated British policies in the country. Not only was maintenance of law and order rendered a much simpler and easier task

3. Percival Spear, *India* (Ann Arbor: University of Michigan Press, 1961), p. 320.

than it would otherwise have been, but the machinations of divisive tactics were given a clear field by the discursive approach of the Indians. Such an approach is not conducive to galvanizing a people into a sense of comradeship and unity; it in fact promotes discussion of differences rather than tending to obliterate them in the crucible of passionate action. Armed activity would have brought together Sikh, Hindu, Muslim, and the others, just as it had in 1857–58.

One might say they were naïve, but it would be truer to say that the moderate Indian leaders of the Congress party, were encouraged by the British system of democracy to think that the logical and natural course of events would be the development of full self-government in India, and that the vast country, as its response to this development, would be firmly a partner of Britain and a devoted member of the self-governing fraternity of dominions under the titular leadership of the British Crown.

But the British, even the best among them, did not look at the future of India in this way. They envisioned remaining in power in India for the foreseeable future. For example, Lord Morley, the Liberal British statesman in charge of Indian affairs in the British cabinet, wrote the following on August 2, 1906, after a conversation with G. K. Gokhale, the outstanding Indian leader of his day, and, in his attitude toward the British, a loyalist: "Yesterday, I had my fifth and final talk with Gokhale. He made no secret of his ultimate hope and design: India to be on the footing of a self-governing colony. I equally made no secret of my conviction that for many a long day to come—long beyond the short space of time that may be left to me—this was a mere dream."[4]

But there was a dilemma involved: constitutional progress in India and the continuance of British dominance in the country were, even in the fairly short run, an impossible partnership. The former would stimulate the demand for self-government, and with each installment of constitutional progress the fabric of empire would weaken. Since this was not the objective of the British, how were they to manipulate constitutional development for India while still maintaining intact the pillars of the empire? A problem indeed.

The "solution" that the British devised to this conflict of objectives ensured the destruction of the Indian world's capacity to make for itself a viable synthesis. The British decided that the wisest course was

4. Majumdar, *Advent of Independence*, p. 12.

to promote divisive forces among the Indian people. In 1906, through their own henchmen, they connived at the creation of a group of highly pro-British Muslims, hardly representative of the Muslims as a whole, to wait on the Viceroy, at this time the Tory Lord Minto. The deputation, which called on the Viceroy on October 1, 1906, was led by the Aga Khan, a well-known beneficiary of British favors, whose loyalty to the throne had been amply demonstrated, and whose desire was to maintain the British empire intact. He obviously could be trusted by the British as leader of the delegation. His group would surely make no demands that would reduce the strength of the British hold on the country, whatever else their impact on India might be.

This is precisely what happened. The deputation led by the superloyalist Aga Khan made two major demands. One was that in any constitutional reforms that might be introduced, the representation of the Muslims should be far in excess of what it would be based on their population. This was asked for on two grounds: because of the loyalty of the Muslims—and this was indeed true of the kind of Muslims who made up the delegation—and because they had ruled in various parts of India immediately preceding the establishment of British power. The second demand of the delegation was truly revolutionary in its way—that the highly inflated representation asked for by the Muslims be elected by exclusively Muslim electorates! This would be equivalent to the creation of separate electorates in the United States for blacks, Hispanics, Jews, and so on. If that were done, separate sovereign communities would grow—which is precisely what the British and the Muslim loyalists were aiming at. They were not thinking of the Muslim people in India but rather of the security and maintenance of the British empire and of the sharing of subsidiary power with a group of loyal henchmen.

There is ample evidence, in spite of the secrecy surrounding the backstage maneuvers, that the deputation, its demands, and the response by the British were all prearranged. Lord Minto could not contain his glee and *immediately* announced to the deputation in reply to its demands: "I am entirely with you." [5] That such extraordinarily important and far-reaching proposals should receive the immediate blessing of the British cannot be explained except by introducing the notion of prior agreement between the two parties. This view

5. Sidney Wolpert, *A New History of India* (New York: Oxford University Press, 1977), p. 278.

was affirmed at the time by Mohammad Ali, a highly respected Muslim leader, with a far larger following than any member of the deputation. He dismissed the meeting as being "a command performance."[6]

Meanwhile, the British rejoiced and by so doing gave additional credence to the view I have advanced. On the day her husband was so responsive to the Aga Khan's deputation, Lady Mary Minto recorded the following in her diary: "This evening I have received the following letter from [a British] official: 'I must send Your Excellency a line to say that a very, very big thing has happened today, a work of statesmanship that will affect India and Indian history for many a long year. It is nothing less than the pulling back of sixty-two millions of people [i.e., the Muslims] from joining the ranks of the seditious opposition.' "[7]

Apart from the handpicked deputation, and their hangers-on, Indians of all regions and religions decried the whole operation. But power was in British hands and British heads, and those hands had decided to fashion developments that would maximize the chances that the Raj would continue. Henceforth secular democracy for India as a whole was an impossibility. The British lost no time. They immediately drew up a constitution that enshrined as law the two demands of the Aga Khan's deputation—overrepresentation and separate electorates for the Muslims.[8] A mortal blow fell on the long-practiced art of synthesizing, which had been the hallmark of several thousand years of what one might call the Indian experiment for peace among peoples. A process that had devised viable relationships among many different peoples was brutally assaulted by these decisions, which destroyed the avenues to political and social accommodation between the Muslims and the rest of the people in the country—not just the Hindus. With one massive cynical imperialistic stroke the fortunes of modern India were rent asunder and the best work of Asoka, Akbar, and many others was ruthlessly negated.

6. J. S. Sharma, ed., *India's Struggle for Freedom: Select Documents and Sources* (New Delhi: S. Chand, 1962), 1:212.
7. *Ibid.*, 1:215.
8. These were the Minto-Morley "Reforms" of 1909.

Chapter Five

USING INDIA INTERNATIONALLY FOR IMPERIAL PURPOSES WHILE CRUSHING IT AT HOME

Churchill is said to have once remarked that 25 percent of the national income of Britain was derived, directly or indirectly, from India, and that he would be no party to the bartering away of the brightest jewel in the British Crown. Moreover, apart from being a great financial prize, India contained a quarter of the world's people, which endowed Britain with enormous international prestige and was conducive to imperial pomp and circumstance.

Over and above all this, India could be made use of in international affairs. Addressing the Indian Legislative Council in October 1900, Lord Curzon stated: "It was the prompt despatch of a contingent of the Indian army a year ago that saved the colony of Natal. They were Indian regiments who accomplished the rescue of the legations at Peking. . . . If our arm reaches as far as China in the east, and South Africa in the west, who can doubt the range of our influence, or the share of India in imperial destinies?"[1] Explicitly, from Curzon's time on, India was made to play a considerable, though of course subservient, role in international affairs. Indian garrisons were sent to the Persian Gulf, while British officers and Indian staff, paid from Indian revenues, manned the various diplomatic and consular posts of His Britannic Majesty's Government in the Persian Gulf, Iran, Afghanistan, and Nepal. These were financially onerous commitments but to some extent they did create, among a small section of Indians, a sense of the country's international importance.

The growing feeling among some Indians that it was fitting that a

1. Durga Das, *India from Curzon to Nehru and After* (London: Collins, 1969), p. 46.

country consisting of a quarter of the world's population should assume an international posture and acquire high international status was not shared by the British government, though Curzon himself had, one might almost say, imperial designs of his own, in the sense that as viceroy he was disposed to enlarge his own jurisdiction, and he saw an expansion of India's role in international affairs as a way to do so. The Russo-Japanese war of 1904–5 was a stimulant to India's renewed interest in international affairs. In that war a much smaller Asian country than India had routed the renowned imperial Russian army and navy and had acquired great prestige in the world, particularly in Asia. People began to think that if Japan could be so important in world affairs, then India, a much larger country, should certainly play a significant role. This thinking gave a further impetus to the developing sentiment in favor of a juridical self-governing status for India.

When the First World War broke out in 1914 there erupted a certain feeling of high adventure in loyalist quarters in India, a feeling that led to the maharajas and other chieftains pledging renewed loyalty to the British Crown and offering their own small contingents of paramilitary forces for service against the enemy. There was also some expression of sentiments of loyalty even among Nationalists, not excluding the Indian National Congress, the dominant political organization in the country. Thus, the President of the Congress, B. N. Basu, in his address to the annual party convention in December 1914, stated:

At the present moment, who would desire or support separation from England? The Indian princes secure in their dignity and status, the Indian aristocracy safe in their possessions and influence, the Indian middle classes free in their vocations, the toiling masses sure of the fruits of their labor, are all moving to one common goal, with the impetus which a Central Government, a common vehicle of thought, a common ideal and a growing sense of unity and nationality have given them. . . . The two extremes, one of separation, the other of subordination, are both equally impossible and must be put out of our mind. The idea which we must pursue, and which the Congress has set before itself is that of coordination and comradeship. . . . We must have a system of government modeled on the lines of the Commonwealth of Australia, or the United States of America, modified according to Indian conditions, and presided over by a representative of our Sovereign.[2]

2. J. S. Sharma, ed., *India's Struggle for Freedom* (New Delhi: S. Chand, 1962), 1:396–97.

Even more significant than this authoritative statement was one made by M. K. Gandhi, the great hero of modern India, soon to be known as Mahatma Gandhi and the Father of the Nation, who returned to India in 1915 after a protracted stay in South Africa. In April of that year, speaking at Madras, he said:

> It gives me great pleasure . . . to declare my loyalty to the British Empire; and my loyalty is based on very selfish grounds. . . . I discovered that the British Empire has certain ideals with which I have fallen in love, and one of those ideals is that every subject of the British Empire has the fullest scope possible for his energies and honor, and whatever he thinks is due to his conscience. . . . Hence my loyalty to the British Empire.[3]

Most significant of all, the President of the Congress Party for 1914–15 declared that not only would the future constitution of the country have a place for all the various regions and peoples of India but that it would also have an honorable place for the British. This echoed the long Indian tradition of synthesis. It envisaged the British as adopting India as their home, as they had done in North America and elsewhere, and as the Scythian Goths, the Greeks, the Mongols, the Turks, and many others had done in India.

Very soon after the outbreak of the 1914–18 war, Indian forces were rushed to France and joined with the British and the French in holding the line against the onslaught of Germany. Thereafter, Indian troops were stationed on the Suez Canal and repulsed an attack against it. They fought through the long campaigns in the Balkans and German East Africa; and they played a significant part, indeed a leading one, in the Iraqi campaign leading to the capture of Baghdad in 1917. They were represented by contingents in the Allied armies which occupied Jerusalem in 1917, and went on to Damascus and Aleppo. Almost a million and a quarter men were recruited in India during the First World War, and so great was the feeling of loyalty that, at one time, the British forces in India shrank to only 15,000 men.

However, loyalty and assistance in the common struggle were but one aspect of the Indian situation. Buttressing these contributions was a growing conviction of equality with Britain, a strong feeling that if the common purpose was being pressed in war it should be likewise pressed in peace, and that the Indian people should in every respect be placed on an equal political footing with their erstwhile

3. *Ibid.,* p. 398.

conquerors. The British too, under the pressures of that first great global conflict, very early recognized that a change was called for in the nature of their relationship with India. In November 1914, a bare three months after the commencement of the war—during which period Indian forces had already made a contribution to the effort to hold the Germans—the Liberal Prime Minister of Great Britain, H. H. Asquith, said: "Henceforth Indian questions would have to be approached from a different angle of vision."[4] But it took some years for the British to translate this changed sentiment into something more tangible. Meanwhile Indian trust in Britain began to diminish. A British historian, at that time resident in India, later recorded his views on the situation as follows:

To India the war was an external affliction. As a people they found little thrill in conflict, and little glory in victory. To cheer on their rulers to victory was pleasant; to extricate them from defeat, and help them through arduous struggle and great sacrifice was much less exciting. It is therefore not surprising that at the end of the war India as a country was not only exhausted and war-weary like Britian, but sour, discontented, and resentful as well.[5]

A concomitant of the sense of equality with Britain was a rise of nationalist sentiment in the country. Apart from the cooperative war effort, another factor contributed to this development. The old generation of more conservative and loyalist leaders of the Congress party, which was growing in strength, were leaving the scene. G. K. Gokhale, who had been a towering leader for a few years, died at the end of 1915, and at about the same time B. G. Tilak, the much more radical leader who had served two long terms of imprisonment for expressing his views, was released at the end of his second, six-year, term in jail. Rousing the people again to demand *swarajya,* he became the leading actor in the Congress party and, in 1916, he signed a pact with the Muslim League, the communal body which, as we have seen, owed its origin and rise to significance at least in part to the promptings and continued support of the British themselves. Tilak was in favor of stronger action—such as an economic boycott—in the drive for India's freedom, but by such action he intended neither to sever the close relationship with Great Britain nor to use violence. Even the radical large-scale organized movements for freedom were not given to the use of violence. This did not mean that

---

4. Percival Spear, *India* (Ann Arbor: University of Michigan Press, 1961), p. 308.
5. *Ibid.,* p. 340.

there were not a few stray acts of violence in India, but that approach never took hold as part of the broad national struggle. This stamps the Indian revolution with a unique character that Barrington Moore recognized when he stated that of modern revolutions it was only the Indian that had remained largely nonviolent. All other revolutions have been accompanied by large-scale violence.[6]

At long last, in August 1917, the British government made a gesture toward self-government for India, at least on paper. It decided, with the consent of the major political parties in the United Kingdom, that British intentions in regard to India would have to be stated clearly. With the Conservatives and Liberals both taking part in its preparation, including among them Lord Curzon, an important statement was drafted. It was read in the House of Commons by E. S. Montague, Secretary of State for India: "The policy of His Majesty's Government, with which the Government of India are in complete accord, is that of the increasing association of Indians in every branch of the administration, and the gradual development of self-governing institutions, with a view to the progressive realisation of responsible government in India as an integral part of the Empire."

This was a more far-reaching concession than any the British had hitherto made in regard to India. It contained at least two hedges— "the gradual development" and "the progressive realisation"—and it did not say clearly that India would join the fraternity of other self-governing dominions such as Canada and Australia. However, this status, widely acceptable to the Congress party and other freedom-seeking Indians, seemed implicit in the statement, and it looked as if India would fairly soon become an equal partner in the British system.

Montague's statement was welcomed by B. G. Tilak, the "extremist" leader of the Congress party, and hopes were high when the secretary of state began a tour of India that was apparently to lead to the implementation of the statement he had made in the British Parliament. However, the exclusive group that miscalled itself the Indian Civil Service, strongly opposed its realization. T. G. P. Spear says of them: "They were therefore unresponsive to the new Secretary of State Montague when he toured India in 1917–18."[7] Spear bases this statement on Montague's own diary kept during his tour of India, which was published in 1930.

6. Barrington Moore, Jr., *Social Origins of Dictatorship and Democracy* (Boston: Beacon Press, 1966). See, for example, pp. 413–14.
7. Spear, *India,* p. 343.

The opposition of the top British administrators was not merely a matter of words. Subtle steps were taken to sabotage the new move of the London government. To the bewilderment of an India that had contributed men and wealth freely during the war, and that through all shades of its leaders had expressed its loyalty to the British Empire, the British Indian government had the insensitivity—or, more probably, they were motivated by sinister intent—to set up a committee, presided over by Justice Rowlatt, proposing that judges alone—without juries—be authorized to try political cases and that the provincial governments in India, the authorities in charge of law and order, be given power to jail suspects (i.e., persons known to be in favor of the rising freedom movement in the country) without due process of law.

Rivaling Lord Minto's spontaneous acceptance of the far-reaching demands made by the superloyalist group of Muslims that waited on him in 1906, the British government of India immediately accepted these proposals and introduced legislation to implement them. This legislation was passed early in 1919 despite the negative votes of all the nonofficial Indian members of the Imperial Legislative Council. There could have been no clearer evidence of the adamancy of the opposition of the administration in India to the proposals of the British government itself. It is also probable that by now, since Britain had come through the war, there was no longer the pressure of grave events to push London to translate wartime promises into action.

Be this as it may, the Rowlatt bills were speedily passed into law, and the provincial governments were reminded that they were already armed with other extraordinary powers, such as the right to prohibit meetings, which meant any gathering of four or more persons, and to prevent open exhortations to the people by the political leaders of India. The provincial governments immediately brought these powers into operation. Never had so vast a section of the world's population been subjected to such glaring and inexplicable contradictions as was India in the period immediately following the First World War.

M. K. Gandhi's protest against the Rowlatt Acts became the basis of his first national campaign in the struggle for India's independence. In his small, reflective, and vibrant voice, never raised in harshness or anger, he went about calling on the people of India to hold meetings to protest the acts. Not even he could have anticipated the response. In all the cities of India the anguished roar of the people went up against the new unjust legislative provisions, even though the independence movement (and it was striving successfully to remain peaceful) now could claim that it had the sanction of the British government, as implied in the official statement of August 20, 1917. Suddenly the streets of Calcutta, Bombay, Madras, Delhi, Lahore, Allahabad, Ahmedabad, Poona, and elsewhere were filled with people chanting the names of their great leaders, Gandhi and Tilak, and calling for the withdrawal of the Rowlatt Acts and of other governmental repressive measures.

The British authorities reacted with what they called "necessary firmness" and what the Indian people could only describe as extreme ruthlessness. Squadrons of police—mounted and on foot—charged into peaceful processions; thousands of persons were thrown in jail, and the army and the police were ordered to open fire on peaceful crowds. The most brutal and sanguinary case occurred in the Punjab on April 13, 1919. On that date some 10,000 unarmed people were gathered in the Jalianwala Bagh, a walled garden in the city of Amritsar, to listen to addresses by national leaders urging them to work, by peaceful means, for the independence of India: they were urged to use only Indian-made goods and develop local handicrafts to supply their needs. There was no danger to "law and order" in a meeting propounding these themes. However, the local administration took an entirely different view—one of unbridled imperialism.

At the head of affairs in the Punjab was the governor, Sir Michael O'Dwyer, a man who believed blindly in the eternal destinies of the British Empire and to whom any voice daring to express a different view deserved only to be silenced. There is probably no name in modern British-Indian history which is less palatable to Indians than that of Michael O'Dwyer. Under his authority, there were brought into the enclosed garden several companies of infantrymen under the command of Brigadier Dyer, an officer who was in full agreement with Sir Michael.

Brigadier Dyer ordered his troops to open fire on the peaceful gathering. It was sheer slaughter. Bodies of the dead, dying, and wounded were carried away by those who were able to do so. The British then made an incomplete count of casualties and announced, with almost gleeful justification, that 379 persons were killed and 1,200 wounded. Those present estimated that over 1,000 were killed and some 3,000 wounded.[8] The reasons for the heavy casualties

---

8. Considerably larger figures were given to me by old citizens of Amritsar. Motilal Nehru used the figure of a thousand dead. See R. C. Majumdar et al., *Struggle for Freedom* (Bombay: Bharatiya Vidya Bhavan, 1969), p. 306.

were, first, the fact that the meeting was held in a space enclosed by a high wall with only a few small gates by which people could exit and, second, that the firing took place without warning.

It will be difficult for the reader to imagine the sharp and baffling conflict in the minds of the Indian people between their wartime fervor for the Allies on the one hand, and the actions of the British authorities in India on the other. The result of this situation was the melting away of all trust between the Indian people and the British government in India. In spite of statements by the Viceroy that the intention of the government was to press on with constitutional reforms that would give some substance to the principles enunciated by the British Parliament, there was no enthusiasm at all in the country for what might be offered by the foreign rulers.

Chapter Six

THE ECONOMIC AND SOCIAL SCENE IN THE EARLY TWENTIETH CENTURY

It seems that the Indian people thoroughly learned one lesson during the period of British rule in India: they could subsist on very little in the way of material goods. It is difficult to observe accurately the transition from a medieval society, dependent almost entirely on unmechanized agriculture, to a society dependent in significant degree on manufacturing industries and large-scale trade; it is even more difficult to observe accurately the backsliding of the economy of a vast country. In the case of India it is particularly difficult to observe accurately such counterprogress because the whole economic situation was subtly distorted during the British regime.

This distortion forced the Indian economy into a straitjacket which was tailored to conform to the needs of the British economy. For example, the trade of India was directed almost exclusively to Britain and it was so rigged that the British Isles were the main beneficiaries. Simultaneously the Indian economy, particularly its manufacturing sector, was steadily weakened. It was easy for the British to arrange this. Freight rates could be manipulated by the shipping lines, all of which were British at that time, so that it was expensive to ship manufactured goods from India to Britain and inexpensive to ship such goods from Britain to India. If one were to look at the British Board of Trade statistics for the year 1800 one would find a significant export to Britain of Indian-manufactured textiles. Then, turning to the corresponding statistics for the year 1900, one would find practically no export of Indian textiles to Britain and, on the other hand, a large import of British textile goods, a manipulation which brought immense benefits to the Manchester industrialists and their workers at the cost of the Indian textile industry and the workers of India.

Similarly for all manufactured goods, and any goods for which the British were seeking overseas markets, the terms of trade were pegged so as to be extremely favorable to the economy of Britain and detrimental to that of India. In the pre-First World War era, 70 percent of India's trade was with the British Empire, and 18 percent was with neighbors such as Burma, Afghanistan, and Ceylon, mostly in the form of petty over-the-border exchanges. Trade with the rest of the world, including such major traders as Germany, the United States, and Japan, accounted for a mere 12 percent of the total. These figures illustrate how India was preserved as virtually an economic adjunct of the British system.

In this connection British policy in regard to the textile industry of England and India is a case in point. In 1894, in order to balance the budget, the government of India imposed a general import duty at the rate of 5 percent *ad valorem*. However, the authorities were not about to let any competitive advantage accrue to the textile mills of India. They therefore imposed an equivalent excise duty on all cotton textiles manufactured in Indian mills. Thus, on balance, a situation was created which militated against the development of India's textile industry. It was the unforeseen interposition of two new factors which came to the rescue of the Indian industry. First, in 1905, Indian political leaders launched the *swadeshi* movement—the movement to buy Indian-made goods and to boycott British goods. The result was a sharp increase in the demand in India for locally manufactured textiles. Secondly, Japanese textiles were driving Manchester goods from the Indian market. In these circumstances, the British authorities acceded to the growing clamor in India for some "protection" for the Indian textile industry by creating a tariff board in 1923 and charging it with the duty of proposing measures that would stimulate the development of Indian industries. It was not until 1925 that the excise duty on Indian textiles was finally abolished so as to encourage the Indian mills to capture the indigenous market. Thus, it took just over thirty years to arrive at this modest degree of equity in regard to the Indian textile industry.

Gone indeed were the days when foreigners visiting India would marvel at the prosperity of such cities as Delhi. And not only of Delhi. Sir Thomas Roe, the first British ambassador to the Mogul court, when he arrived at Surat at the beginning of the seventeenth century, observed that the port city was one of goodly size, larger than London. The fabled wealth of India was no doubt based on a web of fact and fiction which had been woven by travelers from the time of the ancient Phoenicians. However, a British authority, studying the evidence contained in the accounts left by Western visitors of the seventeenth century, pronounces the verdict that "material conditions compared not unfavorably with those of contemporary Europe." [1]

Even down to more modern times, Indian industrial skills were of a high order. Take the example of shipbuilding. The East India Company was the London-based corporation in which was vested the exclusive right to trade between Britain and India until the year 1813. During the last twenty-five years of this monopoly, many of the ships of the company were built on the southwest coast of India by Indian shipwrights. Moreover, some of the ships in Nelson's line of the fleet were built in India by Indian experts. This flourishing shipbuilding industry could have made the move from the grand sailing vessel to the modern steam-powered ships had encouragement been given, and had the market not been preempted by the British for themselves. Indeed, without any such encouragement, in the early years of the nineteenth century a Bombay shipbuilder by the name of Wadia developed one of the earliest known seagoing steam-propelled vessels.

It is difficult to date precisely India's decline from a well-developed country to one which was backward. Certainly the internal political upheavals of the eighteenth century had something to do with the process, but quite rapidly a new stability was being established of which the main elements were the spreading Maharatta domains, the Sikh kingdom in the northwest, thoroughly Indianized fragments of the once Turkic or Persian aspirants to imperial power, and the continuance by wide consensus of the titular position of the Mogul emperor in Delhi as a symbol of a larger Indian unity. But these evolving internal arrangements were upset by a fresh set of traumatic experiences for the Indian people in the eighteenth and nineteenth centuries—the first truly foreign conquest of India. With the completion of the British conquest, India was sealed off from further development and had to accept a new and harsh economic system for the benefit of the new type of conqueror who insisted on remaining outside the system. This brought in its wake a plunge into despair, a

1. Percival Spear, *India* (Ann Arbor: University of Michigan Press, 1961), p. 159.

bleeding away of initiative and confidence, and a general falling off of all standards, including economic ones.

What of education in the country in the context of this new experience of subservience to an aloof conqueror? Never, within the memory of civilized man, had India's population been uneducated. Its people had given birth to such ancient texts of subtlety and literary merit as the four Vedas, widely regarded as being the earliest recorded scriptures of the Aryan people, the Laws of Manu, again among the most ancient of legal texts, the *Mahabharata* and the *Ramayana*, two celebrated Indian epics which have transmitted to much of Asia the mythology of India, and other treatises such as the Puranas—half myth and half history. This vast corpus of learning and the human imagination was added to by the writings of Buddhist monks, scholars, and poets. Even if one adds such literary giants as Kalidasa, Bhartrihari, and the prince who wrote *Shilappadikaram,* "The Ankle Bracelet," one has only touched some of the high peaks of an immensely prolific literature. It is said that when the Buddhists first went from India to China they required 145 mules to carry the learned cargo of texts across the mountains to what was, to them, a land in need of enlightenment.[2]

Thus the tradition of learning, writing, disputation, reading, meditation, and discussion was an ancient one in India. It gave birth to interesting systems of philosophy, many of which have flourished until today, and some of which have gained currency in the West as various forms of yoga and meditation. Other aspects of the lore of ancient India which have found audiences in the Western world have included such diverse collections as the fables contained in the *Panchatantra* and the sophisticated eroticism of the *Kama Sutra*. The continuity of learning has never been lost in India, and by the time the British took over the governance of the country, a significant fraction of the population had had an unbroken tradition of learning stretching back over several millennia.

The British brought a new language to the subcontinent (even though it could legitimately be regarded as a distant relative of the

2. Of the still far from fully explored richness of early and continuing scientific work, particularly in mathematics and astronomy, some indication is available from a publication titled *Census of the Exact Sciences in Sanskrit,* series A., vol. 1, prepared by David Pingree (Philadelphia: American Philosophical Society, 1970). This is but the first installment of a bibliography of writings on Sanskrit texts in the field, and on some of the texts themselves, and it contains some 1,400 entries.

Indo-Aryan languages of India). In the circumstances, the British made new demands in the educational field, opening both new opportunities and challenges and greater difficulties than ever before. Since the British did not bother to learn the Indian languages there had to be brought into being, between them and the people, a large body of Indians who could serve as interpreters so as to keep the British informed about day-to-day needs of the people, and who were also equipped to carry out the subordinate tasks of the administration. All this meant that increasing numbers of Indians had to be taught English. In 1835, after surveying the scene, Lord Macaulay, at the time a member of the Council of the Governor General of India, recorded his famous Minute on Education. That document reached the conclusion that it was necessary to set up a system of education that would teach the Indian people to be brown-skinned Englishmen. It was a typical overstatement of the case, based on the imperial necessities of the situation, and couched in terms which showed both Macaulay's ignorance about India and its own literatures, and his early Victorian belief that England was the fount of superior wisdom in virtually everything under the sun.

However, in some ways the decision was a wise one and it was welcomed by a new generation of Indians who were keen to modernize the country. Indeed, the influential Raja Ram Mohan Roy, over a period of years before Macaulay's Minute had been written, had espoused the cause of a modern liberalized education. He had the wisdom to perceive that the purely traditional forms of education were no longer adequate to prevent the country's falling behind the rest of the world, which was beginning to change radically as a result of the Industrial Revolution.

At the same time, it was a fact that the new educational policy cut the ground from under the indigenous educational institutions in the country. Many British writers had pointed out that all over India there existed village schools. C. L. Prendergast, a member of the Council of the Governor of Bombay, observed in 1821: "I need hardly mention that every member of the Board knows as well as I do that there is hardly a village, great or small, throughout our territories in which there is not at least one school."[3] These village schools gradually died out because of Macaulay's policy and the demand in the new India for a bilingual education, with the major

3. S. N. Mukerji, *History of Education in India* (Baroda: Acharya Book Depot, 1951), p. 45.

emphasis being placed on English. Later the British did take some steps to develop education in the local languages, but success was scant because the old momentum had been broken and the governmental demand continued to be for persons educated in the use of English.

No accurate statistics are now available for the amount of education among the population prior to the coming of the British, but in 1822 Sir Thomas Monroe, Governor of Madras, concluded on the basis of a thorough survey he had ordered that one school had existed in Madras province for every 500 persons. In addition many boys were taught at home, but he found that the education of girls was almost nonexistent. All in all, Monroe concluded that one-third of the boys in the age group of five to ten years were being instructed.[4] In 1901, after a hundred years of "enlightened" foreign rule, the figures were far lower. The national statistics compiled in that year showed a literacy rate for the total population of 6 percent, a sad commentary on the British effort in the field of education.

However, in British times, missionary societies and then the government itself established colleges to impart university-level education in the liberal arts and sciences. By the beginning of the twentieth century there were more than 200 colleges in the country. Similarly, private societies, including a large number of indigenous groups, and the government took steps to develop high school education. In 1902 there were 5,124 secondary schools with an enrollment of 590,129 scholars. The facilities for basic and primary education, however, remained woefully inadequate. In 1902 only a sixth of the boys of school age were enrolled, and the proportion of girls was much smaller.

The total educational picture included a trickle of Indians who were able to gain admission to Oxford or Cambridge, particularly in the nineteenth and first half of the twentieth centuries. Some brilliant men as well as a few oafish young blades went to those great universities, and a number of talented men, and a few women, went to London to qualify as barristers-at-law at the Inns of Court. Those who came back from England—"England-returned" to the envious, less fortunate, and usually less well educated—formed a glittering elite whom the other educated Indians, not excluding the Congress party nationalists, looked up to and secretly admired. To complete

4. *Ibid.,* p. 40.

this aspect of the picture, it must be mentioned that the thin layer of the England-educated in the country created a great gulf between the masses of the people whose lives, in all respects, went on outside the pale of Anglicism, and the new elite. There was a positive aspect even to this unfortunate social rift. A well-known Indian educationist, who was on the fringes of the nationalist movement, has recorded his views on this point as follows: "What the revival of Greek learning had done to usher in the modern age of Europe, that the spread of Western thought did in India. Religious and social reformation, romanticism, enlightenment or rationalism, historicism in outlook and patriotism as a principle of social motivation, were powerful impulses due to the study of European—more specially English—literature, philosophy, and science."[5]

In the next few decades very little was done to expand educational facilities, particularly for the great rural proletariat. The gulf widened between it and the Western-educated elite—one scarcely conducive to the development of a homogeneous community. The reason for neglect in the educational field was not just apathy in political quarters, but deliberate political policy. Witness the sentiments of alarm expressed by Lord Dufferin, Viceroy of India, in 1887. Writing in that year to the Master of Trinity College, Cambridge, he stated: "India is daily becoming a more difficult country to govern. . . . a highly educated and, in certain respects, a very able and intelligent native class has come into existence during the last thirty years, and naturally desires to be admitted to a large share in the conduct of their own affairs."[6] Previously, he had written to Sir F. J. Stephens: ". . . all the arts of radical agitation are coming into use in India. A Celtic Parliament is not likely to prove the home of wisdom, justice or moderation, but imagine a Baboo Parliament."[7] How wonderfully English was the noble lord! He poured contempt on the Irish, and by implication on the Welsh, and of course on the Indians, to whom he referred contemptuously as "baboos" (clerks). He made, however, many references in his papers to the high degree of intelligence and ability of the Indians, but it would seem that the British quite early decided that, in their own interests, it was wisest not to encourage expansion of the already growing class of English-educated people

5. Tara Chand, *History of the Freedom Movement in India* (New Delhi: Government of India, Publications Division, 1967), 2:446.
6. *Ibid.*, p. 508.
7. *Ibid.*, p. 507.

and consequently they went about the development of educational facilities in India at less than a snail's pace.

Those running the incipient but growing nationalist movement for freedom were helpless to alter this state of affairs. They could deplore the situation, but the resources to change it were not available to them. In 1919–20 an attempt was made to establish "national" colleges, but their degrees remained unrecognized and provided their graduates with no leverage in the job market. Expressing sorrow at this state of affairs, in October 1931, Mahatma Gandhi said to his audience in London at the Royal Institute of International Affairs: "Today India is more illiterate than it was fifty or a hundred years ago."[8] Increasingly the politically conscious elements in India felt that while the whole educational system required radical revision and a great push forward, these steps would have to await the return of independence to India, when the matter could be handled in the interests of the country, and especially of the masses who for so long had been given but a meager sliver of educational opportunities.

8. Mukerji, *History of Education in India*, p. 352.

Chapter Seven

THE PERIOD OF TOTAL CONFRONTATION
THE GANDHIAN MYSTIQUE

From 1919 onward, the spreading tentacles of nationalism and the well-organized British occupation of the country were locked in a battle for survival. One party had to give in, and the Indian nationalists were determined that it should be the British. However, the Raj still retained a sense of confidence that it could at least contain, if not turn, the tide which had everywhere begun to rise up against it. The Raj still had formidable assets: the princes, the rich landed class, the seemingly quiescent peasantry, and the large body of those who had by now tasted two generations of British patronage, jobs, titles, land grants, and other favors.

Many, in India and in Britain, were writing or speaking bravely of the permanence of the British Empire. The sentiment was deeply rooted, so much so that Joseph Chamberlain, a prominent British statesman, could proclaim that the British race was "the greatest of governing races that the world has ever seen." [1] It followed that the British Empire would prove to be permanent while others had come and gone. And yet, a bare seventy years after they completed their conquest of India, the British found themselves on the defensive. Not that they openly admitted this to be so—on the contrary, in spite of the promise given in Parliament on August 20, 1917, the British satrapy running the administration of India continued to think in terms of unending vistas of pomp and lordship for themselves. Furthermore, it was made to appear to be a sign of their confidence in their irreplacability that they were willing, though grudgingly and on their

---

1. Tara Chand, *History of the Freedom Movement in India* (New Delhi: Government of India, Publications Division, 1967), 2:472.

own terms, to share the upper, though not yet the uppermost, echelons of the administration with carefully selected Indians. In a sense
they had no choice in the matter, for Indians who were at Oxford or
Cambridge would offer themselves to the Civil Service commissioners
in London for recruitment to the nearly all-powerful Indian Civil Service. The answer of the commissioners was: "There is a competitive
examination, an extremely stiff one. Take it along with your British
colleagues from Oxford and Cambridge and see whether you can get
in." The brighter students at the universities took up the challenge,
and from 1867 on an ever-growing number of Indian names appeared on the list of successful candidates. From 1920 on the rate of
Indian recruitment rose, because the British conceded that eventually
this elite would be recruited on the basis of 50 percent British and 50
percent Indian. As more and more Indians joined the upper echelons
of the administration the appearance of partnership developed. The
reality was very different from the appearance. For the most part, the
Indians who were recruited regarded themselves as belonging to a
different establishment. Some even identified with the independence
movement. They were serving, not the British Crown, but the interests of their own country as well as those of their own egos, which
revelled in the prestige, comparative affluence, and power that went
with the positions they held. They accepted the alien harness with the
knowledge that it would prepare them to hold important administrative positions which would be entirely in Indian hands once independence was gained. So cooperation and partnership between Indian
and British colleagues in the services was largely superficial. There
was also another irritant: a considerable percentage of the British
personnel in the higher services resented the presence of Indians in
the top echelons, which had for so long been their exclusive preserve.
To a degree, although generally below the surface, the British-Indian
administration became a house divided against itself, and this too contributed to the eventual fall of the British system in India.

Though India had sent almost a million and a quarter of its men
into the field during the First World War, the officer ranks of the Indian Army were completely British: apparently no Indians were considered worthy of the "King's Commission." Clearly, this situation
could not continue after a war in which so much Indian blood had
been spilled. Under the force of these circumstances, the British government decided to start a very modest program of Indianization of
the officer ranks. The program was to cover only eight battalions, a

fragment no larger than one-thirtieth of the total force. Even in this small corner, promotions were much slower than in the rest of the army, and though the program began in 1920, in 1936 the highest-ranking Indians in the eight battalions were two officers who had just been promoted to the rank of major. When the Second World War broke out there were no Indian battalion commanders. In the army, right up to the threshold of independence, there was no partnership between British and Indian officers; there were no cases of junior British officers serving under Indian officers, while the latter always had stacked above them several rungs of British commanders.

What of the situation on the political front? Was Britain moving ahead in accordance with its promises? At the end of 1919 a small step forward was taken. A committee was created, under the chairmanship of a distinguished British jurist, Lord Hunter, and with a membership composed of four British officials, three of them jurists, and three Indian jurists. The committee was to inquire into the turbulence experienced and the atrocities committed earlier that year, particularly in the Punjab. In that northern province, not only had there been the terrible devastation at Amritsar, but the British had resorted on several occasions to firing at peaceful Indian demonstrators; they had also bombed people in the countryside, killing scores of farmers whose only crime was that they happened to be at work in their fields when the Royal Air Force planes streaked above them.

The appointment of the Hunter Committee was welcomed in India, particularly the fact that it contained eminent Indian jurists, although all of them were persons, as had to be expected, whose loyalty to the British connection and the British government was above reproach and had been recognized by the Crown in various ways. It was hoped that this committee could reach objective findings on the basis of a consensus; but loyalist and deferential to the British though the Indian members were, they found to their dismay that the attitude of their British colleagues was so supportive of the "administrative acts" of Brigadier Dyer and other members of the army in the Punjab that the committee's report divided along national lines. No agreement was possible between the Indian and British jurists even on clearly criminal acts, though the Indians leaned over backwards to be moderate. There could be no clearer example of the fact that India was now at war, in her own nonviolent way, with Britain. To further heighten Indian dismay, the House of Lords passed a resolution endorsing Dyer's action at Amritsar, and a public subscription drive was launched in Britain which collected a sum sufficient to provide for Dyer and his family. Thus, the wise political act of appointing the Hunter Committee ended in worse than a fiasco.

The primary consideration was the shape of the new constitution under which India would be governed following the high-sounding British declaration of August 20, 1917. That declaration, as we have seen, set out the goal of self-government for the Indian people. Expectations accordingly ran high. However, when Parliament adopted a new constitution for India, the Government of India Act of 1919, it was as if the ostrich had shrunk to the size of a hedge sparrow and given birth to a puny egg. The new constitution fully maintained the powers of the British viceroy to govern India, under the instructions of Whitehall, and to remain at the helm of affairs. The Central Legislative Assembly was expanded in membership and the number of elected representatives (146), was to be larger than the number to be nominated by the viceroy (106). However, the constituencies were so designed that it was overwhelmingly assured that of the 146 elected members more than half would be certain to support the official hierarchy. Therefore, there was no real passing of control in the legislature to Indian hands. Moreover, to render the situation even safer for the British, in a country with a population of over 300 million people, at that time the largest population of any country in the world (India then comprised not only its present territories but also the regions which are now Pakistan, Bangladesh, and Burma), the electoral roll mustered a mere 5 million qualified persons. To be enfranchised, a person had to pay a fairly large annual land revenue or be assessed for income tax. This meant that about 97 percent of the adult population remained disenfranchised. Thus the new constitution brought very little genuine political participation to the Indian people.

In the provincial administrations the electorate was the same restricted one, but in a certain respect the situation was a little better There were to be two categories of departments—"reserved" and "transferred." Among the reserved departments were those of justice and the police, which were to remain the direct responsibility of the British provincial goveror and his appointees. The transferred subjects, such as education, village cooperatives, and public health, regarded by the British to be of lesser importance, were to be administered by the Indians. They covered the vast field of potential nation-building that had been neglected by the British, who now wanted to pass on to others the responsibility for continued failure; and failure was a certainty because finance also remained under British jurisdiction. The ministers placed in charge of the transferred subjects were Indians, but they were nominees of the governor—tried and tested loyalists. Needless to say, none of them came from the ranks of the nationalists leaders or from among those known to be sympathizers of the movement for Indian freedom.

However, in the provincial legislatures there was the prospect of being able to legislate on matters relating to health, education, agricultural cooperation, and one or two other minor subjects. This gave the members of the provincial legislative councils some experience of law-making and a share, although a limited one, in the process of governing the country.

The puny advances enshrined in the new constitution amounted, in the eyes of most politically active Indians, to a mockery of the promise made by the British government on August 20, 1917. This state of affairs, taken together with the events of 1919, gave Gandhi his first opportunity for large-scale, nonviolent agitation against the foreign ruler of the country. He announced that in no circumstances would there be "cooperation in any shape or form with this satanic government." Early in 1920, at a special session of the Indian National Congress, his program was adopted by an overwhelming vote and amid an outburst of great spontaneous enthusiasm, whereas the pleas of those few who advocated cooperation with the government were brushed aside. Gandhi's program was based on the principle of noncooperation with evil. This was to be expressed through resignation from government appointments, an exodus from the schools and colleges of the British-sponsored educational system, and a boycott of the forthcoming elections to the legislative bodies created by the new constitution. The reaction of the British was one of scorn and injured pride, tempered in some cases by a sense of bafflement.

In the country, the movement created among Indians a new mood of self-awareness, an inner independence that made the British presence an unpleasant intrusion. Acts bolstered this new mood: Sir Rabindranath Tagore, Nobel laureate in literature, renounced his British-conferred knighthood. Large numbers of other Indians of renown renounced their medals and titles. Of course, the British could find others who would accept their honors, but they realized that renunciations by persons who were held in high esteem in the country signified that British influence and prestige were suddenly on the wane. There was a considerable exodus from educational institutions, which caused hardship to the students concerned, but these acts of self-sacrifice again bolstered the new mood in the country. Though not all the nationalists boycotted the elections, the most prominent ones did, again creating some feeling in the country that British institutions were no longer an essential element in the life of the Indian people.

In addition there were mass marches and peaceful demonstrations against the authorities. Gandhi insisted that these must remain scrupulously nonviolent, for he conceived his movement to be a moral protest and not an angry confrontation. However, early in 1922, in the province lying to the east of Delhi, a mob of demonstrators became unruly. Unable to contain themselves, they burned a rural police station, resulting in twenty-two police deaths. Gandhi was aghast at this incident. He immediately called off the whole movement, though it continued to create great problems for the British authorities, not least because Gandhi had been able to rouse the enthusiasm of the most prominent Muslim leader in the country, Shaukat Ali, and the two had made extensive tours together. The authorities were relieved at the unexpected demise of the movement, and soon regained their imperial hauteur. Instead of respecting Gandhi for having responded so scrupulously to the Chauri Chaura incident, they took his action in calling off the movement as a sign of weakness, and promptly arrested him and sentenced him to six years' imprisonment for "incitement"—a typical example of the maladroitness of authoritarian governments. This action infuriated the Indian people who, nevertheless, adhered almost without exception to Gandhi's principles and refrained from committing acts of violence against the government.

There is something enigmatic about those few persons whose courage and perseverance are such that they are able to influence the course of history. The enigma exists because one realizes that in addition to their obvious good qualities these persons possess an indefinable capacity to move whole societies. Enhancing the Gandhian enigma was the fact that the methods he chose were both so lofty and so archaic. They were lofty, especially in the sphere of politics, in that throughout he insisted that the end never justifies the means, that any form of freedom for India achieved by methods that were not morally impeccable would be worthless; and he would have none of them. They were archaic in the sense that Gandhi was intuitively and deeply acceptable to a people in whose ancient traditions is grounded the concept of *ahimsa,* or nonviolence, as the most sublime height to which man can aspire. It is to be remembered that Hinduism is not a religion based on dogma, though, of course, there are within its fold subsects that have provided ritualistic dogma for their followers. In its essence, Hinduism confronts man with the lonely task of working out and achieving his own individual relationship with the Universal Self, the Godhead, or the Absolute. Engaging in this lonely venture, one is to bear in mind that all forms of life, not just human life, are sacred and are to be treated with respect. Faced with the harsh necessities of survival, an impoverished society tends frequently to fall away from these ideals; but they never completely die out and continue to be practiced by the more enlightened. When a leader arises who is able to command respect, as Gandhi did, and he calls attention to these ideals while clearly exemplifying them, his call invokes in those who have been brought up in the tradition of nonviolence a fervent hope that they might be able to rise to the demands of the leader. Gandhi brought these ideals very close to the people by embodying them himself to a quite extraordinary degree.

He came from an upper-middle-class family that had held the virtually hereditary position of chief executive in a princely state named Porbandar, in western India. He could have succeeded to this important position, one far beyond the reach of the average person in India. However, though a shy child, he was ambitious, and decided to try to rise even above his father's station. He persuaded his family to send him to London to study law. He qualified as a barrister in 1889 and returned to India, where he started a legal practice; but he soon moved to South Africa (1893) as the legal adviser to Indian merchants there. In his new abode he was confronted with a form of subjugation much more onerous and horrifying than what existed in his own country. It was in this context that Gandhi developed and applied the technique of noncooperation in his attempts to secure humane and fair treatment for people of Indian origin and blacks in South Africa. He achieved some success (1914), which eventually led—after he himself had left South Africa—to the Cape Town Agreement of 1927, under which people of Indian origin were to be treated as any other settlers in South Africa, except that an agreed number of them were to return to India.

In 1915 Gandhi returned to India to use the techniques he had developed in South Africa in the fight for freedom. His first decision was to give up all the trappings of a British-trained lawyer and to live as a humble village Indian. He dressed in the simplest clothing, sometimes clad only from the waist down, and wearing toe-hold sandals on his bare feet. Always a vegetarian, his diet now was restricted to the simplest fare: lentils, rice or unleavened bread, and vegetables. As to drink, he was a "water totaller," regarding even tea or coffee as too strong and harmful for the body.

The Indian people venerate persons who are able to subdue normal passions and desires. Being without the guidance of dogmatic teachers or prophets—and rejecting dogma as being at a lower level of teaching—the guidance of the enlightened and tranquil person whose life reflects high moral disciplines and values is of more significance than in most other societies. Moreover, Gandhi, by adopting the way of life of the vast bulk of the people of India, when it was well-known that he could have remained one of the relatively wealthy, created a profound impression on them, and within about four years of his return to India he had acquired, by common consent, the rarely bestowed and highly prestigious title of "Mahatma," the Great Soul, an appellation awarded only to persons of very high spiritual attainments.

When this man, who had become one of them, called upon the people to join with him in mass peaceful noncooperation with the British, and talked to them of *ahimsa,* it was as if the very spirit of India, the spirit which the people revered but were themselves unable to grasp fully, had come alive and was beckoning irresistibly to them. So, for the first time in modern India, there arose the extraordinary phenomenon of a mass movement based on the application of ancient traditions and the deeply ingrained sentiments and values of the people.

As Gandhi developed, two features became increasingly salient in his spiritual life. One was that he became more and more devout within the Hindu tradition. The second was that he became less and less dogmatic, less and less exclusive in his Hinduism. For example, he made it a practice at his daily evening prayers to read not only from the *Bhagavad-Gita* or other Hindu texts, but also from the Koran and the Bible. In this way he presented his largely Hindu audiences with an eclectic view of religion and called for respect for all other religions.

However, to many Indians who were not Hindu, particularly to the sectarian Muslims, this technique of Gandhi's, based though it was on eclecticism and tolerance, smelled too strongly of Hinduism and became a barrier between them and the national movement. Thus the very strength of his appeal to *ahimsa* and nonviolence became for some Muslims a snare; not for those who were secure, such as the Muslims of the northern Punjab and the North-West Frontier Province, but for those minorities in middle India who saw themselves, mistakenly, as likely to be swamped by a resurgent Hinduism. There were also the more sophisticated Muslims, among those educated in the Western manner, who found the insistence on the Hindu tradition in Gandhi's life a danger signal for the future.

On the other hand, for a few years powerful Muslim forces in the country appeared to fall under the sway of the Gandhian mystique. In 1920 Gandhi made statements in support of the Khilafat demands of a large section of devout Indian Muslims. These demands led to a movement of protest against Allied moves after the First World War to dismember the Turkish empire and consequently to downgrade the Sultan of Turkey, who was still widely regarded as the Caliph of Islam. Gandhi espoused this movement, and the Muslim leadership responded by electing him, a non-Muslim, president of the All-India Khilafat Conference of November 1919. But this interesting combination of devout Muslims and a Hindu saint did not prevent the dismemberment of the Turkish empire or the creation of League of Nations mandates which were interpreted as instituting Western rulership over much of the Arab world. The Indian Muslims dropped Gandhi, having decided that he was, for their purposes, ineffectual. Not only did they drop him, but a few years later, Muhammad Ali, a leading Khilafat leader and a close friend of Gandhi's, made highly disparaging remarks about him. For example: "However pure Gandhi's character may be, he must appear to me from the point of view of religion inferior to any Mussalman [Muslim], even though he [the Muslim] be without character."[2]

It is a dismal commentary on the human situation that the unity of ths Indian subcontinent probably would have been ensured if the leadership of the national movement had fallen into the hands of a doughty Northern Punjabi Muslim and a Hindu of the type of Subhas Chandra Bose, men who believed in violent struggle. If such leaders, drawn from the various communities, had gotten together

2. R. C. Majumdar et al., *Struggle for Freedom* (Bombay: Bharatiya Vidya Bhavan, 1969), p. 336.

and fomented armed rebellion against the British, the resulting comradeship in arms and the struggle shoulder to shoulder for freedom would have further cemented the unity of India. But so powerful was the Gandhian mystique that this route to unity and freedom was closed off.

Perhaps the Achilles heel of the Gandhian movement was inevitable. Without an appeal to karma, ahimsa, dharma, and so on, which were entirely benign Hindu concepts, Gandhi would probably have been unable to rouse the great majority of the masses of India to participation in a movement for freedom. India was caught in a dilemma created by its own background and by its own circumstances. In choosing Gandhi as its political strategist and paramount leader, instead of Bose or Nehru, it served the cause of its own division, which was being sedulously advanced by the British as well as by the inevitable power seekers and obscurantists among the ranks of some of the religious communities. Gandhi's religious appeals—high-minded, and inspiring though they were—had the effect of putting the communities of India into their separate religious compartments. In this century the country would have benefited far more from leadership with a secular outlook, but this was not to be.

A nonviolent national revolution was, nevertheless, a miracle, especially one on the scale on which it developed in the vast Indian homeland, and Gandhi's achievement remains a most remarkable one. At the same time, by appealing to traditional Indian values, Gandhian strategy tended to keep the people embedded in their traditional molds and inhibited the development of a fairer and more mobile society. To some degree Gandhi perceived the nature of the problem and started a movement against "untouchability," the scornful and demeaning treatment given socially and economically to persons belonging to the lowest orders of Indian society. He dramatized his work against untouchability by renaming the untouchables Harijans, or the children of God. However, just to pillory untouchability fell far short of the sociological needs of the Indian people, particularly in the modern world. The whole class structure was holding Indian society back, keeping it from developing in an egalitarian democratic manner; and against the caste system per se Gandhi did not inveigh or carry out a campaign. In almost all of the various communities of India, including the higher social ranks of the Muslims, this divisive and degrading caste-ism prevails. In an oblique way, Gandhi's strengthening of traditional values also strengthened caste values, thus helping to preserve barriers and compartments which fragment Indian society and prevent its vigorous growth.

The profound problem of caste-ism is not faced in Gandhi's autobiography, *The Story of My Experiments with Truth*. In this fascinating and powerful work there are two fleeting references to the caste system, more or less in the same vein. For example, after his return from Britain on completion of his law studies, he wrote: "I fully respected the caste regulations about excommunication. According to these, none of my relatives, including my father-in-law and mother-in-law, and even my sister and brother-in-law, could entertain me; and I would not so much as drink water at their houses. They were prepared secretly to evade the prohibition, but it went against the grain with me to do a thing in secret that I would not do in public." [3]

So, though a strong opponent of untouchability, Gandhi remained largely within the social constraints of caste. Perhaps it was his judgment that, in view of the extreme conservatism of the Indian people, he could go no further and had to be content with wresting small gains in the struggle for social justice. However, the result of his tactics was that he often strained relations in the intricate patchwork of Indian society which, over some four thousand years, had developed the essential rudiments of mutual respect and the practical capacity of the various groups to live together in spite of sectarian and other differences. In this connection, it is relevant that he frequently held up to the country the vision of the return of *Ram Rajya,* or the rule of Ram. To him this was a vision of a return to virtue, the absence of corruption, a high public morality in all respects, and a blissful society, but to many of his listeners his repeated cries of Ram Rajya sounded like calls to set up a Hindu theocratic state, for Ram was an incarnation of Vishnu, a member of the supreme Hindu trinity. This would not suit the complexities of India.

However, under Gandhi the Indian people did succeed in making the brightest jewel in the British Crown much less dazzling, and more and more of a liability to the foreign ruler. Furthermore, the Indian National Congress party alone, of all the political parties in India, under Gandhi developed a coherent movement for independence; it alone paid the price in mass imprisonments, scores of deaths, the sequestration of property, constant surveillance, and economic hardship such as the loss of job opportunities. To this party alone, on the

3. M. K. Gandhi, *The Story of My Experiments with Truth* (Boston: Beacon Press, 1957), pp. 90–91.

Indian side, must be awarded the credit for the freedom which eventually returned to the country. The so-called "Moderates," the Hindu Mahasabha, the Muslim League, the princes, and even the Communists and other firebrand revolutionaries, were not in the vanguard in the fight for freedom. Indeed, many of them played along with the imperial rulers, and then came storming in greedily in the last stages to get a share of the cake for themselves.

Two incidents from Gandhi's life, one involving a close friend of mine, Diwan Chaman Lall, frequently a member of the Indian Parliament and a Congress party leader just below the topmost echelon, and the other involving me personally, will convey to the reader something of the strength, humanity, and charm of this complex and extraordinary man. One of these incidents was recorded by Chaman Lall as he reminisced near the dead body of Gandhi on January 30, 1948:

I had been sent by Jawaharlal Nehru to Lahore, along with Sri Prakasa, to try to restore peace to that city.[4] When I came back after seeing the most dreadful sights of little children with their noses or ears mutilated with knives and a woman raped and then a dagger thrust into her private parts . . . I related these stories to Gandhiji in the same room in which his dead body now lay. I looked at my watch. I had taken an hour and a half of his precious time and suddenly realising this, quickly said: "I am sorry I have taken up so much of your time. I will come again another time and tell you the rest of the story." All the time Gandhiji did not utter a single word. As I walked to my car Gandhiji's Secretary ran after me to say that Gandhiji was going to the Muslim camp in the old Fort and wanted me to accompany him. I said I would do so gladly realising that Gandhiji, having listened to my stories of atrocities committed on the Sikhs and Hindus, wanted me to see the other side as well. When the procession of our cars passed the narrow gate, we went right round to the Eastern Wall when an irate Muslim angrily opened the door of Gandhiji's car and nearly assaulted him. Just then I looked toward the entrance and saw a lorry and a *gadda* [bullock cart] blocking the entrance. I turned the cars toward the entrance in order to get the obstructions removed quickly lest Gandhi should be assaulted or his progress obstructed. While I was doing this I saw Gandhiji getting out of his car and beckoning to me a few paces away. When I got to him he was ready to address the assembled crowd which was in a very hostile mood. Gandhiji said to me: "My voice will not carry" (there were no loud-speakers), "and I will whisper each sentence in your ear and I want you to shout it out to the

4. This was in mid-1947, shortly before the partition of India.

assembled crowds." And he put his arm round my shoulder. The first sentence Gandhiji uttered was:

"For me, Christians, Hindus, Muslims, Parsis, Sikhs, are brothers and the sons of the same God."

There came loud cries of "Utter falsehood" (*Sab jhooth hai*)—all lies.

And then I saw the miracle happen. As Gandhiji proceeded, unperturbed, although I was bristling with anger that anyone should have the hardihood to say such a thing to Gandhiji, I saw the miracle happen. Presently Gandhiji said: "I have come to tell you that I will bring peace to Delhi or else I will perish in the process."

That must have been the moment when Gandhiji decided to fast unto death. Hardly had Gandhiji uttered these words than the audience broke out shouting: "Gandhiji Zindabad"—Long live Gandhi. And some were kissing his hands and some touching his feet. The same hostile crowd had been converted by Gandhiji's gesture. . . . It was indeed a miracle that I saw performed before my very eyes.[5]

The second incident, and one within my personal knowledge and experience, occurred at the end of March 1946, in New Delhi. Gandhi had come to Delhi at that time to be available for meetings between the Indian leaders and a three-man United Kingdom cabinet mission sent out by the Attlee government in Britain to work out a formula to govern the transfer of power from Britain to India. Among those who had come to Delhi to aid communication between the parties was a British Quaker leader, Horace Alexander. Horace was a friend of Gandhi's, and was held in respect by two of the three visiting members of the British cabinet: Lord Pethwick Lawrence, the chairman of the mission, and Sir Stafford Cripps, its most dynamic member. Meanwhile Horace and I had struck up a friendship, and he accepted my invitation to stay at my house as my guest for the duration of the Delhi discussions between the leaders.

In spite of his great poise, Horace was feeling the strain of his efforts; the more so because the talks were not going too well. It seemed to me that a certain avenue of solution was not being explored, and I could see why the Congress leaders felt they could not themselves draw attention to it. In these circumstances, I sketched out a constitutional plan and gave it to Horace. He thought it had some merit and was worth trying on the parties. I typed up the draft plan, and Horace and I took it to two major Congress party leaders—Vallabhbhai Patel, later Deputy Prime Minister, and Rajen-

5. From an unpublished article by Diwan Chaman Lall, in the author's possession.

dra Prasad, later President of India. At this point Horace came down
with a virus. On the third day of his illness he had a very high fever
(106 degrees) and he agreed to a doctor's being called in. News of
the gravity of his illness spread to the leaders, and that evening, at
about eight, Gandhi arrived at our house, without warning, accompanied by C. Rajagopalachari (later the country's first Indian Governor General before India moved from being a dominion to a full-
fledged republic), and a few other Congressmen and women.

By the time of Gandhi's arrival, the doctor had been and gone and
had found that the thermometer on which so dangerous a temperature had been recorded was inaccurate, and that, in fact, Horace's
temperature was about 101 degrees. There was no cause for alarm,
but Gandhi did not pay a purely formal call, busy though he was. He
sat with Horace for a half hour or more, all cheerfulness and laughter. He joked pleasantly at Horace's expense. He also talked about
the work of the cabinet mission. He did not feel very hopeful about
it, but was willing cheerfully to go on trying to get to a solution. He
also mentioned my draft plan, of which he had heard from the other
leaders, though he himself had not yet seen it. He asked Horace a
few questions about me, a newcomer to political negotiations.

I listened in to most of the conversation of the two men and as
Gandhi left I talked with him. He was open-minded about a solution,
which was his way of conveying that perhaps my plan might be the
answer, or point the way to an answer. But the dominant impression
he left on me was of warmth, humanity, good humor, laughter, and
an underlying sharpness of perception. There was no tenseness, and
no pretensions, no standing on a pedestal. How different from most
leaders!

Chapter Eight

A LOOK AT NEHRU AND JINNAH

The case for Muslim separateness in politics was first expressed by Sir Sayyid Ahmed Khan in the second half of the nineteenth century, and was later given philosophical content by Sir Mohammad Iqbal. That these men had been favored with knighthoods by the British government is an indication of the close relationship between Muslim separateness in India and British policies of divide and rule.

Sir Sayyid hailed from a Persian family which had been settled in India for several generations but had not become fully assimilated. It is plausible also that his family, courtiers at the Mogul court in Delhi, resented its loss of prestige, perquisites, and some power, and yearned for the impossible restoration of the old empire, at least in part of the country. Sir Mohammad Iqbal was the scion of a Hindu Brahmin family recently converted to Islam. In his early adult years, he was passionately nationalistic and wrote beautiful verse about the unity of India from the Himalayas and the Hindu Kush to Cape Comorin, the southern tip of the subcontinent. He was thus pro-Indian in the broad sense, and a fervent opponent of British rule. However, with advancing years his outlook narrowed, he drifted to a sectarian position, and came to feel that the Muslims should be allowed to express their destiny in a separate state.

The question still arises as to whether the division of India, which these two men in particular promoted, was the best way of giving the various groups of residents in the Indian fourth of the world a fair chance to express themselves. There cannot be a single view on this matter. On the one hand, one has to accept what has happened, even if the meddlesome hand of the outside ruler helped to shape events. The present Indian people, those who are citizens of the now truncated India, accept the division as a fact which will continue unless at some time and in some form it is succeeded by a loose confederation, or simply a cooperative arrangement, in which the various states of the subcontinent, while not losing their separate identities, embark on a course paralleling the Common Market.

The real creator of Pakistan was, of course, Muhammad Ali Jinnah. He and Jawaharlal Nehru could have averted that development. Why did they not do so? And why did they choose separate paths?

Jinnah was a Muslim, but he was a modernized secular person, by no means narrow-minded, bigoted, or predominantly sectarian. This characteristic is illustrated by an incident which occurred when, as a young lawyer, he paid a brief visit to Cairo in the company of Tej Bahadur Sapru, another distinguished Indian lawyer, who was a Hindu. They went to see the pyramids and were riding on camels led by an Egyptian fellah. Jinnah said to the Egyptian: "I am Muslim." The fellah looked at him doubtfully and said: "Recite the Kalma," which is the major prayer for Muslims prescribed in the Koran. Jinnah was unable to do so accurately! Whereupon Sapru, a learned Brahmin, recited the Kalma perfectly. The fellah turned to him, a smile on his face, and said: "You are the Muslim, not the other."

M. A. Jinnah, the suave Western-educated lawyer, a Muslim whose near forebears had been Hindus, was always uncomfortable with the semi-naked, seemingly primitive Gandhi. He found Gandhi far too archaically Hindu a personality to be congenial. He could not see himself in close relations with a man whose whole life was governed rigorously by religious tenets. Jinnah would have related much more naturally to a modernized Hindu who was willing to concede the need to come to terms with reasonable Muslim opinion.

He was a most unlikely leader for a sectarian political movement. In the winter of 1935–36 he toured the Punjab to assess the political situation there. Dr. G. C. Narang, a prominent Hindu leader, gave a dinner party in his honor at which Jinnah was to meet a group of Hindu and Sikh leaders of the region. It so happened that Dr. Narang invited me to this party. There were about twenty of us, all Hindu and Sikh leaders, except for Jinnah and myself. Jinnah, urbane and immaculately clad in a Saville Row suit and other appropriate finery, smiled wanly at the local leaders dressed in long tunic shirts, loose trousers, and local footwear. All the Sikhs were turbaned, and looked rather archaic with their long greying beards. Jinnah and I, also in Western garb, must have looked like men who had strayed onto a strange planet.

There was a lively political discussion. At that time Jinnah had not espoused the idea of a separate sovereign state for the Muslims. In his impeccable English, he was arguing with razor sharpness in favor of constitutional safeguards which would ensure that the Muslims, especially of North India, would be able to run their affairs, and that their culture and religion would thrive. He was not a person to be satisfied with vague concessions. He demanded effective but limited power for the Muslims, but was not asserting that this could best be achieved by separate statehood. From time to time he would talk with me about London, about current writing, about my own work, and about certain people we knew in common. (At that time I was a young member of the ICS, into which I had strayed after being at Oxford.) Jinnah and I struck up an easy relationship, so much so that though as the guest of honor he was expected to mingle with the other leaders, he insisted that at the dining table I should sit by him. His host was on one side and I on the other. Jinnah spent much of the time at table talking to me rather than to Narang. He was interested in life in a wide sense. He took to me because I too was a westernized Indian and much more congenial to him than the others in the room, who were much more typically Indian. If he had had his way, he would have been content to see India ruled by modernized Indians, rather than by persons claiming power as Hindus, Muslims, Sikhs, Christians, or Parsis. This would have been much more in line with his personality.

In terms of modern education, a scientific outlook, industrial venturesomeness and broad professional skills the Muslims, as a group, lagged far behind the Hindus. It was impossible to construct a modern society on the base they presented. Weighing them down even deeper into a morass of stagnation was the heavy accumulation of superstition and ignorance which closed the eyes of the masses. In this last respect there was little to choose between the Hindu and the Muslim masses. However, among the Hindus, a modern secular leader in the tradition of the late nineteenth- and early twentieth-century reformers—Raja Ram Mohan Roy, K. C. Sen, the Tagore family, Ranade, Dadabhai Naoroji, and Gokhale—would have had enough of a demographic base to create at least the beginnings of a modern society. But this opportunity was lost by the adoption of the humane but regressive Gandhian way. The tragedy of both major communities in India was that they were still so backward, still so shackled, that it was easier for leaders to appeal to regressive attitudes of mind and behavior than to forward-looking, developing, adventuresome, and humanistic aspects, in the largest sense of the term.

Jinnah had in 1916 entered into a deal with Tilak, then the most important leader of the Congress party, to the effect that Muslims would be conceded separate electorates—introduced by the imperial troublemakers, Lords Minto and Morley in their constitution of 1909—in a free and independent India. My own assessment is that Jinnah was not himself wedded to the notion of separate electorates, but was bending to the prevailing wind in yielding to regressive tendencies. After all, he was a politician. At the same time, there was not enough innovativeness on the part of the Congress party. Their position had simply been: "No separate electorates." Since this had got them nowhere, they conceded separate electorates, hoping to resolve their problems with articulate sectarian opinion. It was an impossible hope; separate electorates were far too divisive an arrangement to be made part of any solution aiming at improving relations among the various communities. A wise course would have been to propose to Jinnah a dual system of electorates through which Muslims would enter the legislatures in the country. Half the agreed number of Muslim members might have been elected to the Indian Parliament and the state assemblies by purely Muslim constituencies, while the other half could have been elected by general constituencies. Jinnah could have been persuaded to give this dual system a chance so as to see whether it obtained satisfactory results for the Muslims. Besides, much more should have been made of the point that in general constituencies the Muslim voters could, in many parts of the country, ensure that candidates regarded as hostile to the Muslims were defeated. By no means was this point brought sufficiently into the negotiations. The trouble was that Jinnah was bargaining with congressmen who were themselves often religious zealots, Hindu zealots. This made him very wary.

This brings us naturally to Jawaharlal Nehru, the man who could conceivably have turned the situation around. Nehru was totally modernized. He was a Brahmin, whereas Gandhi was a Vaisya (a member of the trading caste). Yet, paradoxically, it was Nehru who was completely liberated from traditional religion, while Gandhi was steeped in it. Nehru had been educated at Harrow—Churchill's old school—and Trinity College, Cambridge, from where he went to one of the inns of court in London before returning to India as a barrister. Although thus equipped for a thoroughly upper-middle-class life, he was quickly drawn into national politics—in which his father was already prominent—and came immediately under the influence of Gandhi.

This was extraordinary because by training and temperament Nehru, a thoroughly modernized person with a secular outlook and possessing the fineness and sensitivity of an artist, seemed to be totally different from Gandhi. Yet, in a sense, precisely this explains why he fell under Gandhi's spell. Nehru had the uncomfortable feeling that his many years abroad, his education before that under an English tutor, and his upbringing in a family which had consciously westernized itself in almost all details of daily life, had cut him off from India. He at once saw that Gandhi was deeply embedded in those traditions and so had what he lacked. Besides, though thoroughly Indian, Gandhi had learned to communicate powerfully in English and was steeped in much of Western thought and literature. These qualities facilitated the relationship between the two men. Furthermore, Nehru realized that if he was to work in the political field with the Indian people, he must imbibe some of the Indianness which Gandhi possessed. He was far too eclectic and secular a person to espouse Gandhi's religiosity, but that was not the sum total of Gandhi's Indianness. There was his simple way of living, his ability to enter into the life of the people by taking up such a basic occupation as spinning cotton thread, and his participation in a variety of traditional customs and events. All this attracted Nehru, and he wanted it for himself, at least in sufficient degree to establish full communication with the people.

Could Nehru have done otherwise? Could he have become a great leader in India while remaining primarily a westernized personality? In this regard a comparison with Jinnah cannot be made because Jinnah never aimed at succeeding in the role of a mass leader. His leadership was expressed in a certain austere aloofness and dignity, a demonstration of intellectual clarity which won respect, and a reputation for great forensic skill. His intellectual and debating skills had impressed British cabinet ministers and viceroys. This fact was well publicized and contributed to his attainment of an unrivaled position among his fellow Muslims. They accepted him as great because he had shaken the seats of the mighty and could be relied upon to do so again.

Also determining the type of leader required by the Muslims was the success achieved by the British in wooing them away from the mainstream of Indian life by bestowing upon them favors, gifts of land honors, jobs, and other preferments. By and large the Muslims were willing to cooperate with the British. This was true in the Punjab—now the heartland of Pakistan—where the Unionist party, the most powerful political group, maintained a close understanding with the British. It was indeed true of the all-India Muslim party, the Muslim League, which had been founded in close collaboration with the British administration and which continued various forms of collaboration with the British, including cooperation throughout the Second World War. These styles of Muslim politics in India did not call for the emergence of a leader identified with the masses. Thus Jinnah could lead and still remain an aloof Western figure.

Nehru, on the other hand, had to come close to the Indian people if he wanted to play a significant political role. He succeeded in doing so and became a mass leader, loved by the masses of all faiths and able to win their affection and loyalty. At the same time, Nehru was the idol of the young intelligentsia who appreciated his urbanity and his abilities as a writer. His autobiography, which appeared in the mid-1930s, created a great impression among the educated of all communities. I remember how a number of my Muslim friends and acquaintances, on reading the book, remarked that this was the leader that India needed and, by implication, not Gandhi and not the Muslim extremists (at that time Jinnah was not one of these).

Since I got to know Nehru well before he became Prime Minister, and continued thereafter to maintain a very good relationship with him, I feel I should mention certain other aspects of his personality which were relevant to his style of leadership. One was that Nehru believed, intuitively, that decency and fineness were the best foundation for personal as well as political relationships—the two were not put into segregated compartments. He never harbored petty feelings about people. He would never stab anyone in the back, though he would not rescue those who fell because of their own folly or overreaching ambition. In other words, each person had to take responsibility for his own deeds, political and personal. These qualities were not easily understood by many of the Congressmen around him who expected from him a kind of feudal loyalty, noblesse oblige, and backscratching, practices which he despised.

Another characteristic of Nehru's was his tendency to lean on a dominant figure. His own father was such a figure, and Jawaharlal was an only son. The unique Gandhi was also a dominant figure, and it came quite naturally to Nehru to lean on him. When Gandhi died, Nehru wept and said: "We shall feel sad and lonely. . . . We used to run to him for advice and guidance whenever we were confronted with any great problem or when we felt ill at ease or in doubt. There is none to advise us now or to share our burdens. . . . All of us felt that we were his children."[1] He meant all this. Gandhi's death was a staggering deprivation for Nehru.

This characteristic of dependence on Gandhi diminished Nehru's stature, great though it was, in his relationship with Jinnah. The Muslim leader knew that behind Nehru was the shadow of Gandhi, and that shadow dismayed Jinnah. It made him feel that in the last analysis he was dealing not just with Nehru but with the traditional Hindu Mahatma. The real tragedy is that in the final phases of the negotiations with the British—when the cabinet mission was in India, and thereafter—Nehru was much more his own man. He did consult with Gandhi, but not as frequently as he had done in the past, and he did not necessarily follow the advice of the Mahatma. But Jinnah had no proof of this, and even if he had learned it, by now he was riding very high and it was possible that he was not in full control of his own tiger.

All this was unfortunate for India, for here were two men—Nehru and Jinnah—who could have developed a loosely unified entity on the subcontinent, perhaps a confederation or a new type of cooperative arrangement, involving all the people of India. Most prominent Muslims, among them many who later served in Pakistan in important positions, would have been assuaged and found such a solution much more appropriate and natural. Besides, it would have preserved a certain highly important balance in Asia that has been greatly impaired by the division, and this impairment, this weakening of the subcontinent, was precisely what the British were aiming at because from it they hoped to profit. How unfortunate that the leaders of India fell into the trap.

In 1946, while the cabinet mission was in India working, largely through the wily Stafford Cripps, toward a divisive plan for the country, I had a number of private meetings with Nehru on India's future and on possible constitutional formulas. At one of them he said to me in deep sorrow and real anguish:

---

1. *Jawaharlal Nehru's Speeches* (New Delhi: Government of India, Publications Division, 1949), 1:51.

"I don't understand why Jinnah felt he had to leave us. We respect him and he would be of immense importance in India and in our counsels. He was one of us, in the Congress, fighting alongside of us. We expected always to have him on our side. I do not know what happened. Was it that long absence in England? He became out of touch. Maybe he felt that the Congress would not let him have the place he deserved, so he took umbrage. It's such a pity.

Incidentally, these remarks were made following a Nehruvian verbal outburst against Vallabhbhai Patel, later his Deputy Prime Minister. It was an outburst of impatience about Patel's general point of view. Later Nehru grew to appreciate and admire Patel's great contribution to the country and to the fledgling administration of independent India.[2]

Jinnah would have said that he had to leave the Congress because it wasn't Nehru's side but Gandhi's side, and Gandhi was much too obscurantist for him, conjuring up a picture of Hindu Raj and the Vedas, which were out of step with his own secularized modern outlook. The irony is that this modern outlook was also Nehru's. Things could have worked out differently had Gandhi dropped from the scene, through retirement or otherwise, in, let us say, 1932–33, and if Nehru or Bose had asserted himself to his fullest. Either of them, or the two jointly, could have worked out an understanding with Fazl-i-Husain, the Muslim leader before Jinnah, or with Jinnah himself.

It would not have been easy. Nehru was an out-and-out secularist, and in keeping with this attitude, he would have said to Jinnah: "Why does anyone need safeguards—the Muslims, the Brahmims, the Christians, the Parsis, the Sikhs? We are going to have a thoroughgoing democracy, and we will see to it that everyone has a real opportunity to develop and be himself or herself. As for the Muslims, I will see to it that they in particular are safeguarded in the sense that all the educational opportunities which they have neglected are made easily accessible to them, and that their language and customs and all their rich gifts to the Indian tradition are fully maintained. I myself have benefited from them greatly, and I will see to it that they remain a great co-sharer in this country of ours."

But Jinnah, though in his own way an equally secular person, came from a minority community. He demanded safeguards of a

2. *Ibid.*, p. 56.

more specific character than Nehru tended to speak about. He wanted to be sure that in the Parliament of India the Muslims would be guaranteed sufficient representation—at least a third, though by population they were entitled to about a fifth. Nehru would have eventually agreed to this, as well as to other specific demands, provided the fabric of Indian society was not rent down the middle, and equal opportunities for all groups was the agreed objective.

However, time for a reasonable solution was running out. In a situation characterized by mounting pressures all around, reason has little chance to win. Moves and events that can stir the passions of people become the ones that sweep societies; and all too often the passions aroused are those of hate, greed, and lust for power. Still, wise leadership could have roused other enthusiasms.

Certainly, not all the Muslims in India favored extremist trends. In the Punjab, a powerful and dominant group of Muslims did not want the partition of the country; and even less did the doughty Pathans of the North-West Frontier Province want it.

Chapter Nine

TWO AGAINST ONE

As the third decade of the twentieth century advanced, the economic situation in Britain deteriorated, mainly as a result of internal causes such as the growing power of unions to call strikes and the lack of competitiveness in British industry. In addition, the boycott of British textiles by a large section of the Indian market was adversely affecting the exports of the Manchester mills. These circumstances were not conducive to generosity in Whitehall in regard to Indian problems. Perhaps they explain why the British seemed willfully to throw away a major opportunity to brighten their image in India and to lay by for themselves future dividends not only of good will but of more advantageous economic relations.

The opportunity arose in the shape of the impending review of the unpopular and niggardly constitutional reforms of 1919. The British government was about to appoint a commission to inquire into the working of those reforms and to make recommendations for the future of India. In India it was widely felt that much would depend on the composition of the commission, and it was the expectation, even of the moderates and collaborators, that a mixed commission, composed of British and Indians in equal proportion, perhaps under a British chairman to give the ruling power an edge, would be announced. The hope was that the recommendations of such a commission, even if the Indian members were none other than men such as Sir Tej Bahadur Sapru, Sir Fazl-i-Husain, Sir Akbar Hydari, and other knights of the empire, might conceivably be acceptable to some sections of the Congress party and thereby save the country from a great deal of turmoil and perhaps strife.

However, to the dismay of all shades of Indian political opinion, the commission appointed in 1927 by the British government contained not a single Indian. Besides, its chairman, Sir John Simon, was known to be a dry-as-dust English lawyer with no understanding of India and little sympathy toward any non-British people. The only interesting member of the commission was Clement Attlee, at that time a junior member of the British Parliament on the Labour benches. Attlee was Prime Minister of the United Kingdom when Britain did eventually transfer power to Indian hands in 1947. The appointment of a purely British commission of inquiry into the constitutional situation in India was regarded as an insult to the Indian people. The Indian National Congress Party sharpened its opposition to government, and many other voices were raised denouncing the commission and deploring its composition.

Instead of dominion status for India, with which the Congress would have been largely content, there was a strong sense that only complete independence from Britain and her empire would now be adequate. Young Jawaharlal Nehru and Subhas Bose were among the influential voices raised for independence. The older leaders, such as Nehru's father, Motilal were more cautious, but the current was rising against them.

However, Motilal Nehru and others made a last attempt at conciliation by maneuvering to show that there was still a very significant body of opinion in the country that would accept a dominion-status constitution. The group hoped that its maneuver would influence the Simon Commission, bad though its composition was, to recommend the granting of dominion status without any further delay. These Indian leaders convened an All Parties Conference which proceeded to write a dominion-status constitution for India. At this All Parties meeting, the Muslims were well represented, as were all other communities and groups, and the various shades of political opinion.

Jinnah himself sat on the sidelines, to keep his options open. In 1929, the year following the publication of the report of the All Parties Conference, he enunciated a fourteen-point demand which, he said, represented the minimum that the Muslims could accept, and he insisted that the Muslim League alone should be regarded as the vehicle of Muslim opinion in the country. In other words, no Muslims were to be permitted to join the Congress, the moderates, the left-wing parties, peasant parties—such as the Unionists in the Punjab— or new liberal formations! On the face of it, this preposterous notion was a complete negation of the most basic democratic freedoms and indeed nothing short of group exclusivism of the fascist variety. Besides, the fourteen points contained at least one substantive excess. This was that in all the state legislatures, including, for example, Orissa, where the Muslims were 3 or 4 percent of the population, a third of the seats were to be reserved for them. However, there were several good ideas in the fourteen points. For example, they provided India with a federal constitution, with safeguards for the cultural, religious, and other rights of the minorities. Had there been some possibility of give-and-take, instead of a take-it-or-leave-it ultimatum, the fourteen points could have been a working basis for constructive discussion among the various parties.

Jinnah's insistence that the Muslim League alone represent the Muslims infuriated some influential and large sections of Muslims. Those in the Punjab had their own party to which Hindu and Sikh landowners, mostly peasants, had been attracted. In the North-West Frontier they had joined the Congress in large numbers and clearly wanted to retain close ties with the other communities in the country and to have none of the strict compartmentalization that Jinnah was demanding. If only Jinnah had been more reasonable and claimed that the Muslim League was the major but not the only voice of the Muslims in India, communication with other groups could have gone forward. One is forced to the conclusion that though Jinnah had not, at this stage, espoused notions of complete separation of the Muslim community, there was a strong bent of uncompromising exclusiveness in him, a religio-political blinkering that was extremely uncomfortable with cultural and social diversity. One ponders man's narrowness, and wonders with Shelley: "Must hate and death return?"

Though Jinnah was not able to draw all the Muslims under his banner, he had a powerful ally and helper: the British administration, which more and more saw the Congress as the great threat to the empire that might sweep the British out of India. The British were absolutely right. More and more, therefore, continuing and intensifying tactics which they had employed for a half-century or so, they allied themselves with the opponents of the Congress. They thanked God for Jinnah, and hoped that he would succeed in bringing the Muslims into his increasingly anti-Congress fold. Thus nationalist India was now fighting on two fronts. This combination of British favoritism and the increasing narrowness of vision of Jinnah and his ilk was the rock on which efforts to preserve the unity of the country were ultimately to founder.

True, other factors were moving in the same direction. One, which I have already alluded to at some length, was Gandhi's heavy emphasis on traditionalism. But it was apparent, and should have been apparent to Jinnah and others, that Gandhi was advancing in years and that by his side were Jawaharlal Nehru, Subhas Bose, and others who were completely secular in outlook, and who would have been determined to give the Muslims not only a fair share but even a place of great honor in the country. A way would have been found to accomplish this even if these secular leaders and their growing following had found it distasteful to think in terms of preferment for persons who happened simply to be born into a particular faith. There is no doubt that if India had remained united there would have been a much more relaxed attitude toward people of all creeds, as well as to those who did not hold with any particular creed. It went against the grain of the modernizing Indians, no matter what might be their nominal or real faith, that Jinnah should keep harping on the Muslims, their rights, their demands, their goals; just as it went against the grain that the Hindu Mahasabha kept up its talk of Hindu Raj and the glories of India in the pre-Islamic era.

The modernized Indians of course retained a sense of pride in the traditions of their country, whether pre-Islamic, Islamic, or thereafter, including even the era of the British in India, when great persons such as Ram Mohan Roy, Dadabhai Naoroji, Gokhale, Badr-ud-Din Tyabji, Gandhi, and others had come forward. There was pride in the long and colorful heritage of several thousand years. To these Indians, growing in numbers, it was distasteful that so much emphasis was placed on sectarianism by certain leaders. But the more this was distasteful to the nationalist Indians, the more savory it was for the British, who saw in these sectarian demands their own salvation as the rulers of India.

As if to pour salt in India's wounds the two-volume report of the Simon Commission, a highly pedantic and bureaucratic document, discovered new areas of divisiveness in the country. It was wrong to think of the problem simply as one between Hindu and Muslim, in which the poor minority Muslim was putting up a brilliant fight for his rights; nor was the problem being aggravated just by the presence of other communities such as the Sikhs, the Christians, and the Parsis. Then came the great discovery, which was that the Hindus themselves were only a fragment of what had hitherto been thought of as "Hindu India"; there were scores of millions of untouchables and tribes living outside the "Caste Hindu" fold, and seats in the legislatures would have to be reserved for these groups. The aim was clear—the hated Hindu, who made up the great bulk of the population of the subcontinent, was to be reduced to a voting minority in his own country, and then, of course, Gandhi and his Congress would not be in a position to claim that they represented India and the world would be safe for Pax Britannica. Indians who read the Simon Commission report, as I did when a youngster, were puzzled: had they misunderstood their own country? Had they dreamed the unity within diversity? Was caste all that important—did one ask the caste of one's friends, or their religion? It soon became clear: The foreigner was carving up the ancient land of India again, telling the world that it was no entity at all, and encouraging some sons of the soil to do the same.

What helped the British was the failure of Indian leaders to agree on Jinnah's fourteen points. However, the British too had a problem. The Simon Commission had gone too far in its cynicism about the unity of India, even farther than a decent Englishman could uphold, and the Viceroy of India at the time was just such a decent Englishman—Lord Irwin, later, as Lord Halifax, Churchill's foreign minister in the British wartime cabinet, and for some time the British ambassador in Washington. He persuaded Whitehall to let him make a conciliatory statement that might become the basis of reopened discussions between the Indian leaders and the British government. On October 31, 1929, a Gazette Extraordinary was issued at New Delhi to give publicity to the Viceroy's statement. It was to the effect that he had been authorized by His Majesty's Government "to state clearly that in their judgment it is implicit in the declaration of 1917, that the natural issue of India's constitutional progress, as there contemplated, is the attainment of Dominion Status." [1]

This attempt at conciliation by Irwin was dangerously near to being an insult to the Indian people. No one had ever doubted that the 1917 statement meant that India was to achieve dominion status. The new statement, however, sounded as if the British government itself only just woke up to the meaning of the words solemnly pronounced twelve years earlier. It was as if for twelve years Britain had slept on its promises. People asked whether this meant that after another dozen or fifteen years the British government would again

1. *India in 1929–30* (New Delhi: A Government of British India publication), Appendix II, p. 468.

solemnly state: "His Majesty's Government emphatically affirms that its intention remains unaltered." They decided that Irwin's statement of October 31, 1929, was little better than humbug. As a result, at the next annual session of the Indian National Congress, held at Lahore in December 1929—a session that roused young university students, including myself, to new heights of hope and enthusiasm—the crucial resolution establishing complete independence as the goal of the freedom struggle was adopted. Following that resolution, January 26 was declared Independence Day, and it was celebrated for the first time, in spite of governmental prohibition, in 1930. Since then each year India has celebrated January 26 as its independence day, and when the Indian Constituent Assembly adopted its republican constitution in 1949, it was decided to bring it into effect on January 26, 1950, since which date this important day has been renamed Republic Day.

The Congress party did not confine its activities to the declaration of January 26 as Independence Day. Gandhi, in particular, realized that the country had to demonstrate to the British government that it had the determination and the will to assert its right to independence. How was this to be done? One answer was to plan secretly for a sudden and unpublicized—to the administration—demonstration of will through meetings, boycott of government offices and institutions, and nonpayment of the land tax. This course Gandhi rejected. He was equally adamant in rejecting any form of harassment of British personnel in India, and he was of course opposed to resorting to violence, such as the destruction of government property. He decided on a course of action which eschewed secrecy, violence, subterfuge, and personal pettiness. On March 2, 1930, he addressed a letter to the Viceroy, Lord Irwin, beginning "Dear Friend," in which he announced to the head of the British administration, as well as to the people of India, that within a few days he would break the law that imposed an excise duty on common salt. He explained that it was patently unjust that salt, a basic necessity for life, should be taxed by the British government, because this meant that even the poorest of the poor were subject to a heavy imposition on their frugal daily diet. Gandhi went on to say that it was morally wrong that the manufacture and distribution of salt was a government monopoly and he asserted the right of the people to make salt for their own needs. He announced to the Viceroy that in light of these circumstances, he had decided to break the salt laws by going to the sea and making salt for himself.

What a beginning this was to a nationwide movement for independence! He exhorted all Indians to join with him by making salt for their own needs. True to his word, on March 12, 1930, accompanied by almost eighty of his followers, Gandhi set out from his *ashram* on the outskirts of Ahmedabad to walk to Dandi, a small village on the western seaboard of India, north of Bombay. The march was planned as a fairly leisurely one, so as to give the country time to gear up to follow his example.

The British were faced with a sticky problem, the central fact being that by now Gandhi's stature in the country, in spite of the divisive tactics of the authorities, was enormous. A decision to arrest him, especially when he was out to defy a controversial law, would be fraught with serious consequences. In spite of Gandhi's own loyalty to nonviolence, there could be uprisings in various parts of the country that would overtax the capacities of the local administrations. While the governments at Delhi and London weighed the possible alternatives, Gandhi's march continued, and each day the number of those accompanying him swelled, until a stream of thousands of people was on its way to Dandi. As Gandhi's party approached its destination, groups of people all over the country were making their own preparations to manufacture salt.

In certain circumstances, salt can be extracted quite easily from rocks which contain it or from sea water, but it cannot be found in fresh water. In their enthusiasm, however, the people of Lahore decided to march some four or five miles to the river Ravi and to make salt from its waters! Clearly no salt could be made on the banks of the river, but the British authorities became so perturbed that large contingents of police were detailed to stop the people from carrying out their plan. The crowds were broken up by repeated police forays with long iron-headed staves; hundreds were arrested and jail sentences followed, all because of the absurdity that salt could be made from fresh water. Similar scenes occurred in many other parts of the country.

Accompanied by his swelling surge of adherents, Gandhi completed his march in twenty-four days, symbolically made salt, and was duly arrested along with many of his companions. In the whole country there were continuous demonstrations of enthusiasm, peace-

ful marches, and peaceful boycotting of shops that sold British goods
or alcoholic beverages. It was difficult for the administration to cope
with this upsurge of enthusiasm. It was completely peaceful—there
was no attempt at violence, and none of the demonstrators carried
arms of any kind. Nevertheless, on about thirty occasions the authorities opened fire on these groups to disperse them. Hundreds of
people were killed, thousands injured, and within a year and a half
more than a hundred thousand persons were jailed, resulting often in
loss of income, jobs, sequestration of property because fines were un-
paid, and other hardships. Apart from Gandhi, those jailed included
Nehru and his father, Vallabhbhai and Vithalbhai Patel, Abul Kalam
Azad, Ansari, Rafi Ahmed Kidwai, Rajendra Prasad, Abdul Ghaffar
Khan, many other leaders, and tens of thousands of people. Popular
support swelled for the Congress because the charge against it was
simply peaceful activity for the freedom of India.

There followed a couple of constitutional conferences in London,
convened by the British government and euphemistically called
Round Table Conferences; euphemistically because the calling of
these conferences was preceded by debates in the British Parliament
which led to the invitations being so rigged as to make agreement
among the Indian representatives absolutely impossible. All kinds of
loyalists, who had served the British government in various capacities, such as Sir Mohammad Shafi and the maharajas of numerous
states, were brought in as prominent leaders; new categories of invi-
tees were devised, such as the "European Community," the "landowners," and the "industrialists." The net result was that those who
were to represent the major political forces would be swamped by a
host of political nonentities whose only claim to fame was their
willingness to do as bid by the British.

The first of these conferences was a fiasco because by far the most
important political force in the country—the Indian National
Congress—refused to attend a gathering that was so clearly a misrep-
resentation of the aspirations and demands of the Indian peoples.
Gandhi attended the second conference in London as the sole representative of the Congress, but it would have been wiser for him not
to have gone. Another factor in the situation was the adverse temper
of the British to the whole notion of India as an equal partner in the
Empire, or the Commonwealth, as it was coming to be known. The
Tories and Labourites alike roundly criticized Irwin's statement of
October 31, 1929, as having gone much too far, and Ramsay Mac-

donald, the Labour party leader, and for some time Prime Minister, fell in line with the others. On the basis of the rigged representation at the London conferences, he too came to the conclusion that the Indians could not possibly agree among themselves. This was not justified. There had been a striking development in 1927–28. During this period at an ad hoc leaders' conference, Jinnah had agreed to mixed electorates, an abandonment of the vicious separate electorates which the British had introduced, with the help of their henchmen, in 1909. This was an immense gain for the cause of the millennia-old synthesizing forces and trends in Indian society. At last, sanity was reemerging, but by the clever diversionary move of the rigged London converences, the British were able to regain the initiative. The agreement of 1927–28 was overwhelmed by fresh "events," and the British proclaimed that they would have to devise a formula for India—exactly as they wanted to do—setting out a political compromise between the various Indian communities. This so-called Communal Award subverted the progressive agreement of 1927–28, embraced Jinnah's fourteen points, and returned India to the road to division and dissension.

Meanwhile, Jinnah withdrew from the scene. Disgusted with dissensions and the failure of the agreements of 1927–28 to come to fruition, and unable to understand and cope with the vast mass movement for Indian freedom Gandhi had succeeded in launching—in which as many as 12,000 Muslims courted nonviolent arrest and went to jail—he retreated to London and opened up a law practice there. Perhaps he hoped to be elevated to the judicial bench of the Privy Council. He had also been irked by the fact that in two prize Muslim provinces, the Punjab and the North-West Frontier, the Muslims had not taken kindly to his leadership.

So, temporarily, the leadership of the Muslims in India passed to others, among them the extraordinary figure of Mohammad Iqbal, a truly magnificent poet in Urdu and Persian. We have already caught a glimpse of him: the scion of a Kashmiri Brahmin family fairly recently converted to Islam. In the beginning, like all other rational, educated Indians, Iqbal was a staunch nationalist dedicated to the cause of India's independence. One of his earlier poems, "Hindusthan Hamara" ("Our India") was a great favorite at national gatherings. It was filled with sentiments expressing the unity of the Indian subcontinent. However, as he grew older his health deteriorated markedly, and this coincided with his emergence as a person who thought in terms of a sectarian society, where all views are formulated within a tight framework, accepted by everyone. Since Iqbal's great poetic talents had placed him in the vanguard of the cultural and political awakening in the north, his conversion to sectarianism roused a great deal of attention. The British took smiling note and knighted the poet. The extreme Muslims flocked round him, which certainly flattered him, and in 1930 he was named president of the Indian Muslim League.

In his remarks in December of that year, after the tremendously stirring movement for freedom which Gandhi had inaugurated with his salt march, Iqbal propounded the then novel idea that the destiny of the Muslims of northwest India lay in a separate sovereign state, whether in or outside the British empire. He had decided to turn his back on the richness that would be offered by a diversified society, and to choose instead a single-outlook one. In the context of India's history, this represented a profound failure, a profound lack of capacity and energy to share in a multiracial, multifaceted, multiphilosophical, multireligious, multilingual, and multicultural society. Perhaps such failure was inevitable among some people and some groups, but when it infected so great a poet as Iqbal, who gave it the imprimatur of his artistic genius, then the cause of India's synthesizing civilization was in danger.

For some years, no significant adherence to Iqbal's view was expressed. No one of consequence seemed to take it seriously. Nevertheless, it could not be totally ignored, and it certainly gave the British a comfortable feeling because it confirmed that there was a current in Muslim thinking that would rule out joint action with the rest of the country.

Indeed, the mid-1930s saw, in a sense, the height of British power in India. They had succeeded in putting down two large mass movements, those of 1919–24 and 1930–33, mounted by the Indian National Congress against them. The leadership of the Congress had been dispersed in various jails, and there was the appearance of quiet in the land. Moreover, there were more governmental careers open to Indians, and this acted as an inducement to cooperation with the authorities. Much of the Muslim community was either opposed to the Congress, or rather to the Gandhian accent in the Congress, or was willing to accept the lead of the British, particularly as many new job openings were reserved for them. Sitting in his retreat in London, Jinnah is reported to have said, with his characteristic contempt: "The Muslims do not accept my views, for they take their orders from the Deputy Commissioner [the British district officer]."[2]

The superficial apathy in the country did not accurately reflect the spirit of the Indian people. That spirit was expressing itself quietly in a number of activities relating to nation-building. Indian entrepreneurs in and around Calcutta and Bombay were adding to the industrial base of the country. The cotton textile industry had become particularly strong, so that now the Indian market, which had been such a standby for the Manchester mills in the United Kingdom, was almost entirely served by the output from Indian mills. Indian shipping companies were beginning to challenge the dominance of British lines in the trade to and from Burma and Africa. The Tata plant was the biggest steel plant in the British empire. At the same time, the lucrative tea and coffee plantations and gardens, the jute and burlap mills which enjoyed virtually a monopoly position in world markets, and the incoming industrial multinational giants, such as Lever Brothers and Imperial Chemical Industries, were all in British hands, and were, with very few exceptions, making very high profits.

There were no signs that the British edifice in India was cracking. Confidence was characteristic of all British actions, especially regarding the constitution for India which the British Parliament adopted as the Government of India Act of 1935. This anomalous British gift to India conceded the substance of legislative and administrative power in the provinces, as the states were then called, to elected Indian politicians. But there were two important limitations. First, the franchise was still very sparingly given; the voters were the moneyed and landed classes, both in various ways tied to the administration, and amenable to its blandishments and pressures. This ensured that even if the majority of those returned to the provincial legislatures were broadly in the nationalist camp, there would be a strong element present that would voice the views of the administration. And, in some provinces, such as the Punjab and Assam, as well as Sind, and perhaps Madras, the British could hope that the government-making majorities in the legislatures would consist of their trusted friends. The second limitation on the working of democracy (with a small electorate) in the provinces was that the British governors—appointed by the viceroy with the approval of the British government in London—were vested with reserve powers under which they could

2. Durga Das, *India from Curzon to Nehru and After* (London: Collins, 1969), p. 155.

take over the full governance of the provinces, including legislative functions. Not only would this provision frequently be put into effect but even when it was not invoked its very presence meant that the so-called "popular governments" in the provinces had to be constantly mindful that they were not getting out of step with the views of the British government in London. This was devolution of power in two straitjackets; a stifling arrangement.

At the federal center, power remained firmly in the hands of the British viceroy and his appointees. There was no cabinet, but instead an executive council, composed mostly of senior British members of the top satrapy in the country—the Indian Civil Service. These heads of departments of the government were all tried and able in their way—manipulators of the political factors in the country. They knew very well how to balance, provoke, reward, cold-shoulder, instigate, praise, and humiliate, let alone how to prevaricate, that most useful tool of irresponsible authority.

The first elections to the provincial and the central legislatures were held in 1937. The mood of the British showed that they had been mesmerized by their own propaganda. In Delhi, they affirmed, and the Anglo-Indian press loudly proclaimed, that there would be a return by landslide of persons who were proven legislators, or retired administrators, or persons used to exercising authority, such as large landowners. As to the Congress, they were sure that that seditious body would fare very poorly.

Congress was unsure of itself. Its metier was opposition to foreign authority, not cooperation with it. The leaders were of two minds about the party entering the contest. The final decision was that the elections would be contested, but the big names in the Congress party would not run. The results of the election were a staggering blow to both the British and to the Muslim League, now very much the "Jinnah Party." Of the eleven provinces, Congress won outright control of seven, and soon after of an eighth (Sind). The Muslim League did not win even one of the three provinces in which a government dominated by it could have been returned to power. In the Punjab, the Unionists crushed the League and the Unionist party consisted of persons drawn from all the three main communities in the province—Muslims, Hindus, and Sikhs. In the North-West Frontier Province, in which the proportion of Muslims was over 90 percent, the Congress roundly defeated the League.

While the League was electorally humbled, it was not dead. And

Jinnah knew how to take the political initiative. In spite of the poor electoral showing of his party, he proposed to the Congress that in the provinces where the Congress had won the elections, coalition governments should nevertheless be created consisting of the Congress and the League. In terms of parliamentalry practice this made no sense, but Jinnah's demand did make political sense: if the Congress accepted it, he would have established his claim that the Muslim League represented the Muslims and that he had achieved his goal that the League must share in the exercise of power in the country. Many Indians regret that the Congress did not see matters in this way. Had it done so, the demand for Pakistan would probably not have been adopted as the major platform of the League. The Congress turned down Jinnah's proposal, and he then was free to tell his followers, and the Muslims in general, that the "Hindus" were determined to exclude the Muslims from a share of power. It did not matter very much, to those who had come to believe that Jinnah represented the best interests of the Muslims, that the Congress did include Muslims in the governments it set up, and that the Congress government in the North-West Frontier Province was overwhelmingly Muslim in composition. The Muslims in the Frontier Province and those Muslims who had supported the Congress in the elections were strongly opposed to capitulating to Jinnah. But they underestimated his ability to strike back at them.

In the minds of such leaders as Nehru and Gandhi, particularly Nehru, there was another very important issue involved. This was that the Congressites, whether Hindu, Sikh, Muslim, Christian, or Parsi, had fought the British and were now entering the governments in the provinces not to cooperate with them but to make it clear that the Congress could run these administrations and that the British had better quickly complete the process of handing over all power to Indians. In brief, they were entering the government with a view to completing their task of obtaining freedom for the country. On the other hand, a very large proportion of the members of the Muslim League, including those who had succeeded in winning seats in the legislatures, were men who had collaborated with the British, and had often been their stooges. How could the Congress form coalition governments with such people? Would they not wreck the movement to complete independence? The presumption that they would do just this was strongly indicated by past actions. As to the risk that Jinnah would exploit the refusal of Congress to cooperate with him, Nehru's attitude was: "Let him try it. The people, the Muslim people, will not be fooled by him." But Nehru was wrong. Secular himself, a great admirer of much of Muslim culture, and a person who was comfortable with such Muslims as Syed Mahmud, Rafi Ahmed Kidwai, and Abul Kalam Azad as he was with few others, he assumed that the Muslim masses would accept his word that there would be no difficulties at all if the Congress exercised power in the provinces and, eventually, at the center. Loved though he was by countless Muslims, Nehru miscalculated. The masses were too primitive to understand that his word meant more than the words of those who were attempting to rouse religious fears and prejudices.

When World War II broke out, the Congress said to the British: "If you want us to cooperate in opposing Hitler and fascism, then give us immediately the status of Canada, and we will join wholeheartedly in the struggle, but we cannot be put in the position of simply carrying out the behest of London, of not being able to share in decision making, of being reduced to the position of suppliers of cannon fodder." The Viceroy, the Marquis of Linlithgow, was not pleased at the prospect of losing the support of the Congress governments in the provinces, but he was a strikingly unimaginative, rather dull-witted person, and did nothing to push London along a sensible path. But the major blame for the lack of movement in the direction of a decision which would have served the allied cause wonderfully well has to be awarded to London. The main reason for the attitude of the British government was the psychology of successful self-deception. The British had made the crucial declaration of intent to free India as early as August 1917. They did nothing to implement the declaration once World War I was over, and by the mid-twenties they had deceived themselves into dismissing the declaration as an aberration which must be forgotten. When Viceroy Irwin resuscitated the declaration in 1929, London was deeply offended that it was being asked to face up to the forgotten aberration. In 1939, therefore, the Congress demand for dominion status was most unwelcome: "Oh please, please don't bring that up! Why must you? The princes, the Muslims, the peasants, the outcastes are staunchly behind us. Need we worry about those weak-kneed caste Hindus?" Besides, there was a new war with Germany, and Whitehall had no time for India.

While the attitude of London was pig-headed, offensive, and smacking of duplicity, it was one thing for the Congress to make clear to the British that genuine all-out cooperation would obviously require a new relationship of equality between India and the other main partners in the Commonwealth, and quite another matter to refuse all cooperation unless there was an immediate transfer of power to Indian hands. Congress took the latter course—with the full approval of Gandhi, Nehru, and the other leaders—and it was the wrong move. Its basic flaw was that it showed an incapacity on the part of the Congress leadership to put itself in the shoes of the British. No negotiation can move forward unless one can do so. To tell the British bluntly that the Congress would pull out of the provincial governments unless dominion status was immediately conceded was to hold a revolver to the head. It was bound to be interpreted as a dastardly attempt to take advantage of the weakness of the other side. At the same time, it must be remembered that in the fall of 1939 few could have predicted that Hitler was as powerful as he turned out to be, and that he would soon overrun practically all of continental Europe. The Indian leaders assumed that the British and the French, with overt or even covert American assistance, would have no difficulty in holding the Germans in check, and that the war would not necessarily become a major conflict. This was a miscalculation on the part of the Indian leaders. With one or two exceptions who thought differently for tactical reasons, they had no sympathy for Hitler or for fascism. Nehru in particular had joined with the Western European socialists and others in roundly condemning both nazism and fascism.

However, in weighing the demands of antifascism against the demands of national freedom, the Congress party should have come to the conclusion that the Nazi danger was the major immediate threat to the world, and should have unreservedly thrown their weight into the struggle against Hitler and his allies. Had they done this, it is difficult to see how the British, at least by the time that Hitler was marching victoriously across Europe, could have refrained from bringing the Congress leaders into important seats in the government. After the middle of 1940, the British desperately needed all of India's efforts in the war against the Axis powers.

The Congress decision, however, was to pull out of the provincial governments, a decision they put into effect almost immediately following the outbreak of the war, at the beginning of September 1939. The by now long relationship between the Congress and the British—both the London government and the Delhi viceroyalty—had been a stormy and bitter one, with some brief periods of smoother prospects. The refusal now of cooperation in the war effort brought to the fore the anger and hatred of the British and the least responsible attitudes in the Congress. As the war progressed into 1941—with Japan coming in on the side of the Axis—and 1942, Britain's situation became increasingly desperate, but the attitude of Congress remained the same as at the beginning of the war.

The people of India were angered by the fact that the British had not made overtures to the national leaders and had not offered them the substance of freedom. The atmosphere was not improved when in 1942, at the time the Japanese were advancing in Southeast Asia and had actually bombed Calcutta, Churchill hastily flew Sir Stafford Cripps, a member of the war cabinet, in from London with the hope that he could persuade the Indian leaders to lower their demands. This might have worked if Cripps had come and said: "Friends (and being a Quaker he could have used this style, which Gandhi liked), tell me, what would you accept at this very difficult juncture for all of us?" There should have been some humility, and some appeal to the good sense of the Indian leaders. This was not at all what happened. Cripps came with an absurd cut-and-dried offer of dominion status after the war was over and at that time the provinces were to be given the option to secede from India if they so wished. In other words, the break-up of India was to be virtually encouraged by this wartime Churchillian scheme. Besides, what confidence could there be in deferred British promises? No one had forgotten the fate of the promise made during World War I. Cripps, the poker-faced vegetarian, did his best with Gandhi, talked haltingly of mysticism and yoga, and gave his personal word that this promise would be carried out. Gandhi smiled his toothless smile and then with an uneasy laugh said: "No thank you, Sir Stafford. I would not be able to get even a child to accept this kind of offer." Later, he described the Cripps offer as a post-dated check on a bank on the verge of liquidation.

By now the Congress was split. The vast majority remained with Gandhi, committed to nonviolence and mass civil disobedience as the only acceptable method of fighting for freedom, but a younger group, led by Subhas Bose and Jayaprakash Narayan—of the latter we will hear more later—wanted a stronger program, one that did not exclude the use of violence. They became known as the Forward Bloc. They, as well as many others in the country, were furious with Cripps and his typically British offer. It was an empty handout, in their view. The country seethed, except for a fairly large number of Indians who had joined in the war effort. Millions were recruited for the defense services and hundreds of thousands of others joined the ever-swelling ranks of the bureaucracy. And, as we have already observed, the Muslim League was cooperating wholeheartedly with the British. One can hardly blame the British for feelings of gratitude toward the Muslims.

Cripps came and went like a single swallow in the late winter, with no impact on the Indian scene. It was a charade by the Churchill government surrounded by a cloud of scathing fulminations by him against the Congress and its leaders, some of which he passed on to Washington. He was particularly offensive about Gandhi, and there was the usual claptrap about the "martial races of India in the north" (i.e., the Punjab and the North-West Frontier) being solidly with the British, and who did the spindle-legged Hindu Brahmins think they were, anyway?

All this precipitated another and more determined phase of the national movement, under Congress leadership, for the freedom of the country. The argument was that what the British refused to give, we must now take for ourselves and then show the world that we were strongly opposed to Nazism and Fascism and, at the same time, that we had had enough of the imperialism and colonialism of the British and French and others who had joined in the unseemly scramble during the nineteenth century to subordinate large parts of the world. We would settle on honorable terms with all the nations of the world, in the interests of world peace and the equality of peoples and nations all over the globe. If this sounds too idealistic, let the reader ask himself whether the usual language of power politics is really acceptable to him or her, and whether Gandhi and Nehru can be faulted for wanting to raise international relations to a more humane plane of conduct.

In August 1942 the Congress roused itself to action and gave the country the slogan, directed to the British: "Quit India! Quit India!" It was a powerful cry, and the country was deeply stirred by it; but essentially the population was divided into five groupings. First, there were those—the determined Congressites, numbering several hundred thousand, with many times that number of active collaborators—who joined in the action. They made speeches, marched in processions, repeated the battle cry of "Quit India," obstructed trains, and some of them overstepped the limits of the Gandhian rules and cut telephone wires and removed railway lines: all these activities had been declared illegal by the authorities, including the assembly of more than four persons anywhere. All the leaders and over 60,000 activists were almost immediately jailed by the authorities, and demonstrations were dispersed by the use of force. At least another 200,000 or 300,000 took part in these illegal activities but managed to escape detention. Over and above these activists were the legions of more passive sympathizers, who carried messages, revealed governmental plans to the activists, harbored "wanted" individuals, contributed money, food, and other necessities, and in other ways helped the movement. These numbered several million, and included large numbers of people in the governmental services, from the highest to the lowest.

The second group, an even larger one, consisted of interested observers who wanted the freedom campaign to succeed, at least to some degree. They would have liked to have seen the authorities forced to relent and to bring the national leaders into a genuine cabinet form of government. This would have given India its richly deserved place in the sun.

The third group consisted of those who had, in various ways, joined in the war effort. It included not only the several million in the defense services, but also those who had joined the numerous other government agencies that had been created or greatly expanded. In addition there were many people—contracting, buying, selling, manufacturing, and transporting—who were making money out of the war. The economy was working feverishly, lots of money was being printed, and millions of hands were stretched out to grab as much of it as they could for themselves. All told, for millions the war was a bonanza.

The fourth group consisted of the anti-Congress forces. The main component of this group was the Muslim League, and in it too were some of the large landowners and the princes or maharajas and nawabs. This group was the special favorite of the British and all the British apparatus in India. Its members did not want the British to concede anything in its dealings with the Congress. If the authorities and the Congress were to come to terms, this group would suffer: Politically, they would be shunted aside to make room for the far larger and more influential Congress party; economically, they would no longer find the new jobs coming to them.

The fifth group consisted of those in the rural areas who remained unpoliticized. They were not unaffected by the war: prices had gone up, scarcities had developed, and before it was over several million of them were to die of starvation in Bengal. Their lot was deteriorating but, on the whole, they waited patiently for defeat or victory and hoped that in either case things would begin to look up again for them.

Churchill, the British bulldog, was not about to surrender to the mild-mannered, nonviolent Gandhi. He was irked by the effrontery of the Congress. To him war was hard and brutal, whereas the Gandhian movement, nonviolent and unarmed, was soft and irrelevant; those who ran it would no more be able to defeat Hitler and the Japanese than would a flock of ostriches. From Washington, Churchill had sent his cabinet in London a minute on January 7, 1942, which included the following remarks:

The idea that we should "get out of India" by putting the Congress in charge at this juncture seems ill-founded. Yet that is what it would come to if any electoral or parliamentary foundation is chosen. Bringing hostile political elements into the defence machine will paralyse action. . . . The Indian troops are fighting splendidly, but it must be remembered that their allegiance is to the King Emperor, and that the role of the Congress and the Hindu priesthood machine would never be tolerated by a fighting race. I do not think you will have any trouble with American opinion. All press comments I have seen on India have been singularly restrained, especially since they entered the war.[3]

The phrase "the Hindu priesthood machine" shows either how the reports coming to London from the authorities in Delhi had twisted the facts, or how Churchill clung to outworn and silly clichés in respect to India. There was no question of a Hindu priesthood machine running India under the Congress; indeed, there was no priesthood machine running anything in the country! Had the British relented and brought the Congress into the Delhi cabinet, Muslims, Sikhs, Hindus, Christians, and others would have been ministers. If Churchill did not know this, his men in Delhi were deliberately misinforming him because they did not wish to part with power. Nor was it accurate on Churchill's part to describe the Congress as "hostile political elements." Gandhi had dinned into Indian ears that there was no hostility to Britain but only to the continued rule of the British in India. Moreover, there was a strong desire among the Congress

3. Winston S. Churchill, *The Second World War* (New York: Bantam Books, 1962), 3:584.

leaders to cooperate in the effort against Hitler, and they would have jumped at an opportunity to show how well they were capable of doing this. Finally, with reference to these remarks of Churchill's, the reader will have noted that he conceded that if there were anything like democratic elections in India the Congress would come to power. This, at least, he got right, but he found specious reasons for refusing to adopt a democratic course, which would in fact have served the Allies well by gearing up the Indian war effort.

In the late summer of 1942 there was much turmoil because of the Quit India movement. The authorities put it down harshly. There were numerous incidents of shooting into groups and crowds of Indians, and some of the activists departed from Gandhi's strict injunctions that every phase of activity was to be nonviolent. However, there was no doubt that the authorities remained in control of the situation. The net political effect of the movement, in the short run, was that the administration relied more havily than ever on the "loyal" elements in the country, and in this category they placed the Muslim League. This intensified the three-way contest for India between the Congress on one side and the British and the Muslim League, now more firmly than ever in the British camp, on the other.

But there was another, more subtle, effect of the Quit India movement: although the British remained at their posts, many of them had had enough of India, and began to ask themselves seriously whether it was worth their while to stay on in a country in which they were clearly not wanted. Many of them lost their nerve and wanted to leave, and by the time the war ended some of them even said so to their Indian friends. They knew that the era of the empire was over. When I myself was told this by some of my British friends, I was taken aback. I could not quite believe it, but when I questioned them I found a weariness of the soul, a need to go home and and to stop lording it over others who were perfectly capable of looking after their own affairs. It then became clear to me that we were at the end of an epoch, a swift change was about to occur, and nothing now could stop it.

Came the end of the war, and with it the defeat of Churchill's government by the British electorate in July 1945. Clement Attlee, who had been a member of the controversial Simon Commission sent to India in the late twenties, succeeded him as Prime Minister and formed a new Labour government in Britain. After the tremendous suffering endured by Britain during the war, the overwhelming feeling was in favor of curtailiment of its overseas responsibilities and the priority issue was that of India. Having contributed over two million fighting men to the war effort and a vast supply operation to keep the Allies going, India could simply no longer be kept out of the mainstream of political events in the world. Indeed, even before the close of the war, the Churchill government had agreed that India should send an independent delegation to the conference on the organization of the United Nations at San Francisco from April to June 1945.

As soon as it became clear in India that the Attlee government was going to divest itself of the Indian empire, internal politics became increasingly strident on the part of certain groups. This was not the case with the Congress, which had been the vehicle of the independence movement, and now saw that the fruits of its labors were about to ripen. But they also knew part of the Indian tree had withered under the stresses of the last few decades. The rulers of some princely states and the Muslim League began to translate the recent encouragement they had received from the British to keep the Congress movement from their jurisdictions into a basis of independence for themselves. Here again, the designs of British imperialism were despoiling the fruit of the tree, so those who cherished the future of the country had another major problem to contend with.

However, the realization that the British were, at long last, about to leave, resulted in a general mood of euphoria which made it difficult to concentrate on the practical problems that lay ahead. The sense of relief among the Congress rank and file as well as among the top leadership was so great that it was accompanied by a pervasive psychological incapacity to face up to a host of new problems, or new variants of old problems. It must be remembered that all the Congress leadership had just emerged from long jail sentences, a fate which not one of the Muslim League leaders or the princes had shared. Most important of all, the Congress leadership failed to make a supreme effort to devise a new constitutional program for India which could have been acceptable to a large section of Muslim opinion as well as to other elements in the country. A great many of the leading Muslim intellectuals were more sympathetic to Nehru's outlook than they were to that of Jinnah and many of his strident supporters. Worn out by the long struggle with the British, the Congress leadership did not address itself to this urgent need. One reason was that a section of the Congress leadership was lukewarm to the idea of a final and .old effort to conciliate and construct once again a truly national consensus. One way or another, a great opportunity was lost in the second half of 1945. When general elections were held in the early part of 1946—with only a small section of the population given the franchise—the Muslim League did much better than previously, largely because there simply was no appealing alternative plan before the Muslims delineating the future shape of India. The field was left to those who were dazzling them with visions of the benefits of separatism.

In January 1946, the Attlee government announced its decision to send to India a British cabinet mission composed of three senior ministers of the Labour government with a view to discussing with the Indian leaders the convening of a constitution-making body to form the basis of self-government for India. The Muslim League found fault with the terminology of the announcement from London, but had no reason to worry. The most active member of the three-man mission would be Sir Stafford Cripps who, since 1939 (which was before the Muslim League had officially espoused the goal of a sovereign Pakistan), had leaned to the establishment of separate units for the Hindus and the Muslims.

The cabinet mission arrived in the last week of March 1946, and early in April Jinnah convened a meeting of all the Muslim League legislators in the central and provincial legislative bodies. The four hundred or so persons who assembled at Delhi vowed to achieve Pakistan, by force if necessary. Jinnah, presiding over the meeting, said: "We will fight for it, and if necessary we will die for it; but take it we must—or we perish."[4] From Jinnah this was to be expected, but some of the other speeches were surprising. For example, Sir Firoz Khan Noon, all his life apparently a staunch adherent of the Unionist Party in the Punjab, and a consistent lackey of the British—(indeed his family had gained both wealth and prominence in the service of the British) stated:"If the British force on us an akhund [united] government, the destruction and havoc which Muslims will cause will put to shame the deeds of Halaku and Chengiz Khan."[5]

I quote these bloodthirsty words because I knew Sir Firoz well, and had visited with him and his relatives at their villages in the Sargodha district of the west Punjab. He was not a man of firm positions. He

4. Tara Chand, *History of the Freedom Movement in India* (New Delhi: Government of India, Publications Division, 1967), 4:465.
5. *Ibid.,* p. 466.

would have been quite happy if he had secured a place of honor in an undivided India, but in April 1946 he decided that Pakistan was inevitable and thought it wise to climb on the bandwagon with as much rhetoric as possible. I can say this with assurance, because Firoz Khan Noon, when he was later foreign minister of Pakistan and the gilt had worn off his adherence to a much smaller state than an undivided India would have been—probably the most populous state in the world—told friends in New York, where he came to represent Pakistan at a session of the General Assembly, that he had not been in favor of the creation of Pakistan. This was, of course, true for most of his political life, but he had overlooked that frenzied speech he made in April 1946.

The point that emerges is that the tremendous political wave in favor of Pakistan was at once real and artificial. It was not necessarily the firm position of even those who shouted the loudest for it. It represented the worst fears of the Muslims, although many of them had the confidence that they could have lived honorably in and made a great contribution to the strength of a united subcontinent. That the fears eventually won out was largely a result of how the stage had been set and how the players had been cast under British direction.

Chapter Ten

LAST EFFORTS AT UNITY
DIVIDE AND QUIT WINS OUT

Gandhi, who was of course totally against the division of the country, did not seem able to produce concrete proposals for a constitution. The very presence of so towering a figure inhibits those around him, even when there is a clear need for ideas and action to resolve pressing problems. The Congress became quiet, as if "waiting for Godot." Perhaps, its members thought, it is too late to struggle now against the forces unleashed so long ago by the British and the Muslim League leaders.

In a sense the issue was being lost by default, for there was no alternative offered to the country, or to the Muslims in particular. India heard only the cries of Jinnah and his cohorts. It might perhaps have been foolhardy to make an eleventh-hour attempt to reverse the strong currents in the country, but there was all the same a very real dissatisfaction among the politically aware, the technocrats, and some of the politicians, with the way the top leaders were handling the situation.

Most educated Muslims were unconvinced of the need to divide India. Indeed, most were not even certain that Jinnah actually wanted a complete severing of relations between the two entities on the subcontinent. They believed he was pressing hard for the best terms he could get, but for the most part they felt that he would settle for something less than full partition. I heard this constantly from my Muslim friends, many of whom were later to hold high office in Pakistan. Ironically, the majority Muslims of the Punjab and the North-West Frontier generally were not agitating for Pakistan; it was those who were in the minority in their areas who were the most enthusiastic supporters of partition. And, as it would turn out, these people, who were not Punjabis or Frontiersmen, would not be allowed to run the affairs of Pakistan.

In this situation my Muslim friends, a rather broad cross-section of Punjabis, repeatedly said to me: "It's just a matter of window-dressing. The Congress should dress the window attractively, and of course give us assurances that they will follow through, and then among us there would be no enthusiasts for Pakistan at all." In reply, I asked: "But what about so-and-so, and so-and-so? They seem to be sincere enough." The two names I mentioned were those of Punjabi Muslims. The reply was: "So-and-so is a crackpot, and as to the other, he's a politician. What do you expect of him? He thinks he can get a ministership in the new set-up, and he won't get it!" They urged me to try to do something about the situation.

In my own opinion much more than window-dressing was needed in order to produce a real alternative to Pakistan. What was wanted now was some very hard work on the outlines of a constitution for India and the wide dissemination of that outline so that the people could judge for themselves. If such an outline were worked out, in consultation with Muslims, and if it were aimed at meeting the demands to which they attached importance, then it might undercut the strident sectarian cries for separation, particularly since those cries were not getting real support in the Muslim majority areas.

I therefore began to talk to friends on the Congress side, and began to expound to them the need for a clear vision of the independent India of the future, so that the Muslims and other groups in India would be assured that their interests would be fully safeguarded, and that they would have within the Union of India the possibility, indeed the best chance for, their fullest development. Some Congress members were receptive, but the leaders had no time to listen to lectures from me; they were busy formulating replies to the cabinet mission and countering the arguments of Jinnah and others. I decided that the only sensible course left was to draft a constitutional document myself and present it to the leaders, in the hope that they could be persuaded to read it.[1] I first consulted with Horace Alexander, whom I introduced in chapter 7 in connection with Gandhi's visit to my house in New Delhi in 1946. He was in close touch with the British cabinet mission. Horace and I first took my draft document to Rajendra Prasad, later President of India, a distinguished Congress

---

1. My plan for the future of India is reproduced in the appendix to this book.

leader and a close associate in particular of Vallabhbhai Patel, the Congress strongman who was soon to become Deputy Prime Minister in the Nehru government. We asked Rajendra Prasad to read the document and then show it to Patel, whom we were hoping to persuade. I explained that I felt it was very important that the Congress should commit itself to a statement along the lines of my draft, provided we made it absolutely clear that the cabinet mission, too, must commit itself to the statement. I added that the statement took into account the underlying trends of Muslim opinion so that, if it could be backed by both the Congress and the British, it would be difficult even for Jinnah to carry out a successful attack on it. Rajendra Prasad was intrigued by the argument, and promised to read the document and show it to Patel.

My document was in two parts. The first part set out a number of propositions to which the Congress party was to commit itself in regard to the future constitution of India. These included considerably more than the normal rights of minorities, such as freedom of worship, speech, protection and fostering of their cultures, and educational facilities for pursuing cultural ends. Included were, importantly, the commitment to undertake the economic development of the areas of the country which were still unindustrialized so as to raise them to the level of other more developed areas, and the proposition that no part of the country was to be developed at the expense of the development of other parts of the country. Stress was thus laid on the right of the Punjab, Sind, and East Bengal to advance industrially, as well as on taking of steps to implement this right.

The second part of my draft document stated that if an India on the lines set out in the first part were unacceptable to a region, then such a region could opt out of the Union of India provided that it was agreed that any area which might thus opt out would enter common discussions in regard to defense and other matters which might be agreed upon. Second, it was to be agreed that if there were any seceding states, their representatives would join with the representatives of India in drafting a bill of fundamental rights. The importance of these provisions is obvious, and they seemed to me to be especially necessary considering the circumstances in 1946.

Patel and Rajendra Prasad were staying at Birla House, where Gandhi himself sometimes stayed and where he was to be assassinated in January 1948. This was convenient for me, as it was only a couple of hundred yards from the house where I was staying. Time was pressing, and the day following the one on which I handed him my document, I went to see Rajendra Prasad again. I immediately asked whether he had given the document to Sardar Patel. "Yes," he replied. Then I waited for a few moments before asking whether Patel had commented on it. "He doesn't like it," said Rajendra Prasad firmly and somewhat despairingly. I spent the next twenty minutes making all the arguments I could in favor of the approach set out in my paper. Prasad began by listening somewhat perfunctorily, but as I continued he became visibly very interested, and when I stopped he said: "Are you willing to say all this to the Sardar?" I replied that I certainly was. "Wait," he said. He left me alone for six or seven minutes and returned to say: "Come." He led me into a small sitting room furnished with a wall-to-wall soft mattress and bolsters. Patel sat against one wall, with his daughter, who served as secretary, by his side. G. D. Birla, his host—a great Indian industrialist—was in the room. Prasad and I entered and I was beckoned by Patel to sit opposite him. In the conversation which followed, Birla, Prasad, and Patel's daughter were a silent audience, except that toward the end the daughter repeatedly drew the Sardar's attention to the time.

I had expected to be with the Sardar for about half an hour but we argued and talked for a full two hours. To my surprise, he did not raise as many objections as I had expected to the substance of the paper. He would have liked a longer list of subjects for common discussion in the event of any region or regions opting out of India. I pointed out that the subjects could be added to by agreement. "No, they should be agreed on beforehand," he insisted. His major point was that he would not agree to anything unless he knew in advance that the British government was committed to it.

Holding my paper in his left hand and making a gesture of writing on it with his right hand, his rugged voice thundered out: "Will Wavell sign this document?" (Lord Wavell was then the Viceroy of India, after a fairly successful career as a British general during World War II.) "If I am given to understand that the Congress would accept the plan, I will take it to the British cabinet mission. If they do not agree to commit themselves to it, then my effort will have failed." He looked at me fiercely and nodded. *"First* get them to sign it. Then I will consider it."

This was not practicable, but since, in the cource of our long discussion, he had raised specific objections on only a couple of points, I left feeling that there was scope for an approach on the lines of my paper. I felt fairly confident that the reaction of Nehru and Azad, and of the more progressive wing of the Congress in general, would be more favorable than that of Patel. Furthermore, in Patel's camp, Rajendra Prasad, an important figure in his own right, was favorably inclined, and Patel's own reaction had been better than I expected. I should add that as I got up to leave, the Sardar said: "You will see. The British never commit themselves to anything. They will never agree." This was a political insight based on his own long experience.

However, though I saw the force of his observation, I was not deterred. For one thing, Horace Alexander, himself British and a man with a long experience with British politicians, knew the tactics I had adopted and he did not think the British would necessarily balk at my projected sequence of events as regards the commitments of the parties. Second, it was my judgment that in the particular circumstances that existed at the time, the Labour government in Britain was genuinely keen to find a reasonable and widely acceptable solution to the immensely complex Indian problem.

I made a few changes in my document, taking into account my discussion with Patel, and immediately set about taking my next steps. Meetings were in progress between the cabinet mission and the Indian leaders. I realized that I had to move expeditiously.

I had met Nehru several times at small social occasions and at one or two meetings. However, we had never talked politics. I telephoned his hostess, a close relative of his, Rajan Nehru, at whose house I had met Nehru a few times, and said: "I have something very important to discuss with Panditji. Could you please arrange for him to see me for twenty minutes or so?" For two or three days I waited with hope dwindling; time was running out on the type of approach to the problem which I was convinced should be tried by the Congress.

It was on April 23, 1946, that Rajan telephoned: "Come at once. Jawaharbhai has a half hour to spare. If you can get here quickly, you will have your twenty minutes with him." I rushed to their home only to find that Nehru was still engaged in a meeting with a group of thirty to forty popular leaders from the princely (and autocratically governed) states such as Baroda, Kashmir, Mysore, Hyderabad, Patiala. Among them was the towering figure of Sheikh Abdullah of Kashmir. Rajan assured me that the meeting would soon be over, and I was ushered into Nehru's bedroom, which also served as a sitting room for small meetings. I awaited him in tense expectation, completely in the dark as to what his mood would be and how he would receive me.

When he entered the room I was immediately struck by his poise and gentleness. His days and nights were one whirl of appointments and yet there was not the slightest trace of brusqueness in his manner. I was immediately at ease with him. After I had answered a few preliminary questions about myself, I briefly explained my mission, acutely conscious that I might be cut short because my submission was unacceptable. However, Nehru listened and I handed him my document, as revised after my meeting with Patel. I told him that I had had meetings with Patel and Rajendra Prasad. He reacted strongly to Patel's comments and general attitude, brushed them aside, and said "Yes, yes, I would have expected that of him."

Nehru read the document carefully. I watched his face closely. When he concluded reading he looked up, his face reflective and somewhat disturbed. It was not, after all, a document in line with his own thinking, which was strongly in favor of a united, secular, progressive India. "So you want me to accept this?" he asked almost accusingly. I elaborated the case for my document, gently but earnestly bringing out all its implications.

By now my allotment of time with him was over. Was he about to stand up, signaling that I would have to leave? Instead, to my surprise, and in a manner which I later realized was characteristic of him, he weighed aloud, very fairly, the crucial factors involved. He branched off, talking about the general political situation and musing about Jinnah in particular. He was deeply disturbed by Jinnah's position, and deeply regretful. To Nehru, who had grown up in close friendships with Muslims, as close as any he had, the ideas that Hindus and Muslims constituted two separate "nations"—which was now Jinnah's main theme—was both repugnant and absurd. Worse still, it was a highly inflammatory political ploy which no responsible person should indulge in. How had the rational Jinnah got himself involved in this distressing game? Nehru expressed himself equally strongly against some of the other exclusive trends, such as those of the Hindu Mahasabha, which were also guilty of promoting a divisive temper in the country.

I had been with him for over an hour when he pointed to the document and said: "I would suggest you change the sequence of these two paragraphs, and in the event that more than one state emerges at the end the commitment to working out common arrangements for defense and so on should be quite clear, so that there is no misunderstanding." All this was in line with my own intention and I told him that I anticipated no difficulty with the changes he had suggested. "All right, if you can make them, bring me the revised document tomorrow and have lunch with me."

I made the changes. The next day, April 24, 1946, Nehru, Rajan, and I sat down to an elegantly served and delicious lunch. There was a seemingly trivial incident at the beginning that I mention because it illustrates Nehru's innate sense of rhythm and order as well as his capacity to attend to everything down to the smallest details. Above our side plates was a kidney-shaped dish for salad—one for each of us. "That's not the place for them, Rajan," he said and he rearranged them, a little lower and so as to form a harmonious set of lines with the curves of the other plates before us. I might add that artists and leading statesmen share this quality of awareness of detail. It is a sign of a sharper and more illuminated focus.

Nehru talked very informally and pleasantly at lunch, and was even more relaxed than on the previous day. I was pleased because this confirmed that he and I had an easy rapport. He disliked ostentation and criticized a prominent mutual friend who, a few weeks before, had given a large banquet in Nehru's honor at which I was among the guests. "Why all that waste? I can't think whom he was trying to impress. He knows I don't like that sort of affair." He added: "By all means have a party, but none of your elaborate Delhi affairs, my dear Rajan. For example a cocktail party should consist of some sherry and cheese and crackers. After all, it's just a device to bring people together so that they can talk, exchange ideas, and enjoy each other."

I had never felt better than I did when Nehru, having read the amended document, said: "Good. This is all right now. Of course, I don't like the contingency you provide for, but it's something we have to face. Above all, we must make absolutely clear our picture of the India of the future." His eyes were beautifully alight. What he had just said was precisely my own main point, and it was very pleasing that he had espoused it.

He asked what I would do next. I replied: "I have been in touch with the cabinet mission people, mostly through Horace Alexander. Now that you've approved the document, I'm to show it to Stafford Cripps in the next day or two." Nehru said: "Yes, he's the man who's calling the tune on their side." We looked at each other, and I could see that we both had the same fear: Cripps was a difficult man to gauge, and it was not at all clear that he was playing a game that was in the best interests of India. Nevertheless, he was the man to convince on the British side.

When I left there was a cloud on Nehru's face. He was disturbed by the image of Cripps—cold, calculating, inscrutable. I too could not help being wary and suspicious of the man as a result of his attitude when he had visited India on behalf of Churchill in 1942. But I told myself that the circumstances were different now. He was not serving a wartime coalition in which the Conservatives were on top, but a Labour government with a rather different attitude toward Indian problems. But in any stable country how different are the attitudes of the major parties in the field of foreign policy, where the primary consideration always remains national, not party, interests?

I intimated to the cabinet mission, through two of their senior aides, John Short and Woodrow Wyatt, that I had made significant progress with the Congress leadership, and asked to see Cripps. On April 26, 1946, I went to see Cripps, in the company of Horace Alexander. I made a terse oral presentation of my document, told him that it was acceptable to Nehru, and gave it to him to read. Austere, his face parchment-like, he read intently. He reminded me of Jinnah. Both men were lean, hard, and driven, without much of the milk of human kindness. Of the two, Jinnah was the more pleasant and urbane. Cripps took in the document rapidly. Pointing to one word in the text, he said: "I think this should be an 'a' and not a 'the.' Would you agree to alter it?" I looked at the sentence. The change would leave the meaning basically unchanged.

"Yes, and I'm sure Nehru too would agree to the change, but, Sir Stafford, as I have said to you, this is not a document that is open to any significant bargaining or alteration. My approach, evolved after consultation with prominent Muslim friends and others, who think it is fair to all groups and interests, is that if the Congress puts its stamp of approval on this document, then you, or rather the British government, must make up your minds whether you, too, can say yes to it. The Congress will stand by the document. If the British government will also do so, then the Congress party will state officially that it espouses the document and that it undertakes to work out the future of India on the basis it sets out, with all appropriate guarantees that may be demanded by those concerned. By then there could be expressed significant Muslim support for it. I repeat that the document is not a bargaining counter. It is a statement of the utmost that the Congress can do to meet the demands of Jinnah and others like him." I mentioned the names of some of the Muslims with whom I had been in contact. Some of them I cannot mention here because to do so would embarrass them, for they live in Pakistan. But among them were Mushtaq Ahmed Gurmani, a prominent Muslim politician who was later to hold high office in Pakistan, and Manzur Qadir, later foreign minister of Pakistan, but before the partition of India totally unsympathetic to the cutting up of the country.

Cripps did not commit himself but said that, with the change he wanted, the document would be "worth considering." He added: "Whatever you're going to do, do it damned fast. Time is running out, and time is of the essence. If Nehru accepts my change, get back to me as fast as you can."

Though I saw no difficulty about the one-word change, I had to go back to Nehru to tell him about my interview with Cripps. That very afternoon I went to him. Fortunately, Abul Kalam Azad, president of the Congress party and a prominent Muslim statesman, was with him. I told Nehru what had transpired with Cripps, showing the single word I had changed. Nehru read the document again, showed it to Azad, and the two men talked. Both men gave their assent to the document, and as if bracing himself for a confrontation, Nehru said: "Tell Cripps that Azad and I are ready to talk with him on the basis of this document. You have completed your task, Arthur." I thanked him and withdrew. The way seemed clear, if only the cabinet mission would see the reasonableness of the basis now offered, which would also find favor with important sections of Muslim opinion.

Nehru had made it clear, after discussion with Azad, that the Congress wanted to proceed urgently to discuss the future of India with the British cabinet mission on the basis of my plan. This implied that, apart from its own formulations, the Congress had no other plan that it wished to advance at that time. I telephoned Cripps's office to say that the suggested change had been accepted by both Nehru and Azad. They telephoned back to say that Sir Stafford wanted to see me again at seven o'clock the next morning (April 28, 1946). Two cabinet mission aides, Woodrow Wyatt, a member of the British Parliament, and Major John Short, would call for me at 6:30 A.M. In Delhi, in the late spring and summer, one works during the very early hours. Next morning at six I was shaving when Wyatt and Short drove up. I was surprised; they were early. They came in and

John Short said: "Arthur, I'm afraid Cripps is not going ahead with your document. Last night he had dinner with Jinnah and he proposed the idea of a three-tier constitution to which Jinnah reacted favorably. The mission has just issued invitations to the Congress and Muslim League leaders and others to meet with it at Simla on the basis of the three-tier plan. In these circumstances, Cripps feels there's no point in seeing you today."

"Has the Congress also accepted the three-tier proposal?" I asked.

"They haven't really seen it yet. It's Cripps's idea. He developed it last night for the first time."

Astounded, I said no more. The reader can see for himself the extraordinary, and indeed amazing, implications of this news. Unintentionally, John Short had revealed how biased the attitude of Cripps, and of the mission, was. They had decided to adopt, as the basis of further consideration, a plan acceptable to Jinnah, and to brush aside a plan acceptable to important Congress leaders even though the Congress represented many times the number of people that Jinnah and his friends did. This action epitomized the nature of the Indian struggle for freedom: a struggle against the British who had manipulated and engineered into being a divisive movement with which they now took sides in the final disposition of the spoils. It was a cynical move in keeping with the whole divide and rule philosophy of the British—and of other imperialists before them—which they were now obviously hoping would secure for them the good will of the carved-off country they were helping to create. At the same time, by weakening India to the maximum extent possible, they hoped to induce it to become dependent, and even subservient.

The three-tier plan was published, along with the invitations to the Indian leaders, and accompanied by statements of the firm intention of His Majesty's Government to transfer power to the Indian peoples. But the plan itself was a monstrosity: I could see at once that it would be absolutely unacceptable to Nehru and the Congress party; for that matter, it was totally unacceptable to everyone except Jinnah and his friends. It raised the specter of the dismemberment of India in a far more emasculating manner than did the plan I had submitted, or the Mountbatten plan in accordance with which India was finally divided in 1947.

Cripps dreamed up three entities, which were to be held together in a loose federation. Each entity itself could consist of federated states. One of the three entities was to consist of the whole of the

Punjab, Sind, and the North-West Frontier Province, and was thus considerably larger than what became West Pakistan. The second entity was to consist of the whole of Bengal and the whole of Assam, and would, consequently, be more than twice as large as what would become East Pakistan and eventually Bangladesh. The sop to those vast numbers of people—the great majority of the Indian people—who wanted to keep India united was that there was to be no partition for ten years, at the end of which time the enlarged east and west entities, in which Muslims held a very slight majority, could decide to secede from the Indian Union. The intervening period could have been used to increase the Muslim majorities by immigration from among the Muslim population in the central entity. Ten years is not a long time, and it would have been quite easy to maintain and indeed deepen sectarian feelings and the greed for power during the period. The net result would have been to leave India seriously truncated. The three-tier plan was a bad omen for the unity of India; it also did nothing to guarantee full human rights, and it—deliberately of course, in the interests of the departing British—made no mention of consultations for joint defense and other matters of common concern. The whole plan was the work of the crafty Cripps.

In my plan the primary emphasis was on the design for an India which would assure all regions and communities the fullest enjoyment of their rights, liberties, cherished ideas, culture, religion, and the fullest economic development. The powers of the central government were to be few and strictly limited. The Cripps plan was the result of either his narrowness and lack of ability to see the human side of the issue or his determination to foist on the country a plan which best suited the basic and, it was hoped, continuing tenets of British foreign policy. Perhaps both these motivations were operative in Cripps's mind.

Did my plan in any way affect the final outcome of events? Certainly it did not directly. But the eventual division of India in 1947 was precisely on the lines conceded in my plan as the last resort if the equitable design for a federated India and the strongest possible guarantees for all sections and groups in the country were rejected. The lines of division implicit in the Cripps plan were not the ones that were used. Those lines were abandoned basically for three reasons. First, in the Attlee cabinet, Cripps was unable to get his way. Second, Mountbatten was much more deeply impressed with both Gandhi and Nehru as human beings than with Jinnah and his associates, and

Mountbatten was inclined to give India a better deal than Cripps, while being fair to the Muslim majority areas. Finally, the opposition in India to the Cripps plan was rousing the rural people as well as the townfolk—it was much more than the coffeehouse type of protest of intellectuals. It had to be taken seriously.

In my plan the concession of division was linked to a commitment by all parties to enter into discussions on joint defense and possibly other matters, as well as safeguards for the fundamental human rights of all persons in the Indian subcontinent. These important provisions could have been salvaged if Cripps had convinced the British government to support the plan Nehru and Azad had accepted, instead of introducing his too clever scheme that none of the major parties in India were ever able to agree on and which was rejected outright by the Sikhs—the important group from which the British in 1849 conquered most of the territory that now constitutes Pakistan.

Gandhi frequently said that he would like to see Jinnah as the head of the government of a united India, and most certainly by now, had India remained united, the Muslims would have played such a great role in India that they would have had no doubts that the assurances in a plan such as mine were a reality. The hate-love relationship of the British days, which often came out as more hate than love, would have been resolved in much more love than hate.

Unfortunately, the two other members of the cabinet mission could not stand up to Cripps, who was the youngest, the sharpest, and the most active. Lord Pethwick-Lawrence, over eighty years of age, meek and gentle, had to be on the mission because he had been placed in charge of Indian affairs in the Attlee government, but his faculties seemed to function only sporadically. A. V. Alexander, the third member of the mission, the British minister for naval affairs, was totally ignorant about India, and chose not to interest himself in problems that required a lifetime of study. In these circumstances, Cripps was able to persuade Pethwick-Lawrence and Alexander to join him in sponsoring the vicious three-tier plan that would kill any chance of the hate-love relationship between Hindus and Muslims becoming harmonized.

The Cabinet Mission plan had to be abandoned. For a fresh look at India and its leaders and in order to work out arrangements for the transfer of power, Lord Louis Mountbatten was sent to India as Viceroy in March 1947. He was armed by the Labour Government with the widest powers of negotiation with the leaders of India, but by then for months the fires of separatism had been fanned each day by hysterical speeches and there had been some bloody clashes between the communities.

Within two months Mountbatten reluctantly came to the conclusion that to maintain the unity of India was impossible. He saw Jinnah's intransigence as the major reason for this conclusion. Recalling Jinnah's attitude during the crucial negotiations in April 1947, Mountbatten later said: "I never would have believed that an intelligent man, well educated, trained in the Inns of Court, was capable of simply closing his mind as Jinnah did. It wasn't that he didn't see the point. He did, but a kind of shutter came down. He was the evil genius in the whole thing. The others could be persuaded, but not Jinnah."[2]

In May 1947 Mountbatten and his advisers worked out a new plan for India on which the lines of geographic division coincided with those in the plan I had given Nehru in April 1947 and he had accepted. Nehru was thus already attuned to the basic features of an arrangement of that kind. Until the last minute Jinnah fenced, raising fine procedural points, but eventually Mountbatten virtually browbeat him into reluctant assent, and the new plan went forward at a rapid pace, so rapid that on August 15, 1947, the two new Dominions of India and Pakistan were born.

The popular leaders of the Punjab and of the North-West Frontier Province, which would form the bulk of Pakistan, had been opposed to the partition of the country. Khizr Hyat Tiwana, the elected Muslim chief minister of the undivided Punjab, regarded the division of the country as an act of perfidy on the part of Britain, even though he had cooperated with the British throughout most of his political career. Khizr himself, utterly disappointed and shocked, told me later that Attlee had promised him there would be no partition of India. He took up the matter again with Lord Mountbatten as late as 1974, a few months before his death. He asked Mountbatten why the British had gone back on their undertaking against partition. The answer he received, and I quote Khizr Hyat Khan Tiwana's words to me, was that "We agreed to partition because we had come to the conclusion that without it there would be a civil war." Khizr's reply to Mountbatten was: "But it didn't save us from a civil war. There was

2. Larry Collins and Dominique Lapierre, *Freedom at Midnight* (New York: Simon and Schuster, 1975), p. 119.

a civil war. If there had been no partition we would have arranged our affairs among ourselves, and a civil war would have been averted." I do not know what response Mountbatten made, but it is a fact that partition led to over a million deaths, a refugee problem whose dimensions pale that of the Middle East refugee situation, and a property loss that has been too large ever to assess accurately.

Khizr's view was that if a firm stand had been taken against partition from the beginning, the Unionist government would have remained strongly entrenched in the Punjab. It was dominated by Muslims but also contained Hindus and Sikhs. This powerful government could have ensured that little or no violence occurred in the Punjab. Similarly, the leaders in the North-West Frontier Province, and the red shirts of Abdul Ghaffar Khan, who were thoroughly well disciplined, would have certainly seen to it that there were no outbreaks of violence in that province.

Would there have been significant violence in such provinces as Bombay and the United Provinces (now Uttar Pradesh, the largest state in the Indian Union) where some of the Muslims had been shouting for Pakistan? There would not, because the Muslims in these provinces were greatly outnumbered and would have realized the futility of precipitating situations of violence. Moreover, those Muslims in favor of a united India and those who were indifferent to the issue were much more numerous than those who were raising their voices for partition. There would have been stray cases of violence but nothing like the large-scale blood-letting that followed partition.

It is unfortunate and amazing that the advocates of Pakistan did not realize the simple truth that their cry was a cry of hatred against communities other than the Muslim community, and that to fan hatred is a sure way of provoking large-scale violence. A heavy moral responsibility rests on the shoulders of those who preach doctrines of exclusiveness in our world. The analogy in the United States is those who misguidedly preach segregation and by so doing provoke violence and unrest. The fruits of partition were, and were bound to be, bitter for the Indian people, especially those in the northwest and the northeast sections of the country. The only winners were the relatively few who were seeking power and influence by setting up new states. In addition, there were those who sincerely thought they were doing the right thing by their community, but how many of these were happy with the results is another matter. Many of them were pushed aside by those who more successfully competed for the spoils of disaster.

The British hope was that by division of India they would be able to retain a footing in both successor states, which would be weak ones. For about a decade they did manage to do so in Pakistan, but soon they were displaced in world affairs by the new superpowers, and Pakistan and other states in the developing world turned to those powers. The Congress party, which had struggled so long for freedom for India and which had succeeded to power in a truncated country, was determined that the Indian peoples should run their own affairs. They encouraged all the British to leave immediately, and except for a few senior military commands the whole structure of government was immediately Indianized. Very soon, the military chiefs too were Indians. However, the Congress wisely asked Mountbatten, who had won the confidence of Nehru, Sardar Patel and the other Congress leaders, to stay on as the first Governor General of independent India. This was for the period during which the constitution was being framed and before India declared itself to be an independent republic within the Commonwealth. Retaining Mountbatten as the titular head of India was an important symbolic gesture meant to show the British that the Congress government harbored no grudges against its former imperial overlords and was prepared to seek paths of cooperation and even of association in the system of independent states of which the source was an evolving British constitutional framework.

It is apposite at this point to take cognizance of the kind of democratic functioning that Gandhi had in mind for India. His notions had shaped the thinking of the Congress party, and we may fairly assume that they would have continued to be an important factor in an undivided India. In an article published in August 1940, Gandhi wrote:

The Congress policy must always be decided by a majority vote, but it does not cancel the minority vote. It stands. Where there is no principle involved and there is a programme to be carried out, the minority has got to follow the majority. But where there is a principle involved, the dissent stands, and it is bound to express itself in practice when the occasion arises. That means that *ahimsa* for all occasions and all purposes has been recognised by a society, however small it may be, and that *ahimsa* as a remedy to be used by society has made fair strides.[3]

This amounts to saying that in all matters of principle consensus must be striven for and there must be no question of the majority overriding the minority by sheer weight of numbers.

Jinnah and his followers felt they could not put their trust in this Gandhian formulation. Perhaps they did not think the majority would be able to live up to it. Their view cannot be dismissed, but they were mistaken in thinking of the majority in terms of a religious community. A Punjabi Hindu or Sikh has much more in common with a northern Muslim than with an Oriya Hindu or a Tamil Hindu. Conceding that it is difficult to live up to the Gandhian style, it is, nevertheless, the only style that is going to make life tenable in peace for the various peoples on the face of our very small globe. It is a style which is responsive to the trends in our contemporary world that make for ever-increasing interdependence. The British, on the other hand, were essentially lacking in higher statesmanship in adopting a divisive approach to the problems of the subcontinent instead of cooperation and unity in a rich diversity.

3. A. Appadorai, *Documents on Political Thought in Modern India* (Bombay: Oxford University Press, 1976), 2:269.

Chapter Eleven

THE NEW INDIA
INDEPENDENT BUT TRUNCATED

Britain's decision, taken several decades before 1947, to throw its own weight behind the separatists, ensured the success of a double-pronged disruptive movement. India reemerged as a truncated entity. Where did it turn for its political and other guidelines? Largely to those in the Indian community who had been steeped in the British tradition of parliamentary democracy and who, in an even wider sense, had been influenced by the British outlook on life. Nehru was the embodiment of this, but even leaders who are seemingly entirely indigenous products have in fact absorbed British influences. This was so of Morarji Desai, a far more indigenous Prime Minister than the Nehrus. For twelve years Desai served the British administration directly under English superiors, and from them he imbibed much of his sense of discipline as well as his understanding of the importance of an orderly administration and a well-trained administrative machine.

Almost a year before the date of their final withdrawal from India (August 15, 1947), the British placed virtually all power in Indian hands. On September 1, 1946, the government of India was Indianized, with Nehru being installed as its head. He accepted the unusual title of Vice President of the viceroy's Executive Council (the Viceroy himself was President, but acted only as a constitutional head of state and wielded no power).

Nehru at once set in motion steps to evolve a new constitution for India. A constituent assembly was elected by the then provincial legislatures, and it began its task in Delhi in the fall of 1946. Constitution-making reflected the long contact with the British. Though India, being much larger than Britain, necessarily devised a federal constitution, it adopted the conventions of the British Houses of Parliament. The British themselves had created a basically federal structure for India which, in the 1935 constitution, laid the groundwork for the new constitution developed in 1946–48.

The Congress-dominated Constituent Assembly made a brave effort to work out a constitution that would lure the Muslim League back into the fold even though the League members of the provincial assemblies had boycotted the elections to the constitution-making body. With this in view, the assembly very early adopted an Objectives Resolution which was an abbreviated version of the first part of the constitutional commitment that I had been able to get Nehru and Azad to accept in the spring of 1946. The Objectives Resolution set out the commitments which the Constituent Assembly would write into the constitution. It read that there "shall be guaranteed and secured to all the people of India justice, social, economic, and political; equality of status, of opportunity, and before the law; freedom of thought, expression, belief, faith, worship, vocation, association, and action, subject to law and public morality." [1] This was the essential kernel of the Objectives Resolution. Additional safeguards were devised for the minorities, tribal peoples, and the depressed and backward classes.

From the beginning, Nehru envisioned a democracy that would encompass economic rights, making available to the people a better livelihood—housing, food, clothing, education, and skills. He stressed the urgency and importance of working to achieve these ends. In the Constituent Assembly, he stated:

Many in this country have waited for years and years, and the country has waited for some generations now. How long are we to wait, and if we, some of us who are more prosperous, can afford to wait, what about the waiting of the hungry and the starving? This resolution will not feed the hungry or the starving but it will bring a promise of many things. It will bring a promise of freedom, a promise of food, and of opportunity for all. Therefore, the sooner we set about our task the better. [2]

This illustrates the kind of man Nehru was and explains why his popularity reached down to the poorest sections of the nation and why he, at the same time, captured the imagination of the forward-

1. *Jawaharlal Nehru's Speeches* (New Delhi: Government of India, Publications Division, 1949), 1:6.
2. *Ibid.*, pp. 17–18.

looking, educated elites, and won the support of most thinking people in the country.

As to his general vision for India, it comes out in the following words, also delivered at an early session of the Constituent Assembly, in January 1947: "I hope that while India will no doubt play a great part in all the material spheres, she will always lay stress on the spirit of humanity and I have no doubt in my mind that ultimately in this conflict that is confronting the world, the human spirit will prevail over the atom bomb." [3]

The constitution embodied these ideas. It created a federation of the states, or a Union of India, with an independent judiciary. It detailed a catalogue of human rights to give the fullest expression to democracy. In this regard it took into account the Bill of Rights of the U.S. Constitution as well as constitutional practice in the United Kingdom and other parts of the world. Having done all this, how were the constitutional provisions written for the benefit of the common man in India to be implemented with all good speed? How were the masses of the Indian people to be lifted out of the unconscionably low standards of living into which they had fallen in the past two hundred years or so?

These economic problems were gigantic in their proportions, and when it came to dealing with them Nehru was not able to do more than prescribe general guidelines. These guidelines were, as we have seen, admirable. Moreover, he was impressed by the notion of planning, and in 1950 his government set up a planning commission, of which the prime minister, that is, Nehru himself, was to be chairman to underscore the great importance he attached to this organ of the government. The planning commission was to formulate five-year plans covering the development of all aspects of India's economy. The commission got down to its task with enthusiasm and expectations rose high. It consisted of economists who had studied under Keynes at Cambridge, or at the London School of Economics, and they were supposed to be able to evolve plans for the rapid development of India. This was an absurd expectation. These persons, fine and intelligent though they were, could think only in terms of the economic grooves of the academic systems which they had so effectively studied in England and elsewhere. Those systems had evolved largely in the light of the economic facts of Britain—or the U.S.A.—

3. *Ibid.*, pp. 24–25.

with its highly structured economy totally based on banking, trade, and mechanized manufacturing processes. In India, on the other hand, the planning commission was faced with a peasant type of agriculture, a great richness of handicraft skills supported by a specialized manufacturing tradition in metals, such as steel making—which India had developed about two thousand years earlier—and textile weaving. The whole situation was utterly different from that on which Keynes based his theories, and the result was that the well-trained economists who headed the planning commission came up with largely futile, irrelevant, or peripheral plans for the development of the country, plans under which India would move forward at less than a snail's pace and which would bring no relief to the poverty-stricken masses.

Development was not just a Western phenomenon, as was clear from the case of Japan and from what some other Asian countries were beginning to do. The fact was that Nehru did not have the slightest idea of how the economic processes in the country could be geared up to achieve a respectable pace of development. He admired development in the Soviet Union, and he began to look favorably on the efforts toward development in China. But he was totally unwilling to adopt authoritarian methods; and on this issue he had the backing of the Indian people, who are not given to authoritarian systems by their traditional ideas of the duties of rulers, or by their training in traditional village democracy, or *panchayati raj*, which has existed in the country for thousands of years.

So what was Nehru to do? From his point of view the best answer was simply to appoint an able and highly trained finance minister, a Dr. John Mathai or a Dr. C. D. Deshmukh, and also to appoint persons to the planning commission whose qualifications were high in terms of Nehru's own British-educated background. But these steps did not produce the results he desired. Knowing that he did want results, and that results could be produced, I went to him and talked at length about development in India. I pointed out that our main resource was a tremendous wealth of man and woman power, unutilized and waiting to be turned into the sinews of development. Our poor were alive but unused. Why not use them to make, to build, to excavate, to renew? "But we haven't got the money," he said. I tried to convince him that we must break the vicious circle that holds us back—no money, therefore no more work, no more production, no more training, no more hope. "So, what do we do?" he asked. I said we must create thousands of teams of intelligent men and women to search out and identify the local resources in each group of five or ten villages, and then plans must be devised, on the spot as far as possible, to turn those resources into the goods that the people need. "Yes, I see. Go and talk to Dr. John Mathai. See if you can get him to move." I knew what Nehru meant: "Look, I can't do this myself. I don't know enough about it. You must convince Dr. John Mathai, and then we can get going." I telephoned Dr. Mathai's office. He invited me to dinner and we had a long discussion. But his mind was closed to innovative suggestions; he could not help it. He had lived too long in his Cantabrigian grooves.

Some years later, by which time I was India's permanent representative at the United Nations in New York, having just moved over from my previous appointment as consul general of India in New York, I sent Nehru a fifteen-page minute, "Reflections on the Death of Vargas." Vargas had been the all-powerful dictator of Brazil who had unexpectedly committed suicide. From his unfortunate form of exit from the world I was seeking to draw certain lessons regarding the economic life of a developing country, and more particularly India. I heard nothing more about the matter, and decided that Nehru was too busy or not interested enough to pay any attention to my note. However, many months later, the then finance minister, again a very estimable and able person in his way, Dr. C. D. Deshmukh, was visiting New York. At an official reception in his honor, he told me, in a very acerbic tone, "So you thought you could create trouble for us." I was taken by surprise and could not imagine what he might be referring to. I tried to smile and said as good-humoredly as possible: "But no, Mr. Minister. I have certainly had no desire to create trouble for you or for anyone else. Perhaps you have someone else in mind." He came back, even more sourly: "Oh yes, oh yes, you did. You sent that note to the Prime Minister, and he asked me to have the situation investigated. In fact, he wanted a commission of inquiry to be set up. You know, your note about Vargas." "And did you set up a commission?" I asked. He replied, "No, I convinced him that no inquiry was necessary. The whole thing blew over." So much for that effort. Nehru had been impressed with what I had sent him, but the "experts" had shot it down, and no action resulted. I was of course aware that the whole job could not be done by my method of getting on with the local transformation of resources, though I built on this concept an elaborate scheme of local training and learning, of stimulating the adventure of development, of sending the most gifted of the villagers for more advanced technical training, and of drawing up large-scale projects to the extent necessary to meet the needs of the people.

Nehru was the one person who was inclined to listen to what I had to say, and he was very willing to see the ideas I gave him tried out, but his time each day was so overcluttered with administrative minutiae that many highly important matters just slipped away unattended to. Indeed, a massive brake on attempts to move forward was Nehru's lack of any administrative experience; he accepted the machinery of government created and left by the British and tried to use it. But that machinery was designed and trained to maintain law and order, and it was virtually unable to do anything else. Nehru did, of course, face a genuine problem in this regard. When the British left India, the senior departing British officials were whispering to the press, to each other, and to everyone, "The Indians will never be able to administer this country. In three years the administration will break down—five years at the most." Nehru was determined to prove to the British, to the Indian people, and to himself that these slurs were plain wrong, that the administrative machine would not break down, and that the country could go forward better than before.

But the whole point was that the governmental machinery left by the British was not designed to take the country forward. By and large, under the British the condition of the people had not improved; it had even deteriorated in many respects—educationally in the villages, economically in most parts of the country except where modern industry had brought employment and perhaps the hope of more goods and services along with slums. The point that escaped Nehru, because of his lack of experience, was that in undertaking to prove to the world that he could run the machinery he had inherited, he had saddled himself with a highly immobile, blinkered mechanism. Good men indeed were part of it, but they were so encumbered with regulations, conventions, and practices that tended in the direction of doing absolutely nothing to upset the establishment that they inevitably slowed down any effort to quicken the pace of beneficial change. Not that he should have thrown out the machine, though modify it he certainly should have. Essentially, the machine needed a new set of practical guidelines with a view to simplifying procedures and rescuing the mind of the average civil servant from slavish adherence to precedent. Mostly such guidelines were not given, with the result that the machine continued to function in the nonactivist ways instilled in British times.

On some specific occasions new guidelines were elaborated. For example, in regard to the integration into the Indian Union of the princely feudatory states, clear guidelines were issued by the deputy prime minister, Sardar Vallabhbhai Patel, the same strongman of the Congress with whom I had battled in the spring of 1946 about the constitutional future of India. In the Constituent Assembly in 1949, pleased with the response of the higher Indian administrators to his injunctions, he praised them, particularly the British-recruited members: "I have worked with them during this difficult period . . . remove them and I see nothing but a picture of chaos all over the country."[4] But Patel's enthusiasm here was the exception rather than the rule. In other respects he was not at all good at preserving the morale of the administration; he tended to use "his men" in the various ministries to prevent programs which were not to his liking, from going forward, even after they had been approved by the relevant minister or the cabinet. These tactics of course slowed down operations.

One way or another, the rulers of the new India were at a great disadvantage administratively. Nehru heroically kept the machine going, but the machine was running sluggishly and he did not know how to rejuvenate it. It was on the economic and social side that India suffered most in my view. In spite of the five-year development plans, over the seventeen-year period from 1954–55 to 1969–70, the per capita national product (at 1960–61 prices) increased at the rate of 1.3 percent per annum.[5] Considering how low the national per capita product was, this amounted very nearly to standing still. Among the best performances was the increase in the generation of electric power. There was a seven-fold increase in the twenty years from 1950–51 to 1970–71, from 2300 MW to 16,530 MW.[6] An interesting set of comparative figures is that in France in 1970 the consumption of electricity amounted to 20.4 million tons of coal equivalent while in India in 1970–71 it reached 48.6 m tce.[7] Taking

4. W. H. Morris-Jones, *The Government and Politics of India* (New York: Anchor Books/Doubleday, 1967), p. 13.

5. Tarlok Singh, *India's Development Experience* (Madras: Macmillan India, 1974), p. 27.

6. *Ibid.*, p. 38.

7. Leon N. Lindberg, ed., *The Energy Syndrome* (Lexington, Mass.: D. C. Heath, 1977), pp. 123 and 233.

utilization of all forms of energy, in 1970 the figure for France was 225.5 m tce while for India it stood at 309.3. Though in the case of India we are talking of a population at least ten times as great as that of France, the fact remains that power is an important sinew of industry and production in general, and India had, by 1970–71, provided itself with a significant muscle in this regard. When it came to food grains, the rate of increase from 1949–50 to 1970–71 was a meager 2.89 percent per annum,[8] which just about kept pace with the increase in population and left the multi-millions of the hungry just about as hungry as before.

In regard to social change, Nehru was able to get his party to agree to institute a series of laws that protected the right of women to share equally in property, instituted divorce (Hinduism makes marriage an indissoluble sacrament), and raised the minimum age for marriage. Though he was also very strongly in favor of the earliest achievement of free and compulsory schooling for all Indian children and was able to legislate to this end too, he was not able to provide the facilities for universal schooling because his financial experts said there was not enough money to train and pay all the necessary teachers or to build schools for the whole country. As a result, literacy has increased far too slowly since 1947. In that year about 86 percent of the population was illiterate, and in 1979, 70 percent of the population remained illiterate. By now the facilities for primary education have been provided to virtually all villages and towns, and in the lowest grades attendance reaches very high percentages. However, among the large poverty-stricken section of the population, young children soon become an economically useful element in society. They can tend the cattle or goats, fetch and carry for the harried mother in a milieu lacking the labor-saving gadgets that are taken for granted in the United States, and soon join in agricultural activities or work for the richer neighbors and make a little money. They leave school and often relapse into illiteracy. The remedy is not just schooling, but integrated rural and urban development, which would make available more effective tools to the farmer and a variety of skilled occupations to the young villager, for which he would require some education as he advanced in life. In some parts of the country this is happening, but very little progress at the village level was visible in the first twenty years of independence.

In those decades, not only did India virtually stagnate in its econ-

8. Singh, *India's Development*, p. 28.

omy and social outlook but, of a piece with this state of affairs, it failed to develop a realistic view of its defense needs. Here, however, there was a problem unique to India among all nations. Gandhi, and to a great extent the whole movement for independence, had not simply believed in nonviolence but had lived it. The Gandhian philosophy was all along an irresistible magnet for Nehru and for many of the other Congress leaders, including most notably Rajendra Prasad, C. Rajagopalachari, and Abdul Ghaffar Khan. There were others who regarded Gandhi as a brilliant tactician above all, and among these the chief was Patel, who would have played a very large role in India had he not died in 1951. Nehru was faced with an impossible dilemma: how was he to lead the country along the path of nonviolence in its dealings with other countries and, at the same time, develop a defense force capable of discharging its duty to India in a world which had not disavowed war and the use of force in general, the United Nations notwithstanding? The answer adopted was to let things drift, except for a little more spit and polish. Occasionally, the army chiefs and their counterparts in the other services were able to get some peripheral equipment which was almost modern, i.e., just pre-World War II. But the Indian soldier continued to be armed with the .303 Lee-Enfield rifle that had been issued to the British army in the first decade of the twentieth century. This was a slow and cumbersome weapon and reliance on it meant that the Indian army would be outgunned and outmaneuvered on any battlefield by even a semimodernized army, such as that of China which, being a country without any inhibition against the use of force or war arising out of anything comparable to a Gandhian span of history, had equipped its fighting men with a much newer generation of weaponry.

The plight of the Indian army would have been even more ridiculous had it not been for the fact that forces based in and covertly supported by Pakistan invaded Kashmir late in 1947. Since Kashmir had become part of India in accordance with the constitutional arrangements accepted by both India and Pakistan, as proposed and ratified by Britain, it was India's duty to go to the defense of Kashmir. The response of Pakistan was to make its support overt. Pakistan turned out to be mistaken in the view that because most of the Kashmiris were Muslims they would automatically rise up and support the invaders. The invaders were driven out of the major regions of Kashmir, and a ceasefire was negotiated which has remained in effect, except for a war launched in 1965 by Pakistan in another effort to wrest the territory by force from India.

The point, in the present context, is that the early experience in Kashmir brought home to a reluctant Nehru that something had to be done about the equipment of the armed forces, but he was prevented from doing so by other more pressing problems. In 1949–50 there was not enough grain in the country even modestly to feed the population, especially the vast numbers of poor. Nehru concentrated his slender foreign exchange resources on buying food grains and on obtaining credits for shipments. The army could wait, and it did. And, as events in the early sixties were to show, it was made to wait too long, through no fault of its commanders. In the late fifties, when Krishna Menon—a dynamic person if there ever was one, but also a person with powerful prejudices and suspicions—became Defense Minister, the well-liked chief of military staff, General Timayya, went to him with a proposal that India should manufacture under license the Belgian FN 4 automatic rifle with a view to making it standard equipment in place of the old .303 Lee-Enfield. Krishna Menon said angrily that he was not going to have NATO arms in the country. This was a transposition of political views into the realm of technology, and can only be explained by the fact that India's leaders were overpoliticized and hopelessly lacking in administrative experience.

There were two basic reasons why Nehru was so naïve about the administrative machine he had inherited from the British. First, unlike most leaders who come to power in our world, Nehru had had no experience whatsoever of administration on anything near a large scale. He had never been in any position connected with the federal government in India, nor had he served in a state or provincial government. He had no background or knowledge with which to assess the qualities and effectiveness of an administrative machine. In addition, he fondly believed that the British had left a modern stream-lined machine that would serve him excellently. In fact, that machine, was essentially the creation of Lord Curzon, the imperial viceroy at the end of the previous century. Since then, its methods and outlook had remained cast in iron.

In the later Nehru years, from the late 1950s onward, there were signs that some regions and some sectors had broken through the miasma of economic stagnation. In north India the enterprising farmers were adopting changes which led to an upsurge in wheat output, and the same was being done in some of the rice-growing areas of the country. The result was that food grain production went up from about 48 million tons in 1947 to over 72 million tons in

1960–61. This favorable result was also due partly to the enlarging of the acreage served by irrigation works, from 50 million acres in 1947 to about 69 million in 1960–61. However, in most respects, including plans to augment the production of steel, progress remained very slow. Until the mid-1950s, steel production hovered round a million tons a year, which was what it had been during World War II, and thereafter it rose very slowly.

There is some evidence that though economic development in the Nehru era went forward slowly, it was impressive to those who had known India under the British. Let me cite two views from very different sources. In 1956 I was returning after consultations in India to my post in New York as ambassador and permanent representative of India to the United Nations. The chairman of the Dunlop Rubber Company of the United Kingdom was also on the plane, returning from a visit to India. This head of an important British multinational corporation came up to me, introduced himself, talked warmly of his visit to India, and added: "I was enormously impressed with the great strides India has taken in the development of industry and, indeed, generally. I couldn't believe that all this could be done since we [the British] left India. I want to congratulate you and your people." This was an unsolicited testimonial from a person with experience in many parts of the world, who had just traveled extensively in India and had known the country when the British were in charge.

My second witness is an Indian, a villager from the Himalayan foothills near Simla. He had lived in the West with me as my butler throughout the 1950s. In 1960 he went home to India for two months. On his return, I asked him: "How are things in the country, and in your village?" He looked very thoughtful, and said, slowly: "I must say there has been very great progress. We have come 50 percent of the way." I asked: "What do you mean by 50 percent of the way?" He replied: "Half the distance we must go to become like this country." (At that time I was in Vienna as ambassador there and a governor of the International Atomic Energy Agency.) I then asked him to give me the facts on which he based such an assessment. He said,

When the British were there, if I wanted to go to Simla, it took me a whole day's march, about forty-five miles, and all of it climbing. Now all I have to do is to go just below the village to the new motor road and I'm in Simla in an hour. Also, there was no school in our village or in the next village. Our children could not learn. Now there is a primary school in our village and a middle school in the next village. Our children are learning. It's good. There are other things, many. Now there's piped water, clean and good, brought to the village. Before we had to go to the streams, and in the winter they were far away. Now I can sit on my verandah and enjoy the mornings and the evenings. Before there were so many flies, it was impossible. Many things are happening. Houses are improving. My family has built a new house with nice windows.

These facts might fail to impress someone in a highly developed part of the United States, but going back to what my informant had known in pre-independence times, and also to what he had seen in London, New York, and then Austria, he was pleased with the progress back home. He was an intelligent man, educated, and very quick to learn. During his stay in the West he had become something of an electrician, a mechanic, and a full-fledged photographer with his own developing equipment. He was no ordinary domestic. Indeed, he was a Brahmin by caste.

Thus one must concede that even in the Nehru era, economic and social conditions, at least in some parts of the country, were changing for the better. Nehru himself was enthusiastic about the way things were going. Whenever I was in India during his prime ministership, he would ask: "What have you seen? Go to Bhakra and Nangal. See what's happening in the villages too. A new India is coming up." His eyes would light up, but I also still see clearly the dark rings around them, signs of the relentlessly hard work he put in. What an example of dedication he was, and what a pity that there were so few who followed his example.

I went to Bhakra, in the foothills. The massive dam, at that time the highest gravity dam in the world, the hydroelectric works, the wide, lined canals, taking the shining waters out across the land as far as the eye could see—and one knew they went several hundreds of miles farther—were very impressive. In the villages the old mud huts were giving place, slowly and sporadically, to brick structures, but there was still little real sanitation and waste disposal, except for what could be used to fertilize the fields. At a village about forty miles north of Delhi we were driving past fields in which the ripening wheat stood thick and lush. I was accompanied by a senior revenue official who was supposed to be able to correctly assess the state of the crops. I asked: "How much per acre will those fields yield?" He replied: "Sir, the usual yield of eight maunds [672 lbs] per acre or so." "Let's go and find out," I said, suspecting he was way off the

mark. We drove to a shed on the land. The owner of the fields happened to be there with a few of his men. I first had to convince him
that, being in no way connected with the revenue administration, I
was simply curious to know how much wheat he expected from his
fields. After some persuasion, he told me that he would get at least
twenty maunds an acre, which was two and a half times as much as
the revenues officer had predicted. I was elated. "How do you get
these yields?" I asked. He showed me his supplies of fertilizer in his
shed and his improved ploughs. He also had an electrically operated
deep tube well. I shared my delight with Nehru. He was busy at the
time, but his chest swelled a little, and he said. "Keep in touch with
the country. Tell them abroad about it."

Chapter Twelve

NEHRU DIRECTS THE POLITICAL DRAMA

The adoption of the British parliamentary system meant that power would vest in the party that won a majority of seats in the House of the People, the Lok Sabha, of the Indian Parliament. The victorious party would choose the Prime Minister who would be asked by the President to form a cabinet, selected from among the important members of the party in Parliament. The figurehead President of India was to be elected by an electoral college consisting of members of the central and state legislatures.

The first general election under the Indian constitution was held in 1952; under universal suffrage, which had now been introduced, the country had an electorate of about 200 million, of whom over 50 percent cast ballots in the election. The result was a foregone conclusion. The Congress party, hallowed by the long struggle for independence, further sanctified by the association of Gandhi's name with it, and including among its standard bearers Nehru, Azad, Kidwai, Rajendra Prasad, and other national leaders, won the elections to both the central legislature and most of the state legislatures. At the federal center, the Congress party secured 364 out of 489 seats in the Lok Sabha, and a plurality of 45 percent of the vote cast. Nehru was unanimously elected the leader of the party and continued as Prime Minister, in which capacity he had functioned ever since August 15, 1947, the day India regained its independence.

It should be remembered that a major difference between the Indian and the British political scenes is that in India from six to ten parties and a large number of independents contested the elections, whereas in Britain there are essentially two parties. In Britain, both major parties have won elections and formed governments. In India, on the other hand, though many parties competed for the vote, during the Nehru era none except the Congress came anywhere near being in a position to form a government. This was the only party that possessed the characteristic necessary in a national party—the ability to command the confidence of a sizable sector of the electorate all over the country. The Congress party was an amalgam of the nationalist forces in the country, except those of the extreme left and right. On the left was the Communist party of India, which won 16 seats in the Lok Sabha in 1952[1] and at the other end were the Jan Sangh, the Hindu Mahasabha, and the Ram Rajya Parisahd which, between them, won 10 seats in 1952 and did not fare much better in the next two elections.

The next general election came five years later, in 1957, and under the leadership of Nehru, the Congress party did slightly better than in 1952. In some ways it made the best showing it ever has: it secured 75 percent of the seats in the Lok Sabha, 371 of the total of 494, and it polled 48 percent of the vote. Nehru was at the peak of his glory. At home, an era of dire food shortages had given place to one of modest near self-sufficiency, some of the prestigious—as well as highly useful—grand schemes, such as the Bhakra dam, had been completed, and prices were fairly stable. In foreign affairs Nehru had entertained Bulganin and Khrushchev as well as Chou En-lai in Delhi. He had played a useful role in the Suez Canal crisis as well as in the Hungarian problem of 1956. Little wonder then that early in 1962, in the final general election of the Nehru era, his party maintained its clear lead, winning 73 percent of the seats in the Lok Sabha and attracting 46 percent of the total vote. I do not burden the reader with returns to the Upper House, the Rajya Sabha, in the central legislature, because this House, rather like the British House of Lords, has little power. The government takes into account views expressed in the Rajya Sabha, and it uses this house to provide seats for those members of the Cabinet who should not be subjected to the hurly-burly of electoral campaigns. Members of the Rajya Sabha are elected by the state legislatures, a procedure that avoids a long strenuous election campaign.

Why was it that though there was an assortment of parties, a wide range of political thought, and complete freedom of political discussion—more so indeed than in some democratic countries of the West—only one party had developed national stature? The answer

1. In the next two general elections the Communist party did somewhat better, winning 27 seats in 1957 and 29 seats in 1962.

was simply that the freedom struggle had brought together the nationalist forces and they continued to remain together after independence. In the case of some of the individuals concerned the motivation was to secure a share of the rewards. They were able to take advantage of the wide consensus in the country that a national coalition of various views had to be represented in the government.

Who actually made the decisions in this composite government over which Nehru presided? The answer is that he himself made not only all the major long-range decisions, but also many of the minor day-to-day ones. His position and personality towered so high above his colleagues' that none of the ministers stood up to him even if they disagreed with him. Cabinet meetings under Nehru were an interesting study in decision making in that era. Since I had the privilege of attending some of these meetings as well as meetings of cabinet committees, as a senior official of the government, I will give the reader some idea of the process of decision making. At the time when I attended meetings of the Economic Committee of cabinet, the chairman was C. Rajagopalchari. It was a delight to attend the meetings because "C.R.," as he was called, was brilliantly analytical, witty, and serene in all circumstances. He encouraged his cabinet colleagues to speak their minds, but his own brilliance dominated the meetings and generally, though not always, his view prevailed. Most often discussion continued until some consensus emerged.

In the full cabinet, however, the situation was entirely different. Nehru himself presided, and the objective again was consensus. But agreement was reached on the basis of the absence of discussion rather than through it. Each question on the agenda would be presented by the minister concerned. This was done very briefly because a minute on the issue had already been circulated to the members of the cabinet. Members were supposed to have read it—although some had and some obviously had not. Nehru waited for a discussion to start, and occasionally would look questioningly from one minister to another. Sometimes, however, he wore a far-away preoccupied look and simply waited in detached silence. The ministers were extremely hesitant to say anything; they seemed to lack confidence in the presence of their chief. They kept silent unless coaxed by Nehru, in which case the most one would venture to say would be along the following lines: "The proposal put up by the Minister for Labor (or Finance, or Industry, or Education), may not be objected to, if the Prime Minister approves. Let him decide." Thus there was no expression of views. Another minister might then be emboldened to say, "I agree with my honorable colleague. Let the Prime Minister decide."

Sometimes the tone of the phrase "Let the Prime Minister decide," indicated some reservations about the proposal. Nehru would nod his head gently and sometimes might say to the minister who had introduced the proposal, "I take it your ministry has consulted the trade union leaders, and what about the Bombay government?" The minister would look puzzled and turn to the senior official accompanying him, who would then answer: "Those consultations were made and no objections were raised." Nehru would look at the faces in the room. If they were in a state of repose or contentment, he would conclude: "I think we might adopt the proposal." On the other hand, if some silent restlessness could be discerned he might say: "Write to C——— at Bombay, and let me see his reply." There was a minimum of substantive comment and practically no discussion at all. At most two or three ministers would venture to speak on an item. The only one who might make a comment that would open up the issue was V. K. Krishna Menon, but he would do so in a characteristically oblique and involved way that few present understood. Unless the Prime Minister took up the comment, it would be ignored.

Nehru, unlike the British Prime Minister and the heads of other important governments, had decided to be his own foreign minister, and his own minister for atomic energy and for scientific development. Thus in addition to very onerous and vitally important duties as head of the government, he saddled himself with the day-to-day administration of three other ministries and was consequently over committed. He was unwise in so burdening himself, because this clearly meant that he was not able to give enough time to such vital matters as promoting the development of the country, evolving a workable and effective population planning policy, and finding out enough about the administrative machine to see that it needed quite drastic alteration.

Underlying the superficiality of discussion was also the factor of the great difference between Nehru's background and those of almost all his colleagues. Such men as S. K. Patil, H. K. Mahtab, or K. C. Neogy—all significant regional leaders in their own right— were not comfortable communicating with Nehru. They were conscious of their much more limited backgrounds, and feared that they might make some foolish error of judgment or express some immature view in his presence. Discussion was therefore inhibited.

On the other hand, the top officials in each ministry, who prepared the minutes on the subjects to be discussed in cabinet, were often more like Nehru than were the ministers. All of them had spent a part of their lives as students in England. Nehru tended to feel that a proposal that came from this group of senior civil servants was likely to be sound. In some respects, the administration was a tacit coalition between Nehru and certain of the senior officials. The forms, however, were meticulously observed by Nehru. He never went over the heads of his political colleagues. The dignity of the important political figures had to be maintained, and they often proved useful, particularly in handling regional problems, though their role in actual decision making in the administration was generally a minor one.

In the state governments, the process of decision making was more analogous to what has been described in regard to committees of the central cabinet. The cabinets of the state governments tended to be homogeneous. Communication was easy and was so often protracted interminably that decisions were very difficult to reach. When the overstrained machinery seemed to totter, the chief ministers would rush from their state capitals to Delhi to obtain the support of Nehru or some other central cabinet minister designated by him and important in the region concerned. Armed with this support, they would return to their states, the troublesome elements subdued by the weight of central authority. In this way, the states were helped by the central government to keep their own governments going. At the apex of the system sat Nehru himself, increasingly remote from the political fray, whose word, though not law, was so weighty that it could keep the country stable and viable.

Chapter Thirteen

INDIA AND THE WORLD IN
THE NEHRU ERA

While Nehru was not significantly innovative in domestic matters he made a number of outstanding contributions in the field of foreign affairs. Both by inclination and training he was best prepared for and suited to this aspect of governmental work. He had always been fascinated by world trends and movements. During one of his jail terms served under the British—his crime being nonviolent work for the freedom of India—he wrote a long series of letters to his daughter, Indira, which were later published as a thousand-page volume, *Glimpses of World History.* Scholars and others have been amazed at this work. Dr. Saul Padover has written that it "is a remarkable achievement on any level, but it is particularly striking as having been written by a prisoner who had to rely to a large extent on his memory. . . . in its scope and universality it is comparable to H. G. Wells' *Outline of History.*" [1]

Nehru had been impressed in some respects by the early phases of the Soviet experiment in Russia, a country he visited in the late 1920s, and he had been stoutly and vociferously opposed to fascism and nazism. He had also taken a strong stand on the question of freedom for colonial territories. However, for all his interest and concerns, he had no direct experience in handling foreign policy or other governmental affairs.

He began to mold the foreign policy of India as well as that of a large spectrum of countries from the very commencement of his accession to power in India. As early as September 7, 1946, a week

1. Saul K. Padover, ed., *Nehru on World History* (New York: John Day, 1960), pp. vi–vii.

after he was appointed head of the provisional government, he made his first national radio broadcast to the Indian people. In his brief talk of some twenty minutes, he spoke without any notes and without any briefing from officials or conferences with his aides. He laid out the main features of a foreign policy and an outlook on the world which, in the course of the next two or three decades, became the most widely espoused foreign policy among states, and today is professedly adhered to by over ninety sovereign states. This policy and outlook, now known as nonalignment, was a most remarkable and profoundly important contribution by Nehru to world politics, and it is one for which he must be placed in the very front rank of international statesmen. There have been other great contemporary leaders who have been acclaimed for their signal contributions to advancing the power and prestige of their own nations. But very few have made their main objectives the betterment of the world, the development of a philosophy whose central aim was peace, disarmament, and world cooperation leading to the achievement of an era of "One World." Nehru's whole outlook was different from that of a chauvinistic leader. To quote Professor Padover again: "Although an Indian patriot, he has no chauvinistic or racial bias . . . Nehru is neither Asio-centric nor Europo-centric. His is truly a world view. He thinks in terms of humanity and not of nationality."[2] His policy of nonalignment has been basically adhered to by both the Congress and the Janata parties for the last 35 years, a fact which shows how accurately Nehru, governmentally unprepared though he was, foresaw the trends in much of the world and the needs of his own country on the plane of mutual advantage rather than on the basis of a narrow concept of national interest.

The elements of nonalignment were all contained in that statement which he made on September 7, 1946: India would take a full part in international affairs, "not merely as a satellite of another nation"; it would cooperate with all countries for the furtherance of world peace and freedom; it would "keep away from the power politics of groups aligned against one another"; it would work for "peace and freedom . . . the emancipation of colonial territories and dependent countries and peoples" and for "the recognition in theory and practice of equal opportunities for all races." He went on to say: "We repudiate utterly the Nazi doctrine of racialism," and as a general

2. *Ibid.*, pp. vii–viii.

proposition he stated: "The world . . . moves inevitably toward closer cooperation and the building up of a world commonwealth. It is for this one world that a free India will work, a world in which there is the free cooperation of free peoples, and no class or group exploits another." Bear in mind how Britain had treated the Congress over many years and let us then listen to what Nehru said about future relations with that country: "In spite of our past history of conflict, we hope that an independent India will have friendly and cooperative relations with England." He then mentioned India's desire for friendly and cooperative relations with the Commonwealth, the United States, the Soviet Union, India's neighbors in Asia (including Afghanistan, Iran, Indonesia, and the Arab world), and he made special mention of China, "our neighbor which has been our friend through the ages, and that friendship will endure and grow."[3]

Though some of the statements sound platitudinous now, at the time Nehru put them forward they were crisp and fresh and farsighted. The world was on the brink of the Cold War and a division into two blocs in dangerous confrontation. It took some courage for Nehru to enunciate a policy which would not be to the liking of the leaders of either of the two antagonists. Apart from courage, what else explains this extremely creative formulation of policy? First, Nehru was deeply aware of the dominance of the trend of synthesis, as opposed to the trend of confrontation, in the history of Indian thought and action over a course of some five thousand years. In promoting this trend, perhaps a score of different groups of peoples had played a role. Anyone who has become aware of this prominent strand in India's history, and feels himself or herself to be part of it, tends strongly toward being a universalist, one who seeks to arrive at syntheses and understandings between potentially conflicting groups and views. Second, the ideas formulated by Nehru on September 7, 1946, showed the influence of Gandhi's thinking about nonviolence and resistance to evil. Third, Nehru's remarks were parallel with the best traditions of humanitarian liberalism, a ground on which Gandhism and much of Western thought stand together, and in this sense there was also present in these remarks the influence of his Western education.

A few months later, speaking in the Constituent Assembly of India, Nehru said: "I have little doubt that the free India on every plane

3. For text of the speech, see *Jawaharlal Nehru's Speeches,* 1946–May 1949 (New Delhi: Government of India, Publications Division, 1949), 1:1–5.

will play a big part on the world stage, even on the narrowest plane of material power."[4] This statement reflected Nehru's belief that India would make rapid progress in economic development, but the facts did not catch up with his statement. Besides, he did not realize that the operative powers in world affairs would leave out of account such a country as India, no matter that it contained a sixth of the world's people, simply because it was not a power. Later he came to see this unfortunate verity, but for many years his vision of nonalignment was to put into practice, as the only reasonable basis for worthwhile relations among sovereign states, big and small, a nonpower system of political discourse. Indeed, Nehru, based on Gandhi and a deeper Indianism, presented the notion of a world which rejects power, the case for a balance not of power, but of nonpower. This is the underpinning of Nehruvian nonalignment.

Nehru's conceptualization of foreign policy was so clear that he did not need policy advice, and on this basis he came to the conclusion that he did not need a foreign minister. In practical terms this was a bad decision. Any utterance he made had a finality to it. There was no room for a subsequent shift of emphasis, a lack of which robbed Indian foreign affairs of a depth of treatment. It would have been an advantage to India, especially at crucial moments, to have had a skilled foreign minister. Nehru could then have directed his minister to take up an issue with his opposite numbers in the countries concerned (for example, discussions on a common market among a group of Asian countries). The foreign minister would have worked out a strategy, relieving Nehru of a considerable chore. Reactions from two countries, let us say, might have turned out to be favorable or at least interested, but a third country, for instance Pakistan, might have given vent to the view that this was merely a scheme to establish Indian hegemony in the region. The Indian foreign minister would then have tried to get other states in the region to inform the foreign minister of Pakistan that in their view the proposed common market would in fact bring India into real partnership, on terms of equality but not superiority, with the other countries in the region, and this would be in the best interests of all the countries concerned.

Let us assume that Pakistan was still unconvinced. At this stage Prime Minister Nehru could have sought an occasion to make a general reference to India's fervent desire to improve relations with its neighbors, and more particularly with those on the subcontinent. He

4. *Ibid.*, p. 24.

would not need to mention Pakistan to make his point. He might have added that he would hope that arrangements could soon be worked out to ensure regular personal contacts among the foreign ministers of the countries concerned. A process such as this would have protected him from the day-to-day negotiations and given him the opportunity to make the conciliatory, synthesizing statements which could have prevented situations from festering into conflict. This would have given a needed flexibility to the implementation of foreign policy. Without such flexibility the course of relations with China, the United States, and even with smaller countries such as Nepal, was adversely affected.

Nonalignment immediately earned black looks for India's representatives as early as the very first session of the United Nations General Assembly. John Foster Dulles, Secretary of State under President Eisenhower, exemplified this misunderstanding. He made frequent sour references to Indian policy. For example, in a speech made on June 9, 1956, Dulles incorrectly labeled India's foreign policy as "neutralism": "This [neutralism] has increasingly become an obsolete conception, and, except under exceptional circumstances, it is an immoral and short-sighted conception."[5] A few weeks later (July 3, 1956) Richard Nixon, then Vice President, criticized a "neutralism that makes no moral distinction between the communist world and the free world."[6] Nehru responded by questioning whether "the world can be divided up into good and evil. . . . To say that we should all think alike is not at all possible. It is not democratic, either, to want all people to think the same as you do."[7]

Two other tenets of nonalignment were already causing friction between India and some leading countries. From the outset, Nehru had taken a stand against any state's having military bases outside its own territories. Nehru was referring both to the USSR and the U.S. However, since it was then very much part of American policy to contain the Soviet Union within a ring of bases run by the U.S.A. and its allies, India's repeated opposition to foreign military bases was strongly attacked by U.S. spokesmen in many forums.

In April 1954, Nehru took the very first initiative to end the testing of atomic weapons, by requesting the UN General Assembly to take

5. Quoted by D. J. Fleming in *Annals of the American Academy of Political and Social Science,* Nov. 1965, p. 20.
6. *Ibid.,* p. 21.
7. *Ibid.,* p. 27.

up the matter. This step was in keeping with India's desire for a lower military profile in the world. Somewhat to our surprise, this initiative was resented by the nuclear powers. "Why do you poke your nose into our affairs?" they said. But we insisted that nuclear weapons were everyone's affair because the destruction they could cause, and the radiation from testing them, would extend over wide areas. Besides, nuclear weapons could be used against countries which were militarily in no position to defend themselves against their effects.

Then again, the espousal by Nehru and his spokesmen of the cause of freedom for colonial peoples became an irritant to the West, though not so much to the United States as to its European allies. The European colonial rulers contended that colonial territories were within their sovereign jurisdiction. V. K. Krishna Menon, however, contended that colonialism was a state of continuing aggression against people who had been subjected to foreign rule, and this formulation became a rallying point at the United Nations.

The support the United States often felt obliged to extend to its European allies on colonial questions sometimes resulted in bizarre and even humorous situations. I recollect one occasion when, as India's delegate to the Trusteeship Council, I was able to convince the U.S. delegate, Mason Sears, of the reasonableness of a step that we were advocating in order to hasten the program for terminating a trusteeship in Africa. He agreed not simply to support our proposal, but actually to cosponsor the draft resolution which would be brought before the Council. We agreed on the language of a resolution which was duly circulated under the joint sponsorship of India and the United States. It was to come up for discussion and a vote the next day. On that day, however, Mason Sears came to me before the meeting began, looking very worried. He informed me that he had received instructions from the State Department to withdraw the name of the United States from cosponsorship of the resolution, and to vote against it! When the draft resolution came to the vote, it was defeated.

However, there were also issues that provided the opportunity for significant cooperation between India and the United States. One such occasion was during the efforts to end the fighting in Korea. India had made an early attempt in this direction by conveying to the American government the considered view of the Indian ambassador in Peking that, if the U.S. forces and their allies were to advance across the 38th parallel into North Korea, China would regard this as a threat to its security and would feel obliged to enter the conflict. This accurate information was rejected by the Western powers, who chose to place reliance on their own intelligence reports, which were sending signals different from India's on the question of Chinese intentions. In the event, the information given Ambassador Panikkar of India had indeed been an official warning from Peking to the Americans. The Chinese did come into the war when the 38th parallel was crossed and the military conflict escalated to major proportions.

Later came the Panmunjom negotiations. They stalled because agreement could not be reached on the question of the exchange of prisoners of war. Meanwhile, the fighting continued to rage in Korea. The Western position was that the prisoners of war should be free to go where they wished to go. The communist states took the view that under existing provisions of the applicable Geneva Convention the prisoners were to be repatriated to their respective countries of origin. There was a deadlock which seemed unbreakable. In these circumstances, the Western countries prepared a draft resolution for the UN General Assembly in the fall of 1952 which called upon the world body to put its imprimatur on the Western proposal in regard to the prisoners of war. They felt confident that they had the voting strength to give them the endorsement of the General Assembly, which would have vindicated their position. They were, however, aware that such an exercise was substantively futile because it would not end the fighting in Korea. Nevertheless, the United States presented a draft resolution, setting out the Western position, and it was backed by a formidable list of cosponsors, almost half the total UN membership. In this deadlocked situation, Krishna Menon made a historic speech to the Assembly, unraveling the complexities of the law and the facts surrounding the issue, and he closed by introducing a draft resolution sponsored by India alone, which proposed a formula for resolving the problem of the prisoners. It interposed a neutral commission to oversee the operation of repatriation of prisoners, which would ensure that there would be no forced return to any country. Andrei Vishinsky of the Soviet Union blasted the proposal, but the West saw that it perhaps had a chance of being accepted by China. The Western resolution was withdrawn, and the Indian draft was adopted by a very large majority; only the Soviet Union and its then very small band of supporters voted against it. A couple of months later, Peking announced acceptance of the Indian proposal.

The prisoner of war issue was sufficiently resolved to lead to a cessation of hostilities in Korea.

Another striking example of cooperation between the U.S. and India occurred in the fall of 1956 and in the succeeding months in the difficult period of the sudden attack on the Suez region by Britain, France, and Israel. The crucial factor became the firmness of the United States in opposing the invasion, but this posture was greatly assisted by the restraint of the Egyptians and their nonaligned friends, at that time led by India, in rejecting extremist formulations at the United Nations. The head of the Egyptian delegation, Omar Loutfi, and I worked extremely hard to maintain a moderation which helped the United States. Though Egypt was naturally incensed and gravely concerned for its very existence, I was able to get Omar Loutfi to agree, against the urging of others, that the draft resolutions we were introducing in the first emergency special session of the UN General Assembly should not condemn the invading countries, but simply demand their withdrawal. My point was based on two considerations of importance. First, I knew that Nehru did not believe in a diplomacy of condemnation, and that India had even refused to condemn South Africa for its contemptible apartheid policies. In my own view, too, condemnation is a word which should not appear in a diplomat's dictionary. Second, I felt certain that if we were to ask the General Assembly to condemn Britain, France, and Israel, the United States would be unable to vote with us. This would greatly weaken the United Nations effort to get the invaders to withdraw, and it was withdrawal, after all, that was our objective. When I talked to Henry Cabot Lodge, then U.S. Ambassador to the world body, he confirmed that it was most statesmanlike of us to insist that condemnation be excluded. Even though the British and the French dragged their feet, and the Assembly had to go on repeating its demand for their withdrawal, none of the dozen or so of resolutions introduced by the nonaligned states, which were all drafted by me and were adopted by the first emergency General Assembly session and the succeeding eleventh regular session, condemned the aggressors. At one stage, as time passed without withdrawal, it became so difficult to hold our nonaligned friends to the noncondemnatory line that Krishna Menon and I took Cabot Lodge to a meeting of the nonaligned countries so that he could assure them that the United States was indeed using its influence to effect a full withdrawal, and that progress to this end was being made. That was the first and only time that the representative of the United States has attended a meeting of the nonaligned at the United Nations! During the whole of that grave crisis, until it was resolved, the unswerving cooperation between the United States and India was of prime importance especially as at that time India was able to speak for the growing number of nonaligned states.

Ironically, that occasion was immediately succeeded by another, in which Indo-U.S. cooperation broke down and caused some bad feeling that could have been avoided. News came through of the dramatic uprising in Hungary which Soviet troops put down. The U.N. Security Council, as expected, was not able to reach a decision acceptable to all the veto-wielding powers, and the UN convened its second emergency special session. The United States immediately prepared a draft resolution condemning the Soviet action, and Cabot Lodge came to me and asked that India join with the United States and others in cosponsoring the resolution. I replied by reminding him that just a few days previously he had told me that India was very wise in not agreeing to go along with any draft resolution condemning Britain, France, and Israel. I said the same principles were applicable to this situation and we would not be able to cosponsor a condemnatory resolution, but would gladly consider doing so if the resolution would call only for withdrawal of foreign forces. Cabot Lodge countered by saying that the Soviets were much worse than the British and French, and that condemnation was justified. He apparently did not understand, or rejected, our difficulty with condemnatory diplomacy. I pointed out that who was worse than who was a matter of opinion, but the UN should go by the facts of the case; and on the face of it, the invasion by Britain and France from thousands of miles away was reminiscent of the heyday of colonialism and was an extreme case of aggression. It could be argued that the Soviet troops were already in Hungary—not that this made their action any less reprehensible, but at least it was not a coldly planned invasion— and it was also claimed that the President of Hungary had asked for Soviet assistance. In all these circumstances, if condemnation was out of place in the Suez situation, it was also out of place in the Hungarian imbroglio. Besides, I pointed out that a noncondemnatory resolution would command a much wider spectrum of support and would be more effective. However, the United States insisted on a condemnatory resolution and brought it to a vote in the General Assembly. By that time Krishna Menon had arrived in New York and, to my surprise, he voted against the U.S. resolution, thus giving the impression that he favored the Soviet action in Hungary. In doing this he was not in step with Nehru, who had appealed to the Soviet Union to withdraw from Hungary and would have had Krishna Menon abstain. A consequence of Krishna's vote was that almost each day, at the unearthly hour of 3 or 4 A.M., I would be awakened by a telephone call from Delhi conveying Nehru's latest instructions on the Hungarian situation, which I had to pass on to Krishna Menon, much to his displeasure. Krishna Menon was highly intelligent but also impetuous. Moreover, his health played great tricks with him, and on a bad day his impetuosity was as swift as lightning. Galled by the instructions from Nehru conveyed via me, he nevertheless carried them out faithfully. But he continued to defend his vote on the first resolution on Hungary, which rubbed salt into the wound of the Americans.

Meanwhile, India continued to press for a ban on nuclear weapons testing. In 1957 I devised a formula I thought might be acceptable to the U.S. and the Soviet Union. It introduced a commission of scientists from neutral nations such as Sweden, Austria, Switzerland, India, and others that might be acceptable, to pronounce on cases of suspected weapons testing once the ban was instituted. Krishna Menon pleaded eloquently for such a system at the 1957 session of the General Assembly, and some members of NATO even came to us and said that our proposal was very reasonable; but for reasons that were not made clear, the United States opposed the proposal. In the vote, the Indian proposal was defeated, but of great significance was the fact that the votes in favor of the proposal plus the abstentions exceeded the votes against the Indian draft resolution. Among the abstentions were one or two Western European states. From now on, the weapon testing states had to take the opposition more seriously, and it is significant that in the next summer the two sides met in the first conference to study the technical feasibility of detecting violations of a possible agreement on the suspension of nuclear tests. The pressures initiated by India and supported by an increasing number of countries were beginning to bear fruit. But countries do not like gadflies, and India gained the opposite of thanks for its persistent efforts for a ban on nuclear weapon tests. They were looked upon as a moralistic expression of Nehru's sense of supercilious superiority.

The salient fact during the Nehru era in India's foreign relations was that more than any other single country, it was India that took important initiatives on matters of international concern. The militarily powerful states looked upon these matters as their proper domain, and the Indian expressions of concern, coming as they did from a country which was not a leading military power and had no intention of becoming one, were looked upon as unwarranted intrusions. Did it not occur to the great powers that they were, in a sense, strengthening the forces in India that believed the country should, in view of the values of the real world, develop a major military posture? After all, India was still, after the partition, a very large country, far larger in population than any other country with the exception of China. Why should it not join the ranks of the self-styled Great Powers? Indeed, China was faced with just this question, and it decided, to become a great military power; it is at present busy doing precisely this.

India, on the other hand, because of its particular and one might say peculiar sense of values, was not embarking on the path of militarism, though it could have done so just as effectively as China, perhaps more effectively because it possessed advantages, such as a far more cohesive, disciplined and properly trained army, rather than what was essentially a militia force. In Indian eyes it is puzzling and paradoxical that, in order to be an acceptable worker for peace and human well-being, a country had better first join the international elite club, which has come, by tacit agreement, to consist of those countries that have arsenals of nuclear weapons. Of course, many in the leading nuclear weapons states will deny that this is the case, but such a denial will not wipe out the perception that exists in such countries as China, India, and I believe also Brazil and a few others. The salient point is that India, especially during the Nehru era, looked at matters this way, and decided that it would not raise its military profile, even if this meant exclusion from the councils of the great to which it was entitled not only because of its population but also because it has been for several millennia among the world's major civilizations.

In the mid-fifties there was a very instructive and rather amusing case of Indo-American interaction. In a world which was lining up on one side or the other in the great confrontation between the United States and the Soviet Union, I looked at the globe and decided that an attempt should be made to exclude Antarctica, from becoming a scene of power bloc rivalry. I suggested to Nehru and Krishna Menon that India should propose an item for inclusion in the agenda of the UN General Assembly on the neutralization of Antarctica. I asked my staff to do some research and did some myself, as a result of which I wrote the prescribed explanatory memorandum to accompany a request for inclusion in the agenda. Krishna Menon approved the memorandum, and we put in the request which, together with the fairly extensive memorandum, was circulated as a General Assembly document. We made it clear that our purpose was simply to achieve exclusion from the cold war and not to enter into any discussion of jurisdictional questions. However, both Chile and Argentina were most unhappy about our move. They insisted that it would impinge on the matter of jurisdiction and that they would be greatly embarrassed. We set about convincing them that their fears were completely groundless, and I believe we could have done so had it not been for two other factors. One was that the United States' representatives said that this was not a matter that should be dealt with by the UN General Assembly, and that the treaty India envisaged should be drafted in another forum. We pointed out that we were not asking the Assembly to draft the treaty but simply to give its approval to the drafting of a treaty, as had been done in other cases, but the U.S. continued to insist that the United Nations was not the right forum. The second factor, and the one that determined our decision for the time being, was that we were very busy with the 1956 Middle East and Hungarian crises. We decided not to pursue the matter that year, but to bring it before the Assembly the following year, by which time we felt reasonably certain that we could reassure the Latin American countries concerned about the restricted nature of our proposal and its benefits to them. We informed the U.S. of our decision, for which it expressed appreciation.

Then came an amazing development. A few months later, the U.S. issued invitations to nine other states, asking them to meet in Washington to work out a draft treaty on the neutralization of Antarctica! But that was not the only surprise. The second was a classic piece of diplomatic plagiarism: the invitation that the U.S. sent to the countries it chose for the Washington meeting included a memorandum which lifted parts of my own explanatory memorandum to the UN General Assembly without, of course, quotation marks or any other acknowledgment of my penmanship! And there was a third surprise: India, which had been the first to bring up the question of the neutralization of Antarctica, was not among the countries invited to the Washington conference. The Union of South Africa, already barely an acceptable member of the international community, was invited.

India dips far into the Indian ocean, and that body of water extends to the Antarctic circle, but still India was not considered as appropriate an invitee as was South Africa. I laughingly chided Jerry Wadsworth, ambassador and deputy representative of the U.S.A. to the United Nations, one of the best American diplomats of recent times and a good friend of mine, about the use of my language without acknowledgment. He laughed charmingly. And on not inviting us, he said: "Ask Washington. I guess they don't like you!" "I guess not," I said. "Hey, cool it. They thought ten countries were enough for the negotiation of the treaty," he added. True, but it was an odd anticlimactic ending to our unveiling before the world the neutralization of Antarctica.

An interesting, and ultimately cooperative interaction between the U.S. and India took place in 1958 over Lebanon. In the summer of that year the United States Marines landed on the shores of Lebanon when it was feared that the government of that country was being subverted by some neighboring states, and that such subversion might assist the policies of the Soviet Union in the Middle East. Most of the Arab states and some others, including India, were upset about the landing of the marines, fearing that it portended Great Power domination of a small country and also because it could escalate the conflict in the region. Moreover, very recently the Security Council, with the full support of the United States, had sent an observer group to Lebanon, and the reports of that group indicated that the situation was steadily improving. An emergency special session of the UN General Assembly was convened to deal with the very tense situation. The United States took an unusual step: President Eisenhower himself addressed the Assembly on the issue, announcing the conditions under which he would withdraw the marines. Intense diplomatic activity followed, and Dag Hammarskjold, then at the height of his prestige, drafted a resolution which reflected most of the points contained in the President's statement. This draft gave the UN's tacit approval to the landing of the marines in Lebanon. Since a large number of states had made it clear that they were opposed to that landing, it was unrealistic to expect that the Assembly would give its approval to this action. However, the United States, through Dulles (who was present in New York for the special session of the Assembly) and other diplomats made it clear that they favored the Hammarskjold draft resolution. As the leader of the delegation from India, I had to explain that we could not support the draft, and would have to vote against it, because of India's opposition in principle to the sending of military forces to countries without the approval of the UN. The Hammarskjold draft had meanwhile been cosponsored by Canada, Colombia, Norway, and a few other countries. I was called in for frequent meetings with the Canadian foreign minister and my old friend Hans Engen, the deputy foreign minister of Norway. Though I liked and respected these colleagues, I had to maintain my position. Meanwhile, the sponsors were delaying the vote on their resolution while seeking support. There were rumors of strenuous efforts in the capitals of certain countries. Time was pressing; the issue had to be resolved one way or another. The Arabs held daily meetings, and I was in close contact with most of them, and with other representatives. In a last effort to win the support of India, which would probably have influenced another half dozen or more votes, one midnight Sidney Smith, the foreign minister of Canada, asked me to come to his hotel. He accused me of being more difficult than the Arabs, and said that Hammarskjold had told them emphatically that Fawzi, the foreign minister of Egypt, had made it clear that Egypt would not oppose the Western draft resolution. "But I'm in almost hourly contact with Fawzi and Omar Loutfi on the Arab position, and Hammarskjold's interpretation of that position is not what I've been given to understand," I said, adding: "Do you mind if I ring Fawzi now, from your room?" Sidney Smith was surprised that I could get in touch with the foreign minister in the middle of the night. "Go ahead," he said. In the presence of Smith I told Fawzi what the Canadian had said. Fawzi said: "Tell him tomorrow I will spill the beans. Come to me and I will explain the position."

I crossed Park Avenue to Fawzi's hotel and, his head nodding characteristically, he said in his quiet but firm voice: "How can they think these things? Do they imagine that I have been saying things to Hammarskjold that differ from our position? It's nonsense."

The Western powers seemed to think there was still time for a last desperate effort to get the Assembly to accept their position. The next day, unusually early in the morning, Cabot Lodge telephoned me: "Arthur, the Secretary would like to see you urgently. Can you come over at once?" I rushed through my morning bath, and when I arrived at the UN, there was Cabot Lodge himself waiting at the delegates' entrance to escort me to Dulles's office. "We know who counts here now. Not the English and the French. You've been influencing votes so that now the Canadian resolution is in difficulties," he said as we went toward Dulles's office. I laughed. "Naturally, when others ask me, I explain my position. They're entitled to know it." He complained that I had swung around the votes of several countries, which he named. In Dulles's office, Cabot sat in silence while his chief and I did the talking. Dulles asked for a precise statement of our position. To my surprise, the Secretary of State showed much more understanding of India's position than had Cabot Lodge and other members of the American delegation, or the Canadian foreign minister and other sponsors of the draft resolution. Of the powerfulness of his thought there was no doubt. He proceeded to give me his views on the Middle East in general, and in the course of his remarks said that Ernest Bevin had boasted to him of the success of British diplomacy in creating Jordan, but that he himself was of the view that it had been a mistake to do so, describing the country as a nonviable entity, a perpetual client state that had cost the British a large annual subvention that they were no longer able to keep up, so that the burden had fallen on the United States. Dulles was, as I expected, enormously concerned about the problems of law and order in the whole of the Middle East, and it was in this context that he looked at the Lebanese situation, to which we returned in our discussion. I explained Nehru's thinking in some detail. Dulles said: "I think we should be able to find some way out." This led me to think he was not inflexible about the resolution that his delegation and others had been pushing so strongly. That meeting of ours turned out to be a watershed. The American delegation stopped pushing the Hammarskjold resolution, and the Arabs saw that the situation had changed. I had shown them an alternative draft resolution I had prepared. Taking into account both the Hammarskjold draft and mine and, of course, adding their own thinking, they were able to forge a unity on the issue of Lebanon, and it was their draft that was adopted unanimously, with even the United States voting for it. The only one put out was Hammarskjold, who went into a big sulk. This was a far superior ending to the crisis than could have been achieved by the Hammarskjold draft. Indeed, that draft would not have resolved the situation, which Hammarskjold and most of the West, including the United States, had misjudged. It was to Dulles's credit that he came to realize this and saw the wisdom of altering course. In the best constructive sense, there had been a late and very useful converging of views between India (myself) and the United States (Dulles) which bore good fruit.

Another area of conflict during this period was in Southeast Asia. The bowing out of the French was inevitable, and the situation had been complicated by the communization of China. Dulles particularly was angry about this, and he did not agree to sign the documents that emerged from the Geneva conference of 1954 on Southeast Asia. Though the British had proposed that India be invited to participate in that conference, Dulles had not agreed. The British view was that India had earned a place at the table by its successful effort to end the fighting in Korea. Denied such a place, Krishna Menon was nevertheless in Geneva during the 1954 conference, seeing all the delegates. He sufficiently impressed Bedell Smith, Dulles's deputy, to earn for India the chairmanship of the International Control Commission, which the conference created to supervise the implementation of the 1954 Southeast Asia agreements; the two other members designated were Canada and Poland.

The 1954 agreements broke down first in Laos. As a result, the United States eventually concurred in the proposal, made persistently by Nehru, the Chinese leaders, and Prince Sihanouk of Cambodia, that a Geneva conference should be convened to try to get agreement on the independence and neutrality or, as Nehru preferred, the nonalignment, of Laos. The prospects were not good. The U.S. had introduced a large military assistance group into the country which was supporting Prince Bon Oum, the easy-going, self-indulgent right-wing leader and his well-trained general, Nousavan, against Prince Souvanna Phouma, the leader of the nonaligned group. Western-supported military power drove Souvanna Phouma from the country, but this settled nothing. Turmoil increased, and the extreme left wing, the Pathet Lao, began to gain military victories over the right wing, so as to raise the specter of a Communist government's coming to power. On May 14, 1961, the Geneva conference on Laos met in these confused circumstances. Immediately, there was a major confrontation between Dean Rusk, U.S. secretary of state, and Marshal Chen Yi, the Chinese foreign minister. Each accused the other of subverting the independence of Laos, while India—this time a participant in the conference (being chairman of the International Control Commission, it could hardly be excluded) spoke for the independence of Laos outside the framework of big power alliances and foreign military bases or assistance.

Fortunately for the conference, very shortly after it convened President Kennedy and Premier Khrushchev met in Vienna and agreed that Laos should be independent and neutral. The Geneva conference was then faced with the seemingly simple task of translating the Kennedy-Khrushchev agreement into international documents. The task proved anything but simple, because arrangements to safeguard the independence and inviolability of Laos had to be worked out and agreed upon. What had been envisaged as a negotiation lasting about six weeks actually took fourteen months, during which time Laos came near to being partitioned. The role of India at the conference was crucial. The United States and France had drafted and introduced documents which placed before the conference the Western approach to defining Laotian independence and the methods of preserving that independence. The Soviet Union had introduced documents that set out their approach which, at that time, was acceptable to Peking. I drafted a third set of documents, setting out a nonaligned approach. Krishna Menon and I discussed these papers with Souvanna Phouma before they were presented to the conference, and they helped, throughout the long negotiations, in getting a result which the nonaligned countries, among which we hoped to count Laos itself, could endorse. At this conference there was excellent cooperation between Kennedy's representative, Averell Harriman, and myself. I recall one instance in particular when, in his office, he said to me: "Arthur, let's get agreement on this. I'm to call President Kennedy about it at two today." We did reach agreement, which was on the degree of authority of the Control Commission—of which India was to continue to be the chairman—to investigate charges of violation; a touchy subject not only because the sovereignty of Laos was involved, but also because the Chinese and the Pathet Lao feared that Laos's pristine neutrality would be violated by unpredictable foreigners acting in the interests of the United States. Averell Harriman was ably assisted by a very promising younger officer of the U.S. Foreign Service, Bill Sullivan, most recently Ambassador in Iran through the difficult period of the fall of the Shah. It can be fairly claimed that the results of the Laos conference vindicated the nonalignment which Nehru had formulated in 1946. It took constant effort throughout the long negotiations to wring concessions both from the Western powers and from the Communist states with a view to maintaining Laos as a nonaligned country. This was without doubt the best way of assuring the future of Laos, and it might have succeeded but for the sad mess which was made of the Vietnamese problem.

It was no proselytizing zeal which led Nehru to perceive a non-aligned role as the best one for Laos. He saw such a role as the most effective way of preserving the national ethos of a people who were likely otherwise to be swallowed by one great power or another. Nehru's intuition was against the notion of an institutionalized non-aligned movement. For long he resisted the drive of the flamboyant Sukarno of Indonesia and the ambitious N'kruma of Ghana for a concourse of nonaligned countries with a view to establishing some kind of framework for a movement. He ultimately yielded to the wishes of Yugoslavia's Tito, because he realized that a nonaligned conference in Belgrade would remind Yugoslavia's neighbors of its international stature. So Nehru became one of the sponsors of the first conference of nonaligned heads of state and government which convened in Belgrade in September 1961. He kept the conference from extreme courses, not because he was wedded to moderation but because an extremism born of anger or hatred was not his style. At the Belgrade conference, the delegations were at work almost all night for several successive nights. The result was that sometimes we did not have time to tell our chiefs the tentative conclusions at which we had arrived. The heads of government were looking at a draft on the Middle East. The Arab draft condemned Israel in vehement terms. Fortunately, U Thant had had time to brief U Nu the head of the government of Burma. U Nu told his peers at the conference table that he was unable to accept the Arab draft, but that he could go along with the Indian draft. I had not been able to tell Nehru the language I had suggested. I hastily scribbled the two sentences and handed them to him in reply to the question which he, turning round, shot at us: "What draft?" With U Nu's support, the language I had proposed prevailed. Since Nehru's death, conferences of the heads of nonaligned governments have become much more frequent. Perhaps they are more necessary now as occasions to remind the very large membership of some of the essentials on which nonalignment is based. Without the leaders concerned being aware that this is the case, their main value is educational and normative.

The one major aspect of foreign affairs Nehru was unable fully to control was the international economic dealings of India. He was too dependent on the lack of economic wisdom of successive advisers in this field. The conventional wisdom was that India needed vast amounts of imported capital. My view, a minority one, was that we were not making nearly enough use of our great reservoir of capital: the unutilized labor of tens of millions of our people. Also, we had a greater fund of indigenous capacity and trained talent than Delhi took account of. Here is a glaring example: in the early fifties, India decided to build a complex which would manufacture the major types of heavy electrical equipment. Tenders were invited on a turn-key basis for what was, at that time, and in view of our foreign exchange resources, a very expensive project. Westinghouse was interested in the venture and submitted a proposal that the government of India eventually selected. To conclude the negotiations, a technical team of senior men was sent out by Westinghouse at the end of 1953.

I knew well the senior official who would lead the negotiation for India. He was a charming but arrogant person. The straight-from-the-shoulder Westinghouse engineers found him impossible to deal with, and the negotiation collapsed. Westinghouse decided against going ahead with the project. That decision taken, the leader of their team and some of his colleagues came to see me on their return to New York from Delhi. I was at that time the consul general of India in New York. They said that now that Westinghouse was no longer interested in the venture, they would tell me the real facts about the Indian government's project. "You don't need this integrated heavy electrical equipment plant," said the leader. "Don't need it?" I asked, incredulously. "No, you don't. It's a waste of your money. You already have first-class facilities to build three of the six types of heavy electrical equipment. We've been to the workshops. They do just as good work as we could do. All you need is the balancing equipment to build the three types of heavy gear which you are not making in the country. And some of the machinery you need you can fabricate in India. All you need is a project which would cost about a fourth of the big one."

I reported these facts to Nehru in my note, "The Death of Vargas," to which I have already referred. He ordered an enquiry to be made but inevitably, because he was too busy to follow through, and because he trusted his top advisers, his government went ahead with the whole of the original, very costly project with the collaboration of English Electric. I can cite other instances, within my personal knowledge, of waste of our resources in international economic exchanges.

It would be wrong to blame Nehru for these failures. The root cause was the habit of dependence that the bureaucracy and the top advisers had inherited from the colonial era, when dependence was taken for granted and when the foreign ruler inculcated the mentality that the subject people of course could not do this, that, or the other. During the Nehru era India received development loans totaling about $7.5 billion (just under a third being from the United States) and grants totaling about $750 million (over $300 million from the United States).[8] In per capita terms these were not large amounts, and they were considerably less than the per capita intake by almost all other developing countries, but India, given its resources and its philosophy of life, should have resorted to loans only when there was dire need, such as scarcity of food; it could have asked for grants in the event of natural calamities. In such circumstances, wherever they might occur, the nations of the world should assist one another. But to depend on other countries for even a small fraction of the resources required for normal developmental activities was to continue the mentality of the person who expects alms. This mentality persists. To this day, some of the leaders of the government in India think in terms of how much aid they can get from the United States, or Sweden, or the USSR. Only a slight shift of vision is needed. For productive capital investment, it is clearly permissible to borrow in the lending markets of the world, and to pay the going rate. This is what India should aim to do, rather than annually taking its case to a consortium of "aid"-giving countries who decide how much they can lend India in the coming year. In a real sense most of the funds made available do not amount to aid; they are commercial loans which India duly repays, and its record of repayment is a good one. Then why does India agree to the lending countries calling the funds advanced "aid?" It is not aid because it consists of mutually advantageous financial transactions. Just to complete the record, I should add that in the period covered by the "aid" figures I have included in this paragraph, India also received, against payment in rupees, about $3 billion of U.S. Public Law 480 food and other commodities from the United States. A great part of the large rupee holdings which accumulated to the credit of the United States was later cancelled by agreement between the two governments.

Could Nehru have helped to avert the unnecessary war in Vietnam? Probably not. But he did miss two opportunities which are

8. Tarlok Singh, *India's Development Experience* (Madras: Macmillan, 1974). These figures are extrapolated from the table on page 323 of that book.

worth recalling. The first occurred at the end of the Laos conference, in July 1962. The deterioration of the situation in Vietnam had begun. U.S. involvement was increasing. In his final statement to the Laos conference, Marshal Chen Yi, the deputy prime minister and foreign minister of China, said correctly and bluntly that the Laos agreements would not stick unless the flames of war which had been ignited in Vietnam were also extinguished. This was both an assessment and a warning. India was ready to heed these words, and to go into another conference on Southeast Asia, this one on Vietnam, but the Western powers, and particularly the United States, paid no attention to the Chen Yi's words. This was unfortunate, and a crucial opportunity was lost. Nehru should have pressed harder for a conference.

It was not that the United States was unaware of the dangers of the situation in Vietnam—and this takes me to the second occasion, earlier than the occasion just mentioned, when Nehru could have contributed to an early defusing of the Vietnam situation. In November 1961 he was on a visit to Kennedy in Washington. The American president was young, vigorous, and ebullient; Nehru was a sick man, tired out after a long journey, and he was used to a quite different tempo of human communication than that of Kennedy. The President turned to Nehru and said: "Mr. Prime Minister, we would be glad to get out of Vietnam. Tell me, how can we accomplish this? I want to avoid a major flare-up." Nehru listened, smiled wanly, but made no response at all. He needed time to reflect, but the President had other matters to attend to, and he expected a reply immediately. The meeting with Nehru was not a success from Kennedy's point of view. It need not have failed if he had known better how to put Nehru at ease, and if he had known how to wait, taking into account Nehru's physical condition. The salient fact, however, is that Nehru was given an opportunity to help Kennedy out of Vietnam, but he did not make use of it. Already a major preoccupation of Nehru's was China. He had expected very friendly relations with China but he had come to the conclusion that Chinese intentions were different in this regard from his, and as Kennedy sought his advice, he was undoubtedly fitting China into the picture on which Kennedy was focusing his powerful spotlight. Relations with China had developed in a manner which made them the least successful of all India's foreign relations, excluding those with Pakistan, which fell within a completely different category of problems.

Chapter Fourteen

INDIA AND CHINA IN THE NEHRU ERA

We have noted that in his remarkable seminal statement made on September 7, 1946, Nehru referred to the long friendship between India and China and expressed his certainty that the friendship would endure in the future. When India regained its independence, it was not immediately possible for close relations to develop with China, which was still in the throes of its long civil war. However, when the Chinese Communists gained control, India immediately recognized the new government in Peking, and exchanged ambassadors with it. The Indian embassy was accorded especially favored treatment in Peking, and in Delhi the largest plot in the new diplomatic enclave was deliberately allotted to China. Things seemed to be going in accordance with Nehru's prognostication.

Furthermore, in 1954 a treaty of friendship was entered into after the Chinese government forces had mounted a massive attack on Tibet and taken it over. This act was not one the Indians particularly appreciated, because Tibet had long been a Buddhist state with very close and friendly relations with India. It had, from time to time, been completely independent of China, and at other times it had recognized a loose Chinese suzerainty. India was perfectly willing not to quarrel about Chinese suzerainty over Tibet, but suzerainty is a concept which implies autonomy, and India would have liked to see the autonomy of that rather special territory maintained under the umbrella of general Chinese authority, and within the framework of the new Chinese system. Nevertheless, India accepted the new dispensation established by Chinese arms, and it negotiated with Peking the treaty of 1954 which included, for the first time in a treaty, the concept of *panch shila* (or five pillars) governing relations between independent states. These five pillars are mutual respect for each other's territorial integrity and sovereignty, mutual nonaggression, mutual noninterference in each other's internal affairs, equality and mutual benefit, and peaceful coexistence.[1] *Panch shila* is Sanskrit, and its use in connection with the five-point formula evolved for inclusion in the Indo-China treaty seems to continue the long historical process of the outward flow of Indian culture. Moreover, the five points of the panch shila closely reflect Nehru's nonalignment policy.

I have referred in previous chapters to some aspects of India's peaceful cultural penetration of China which became a massive influence there. It is also relevant that for some seven hundred years, until the end of the eleventh century, a steady trickle of Chinese monks and scholars came to Buddhist places of pilgrimage in India as well as to the great Buddhist university at Nalanda in Bihar. Some of them left records of their visits inscribed on stone plaques which refer to India with affection and respect. There was no question of India's being regarded by them as a country of lesser standing than China. Some of them wrote of it as the heavenly country and others as the western kingdoms. Chinese envoys also came to the main kingdoms during the same period. India under Nehru looked forward to the resumption in the Maoist era of the old warm relations between the two countries which had been interrupted by the sealing off of India as a result of conquest.

However, there were several clouds on the horizon. For one thing, the Chinese had been upset by Nehru's outspokenness on Indian values, just as the Western powers frequently found some of his pronouncements on armaments and nonalignment to be irritating. In the early fifties, Nehru stated in the Indian Parliament that India regretted deeply China's use of massive force to take over Tibet. The Chinese reaction was that this was none of India's business, but this view overlooked India's long and close ties with Tibet as well as the ups and downs of Tibetan fortunes. An analogy is perhaps to be found in President Carter's outspoken stand on human rights, which has sometimes drawn critical comments in various parts of the world.

Second, a little research by Indians would have brought to light that Mao, at that time the supreme and unquestioned prophet of the new Chinese religion, had established that it was impossible for any

1. Quoted by Nehru in Parliament from the text of the treaty. See Jawaharlal Nehru, *India's Foreign Policy* (Speeches) (New Delhi: Government of India, Publications Division, 1961), pp. 303–4.

country to remain neutral in the great confrontation between Marxism or socialism and capitalism or liberal democracy.[2] In brief, he dismissed as completely unreal Nehru's posture of nonalignment. This was going one full step further than Dulles. The American statesman believed that nonalignment was immoral; Mao said it simply could not exist. Therefore the new leaders of China, far from continuing to respect India, had no patience whatsoever for the Indian point of view. On the other hand, though not espousing Marxism, the Indian sense of tolerance did not take China's political and economic beliefs as concepts to treat with contempt. There was thus a basic dissimilarity in the attitudes of the two societies toward each other which could not help the development of good relations.

Third, Indians were baffled that while China ostensibly sought good relations with India, it made special efforts to court Pakistan. India had no objection at all to good relations between China and Pakistan, but it became clear that this relationship was to be pursued at the cost of India's known interests. For example, China favored Pakistan's point of view in regard to Kashmir. Moreover, when the glow of mutual affection between China and Pakistan began to appear, the latter was not only avowedly anti-Communist, but had put behind bars any suspected Communists, and was also a firm supporter of the United States' system of military alliances which was anathema to the Chinese. In 1961 I asked Marshal Chen Yi how one was to understand the warmth between Peking and Karachi in the light of these considerations. The Marshal bridled and spluttered angrily, fanned his face, and offered me a cup of tea.

However, whatever the Chinese attitude toward nonalignment—which, of course, has greatly changed since the 1950s because Peking could not possibly continue to regard as impossible a posture which was being adopted by a majority of the world's states—and no matter how sweet the music between Peking and Karachi, India's relations with China could have remained "normal," to use a diplomatic cliché, but for an outbreak of rebellion in Tibet against the new regime in Peking. The young Dalai Lama, the traditional spiritual and temporal head of his people, became the rallying point of the rebellion. His followers feared for his life, and that he should be done to death by the interloping irreligious Chinese was unthinkable. In spite of the presence of hundreds of thousands of Chinese troops to

2. For an example of Mao's actual words on the subject, see Arthur Lall, *How Communist China Negotiates* (New York: Columbia University Press, 1968), p. 28.

contain the rebels, the Dalai Lama escaped and, guarded by his people, he made the long journey from Lhasa to the Indian frontier, evading capture by the Chinese. In India there were manifestations of typical Indian veneration for a spiritiual leader, and an outcry against Chinese policies of repression in Tibet. There was little that the authorities could do to curb the free press—short of declaring a constitutional emergency, which would have been regarded in India as an excessive reaction—but to the Chinese, who had nothing approaching a free press, the outcries and enthusiasm for the Dalai Lama looked like very unfriendly acts and were so interpreted, as events showed, by Mao, Chou En-lai, and the other leaders.

To make matters worse for relations between the two countries, the Dalai Lama and his entourage were given political asylum, and the party was treated with conspicuous respect. This was natural enough, since that the Dalai Lama was held to be a reincarnation of the Buddha, and the Hindus regarded the Buddha as a reincarnation of Vishnu, or God himself. But what was natural for India made the Chinese furious. The immediate result was a very stiff note from Chou En-lai to Nehru in which, for the first time—though there had been exchanges of notes for years about the border—China claimed large areas of Indian territory. The logic of the claims was not apparent, but the timing spoke eloquently. It seems that the Chinese espoused the view that wherever the Tibetans had gained military successes at any time in the past, the areas then under dispute had become part of China! This is analogous to the old Hohenzollern doctrine in Europe that wherever a Hohenzollern has trod is Prussia. In the older parts of the world, to dig up isolated historical events to justify claims to territory is simply not a tenable position. On this basis India could sustain claims to territories as far as Lop Nor in Sinkiang as well as parts of Afghanistan, which would be totally absurd, but the Chinese were completely oblivious to the unreality of their claims, both on this frontier and elsewhere.

Chou En-lai's note was immediately followed by insistent and frequent probings by armed Chinese detachments all along India's northern frontier with Tibet. There had been a few minor incidents before the note, mainly related to Chinese action against fleeing Tibetan rebels. Some of these Tibetans crossed the border into India, re-formed in the high secluded mountains, and again made raids into Tibet. These forays were certainly unwelcome to the Chinese, and should have been the subject of discussions between India and China.

The problem was that these deeds were performed in the high mountain fastnesses of the Himalayas where no continuous surveillance was possible; and in any event the Tibetan forays were extremely ineffectual—or so the Chinese claimed.

The matter was none too well handled by Delhi, because of overconfidence that India was right and the Chinese wrong, and that Peking was merely seeking pretexts to repay the Indians for having given sanctuary to the Dalai Lama and for other annoyances. A major instance of poor handling was the way the Indians presented their case for the border. They based their claim largely on what the British had called the McMahon Line. In fact, there was no such thing as the McMahon Line. There was only the watershed line, and McMahon, who had been a British official, had drawn a line along the watershed in a conference with Tibet and China in 1913. It was not without significance that Tibet attended the conference, and so did China—two entities. China recognized that line, as drawn by McMahon, in its negotiations with Burma (1956–60), as well as with Nepal a few years later. But it was unwise of India to claim so "imperialistic"-sounding a border as the McMahon Line. The Chinese spurned any reference to it. What should have been a persuasive claim on the basis of the watershed became distorted.

Shortly before the escape to India of the Dalai Lama, Delhi discovered that the Chinese had, in a very remote area of Indian Ladakh, quietly widened for use by vehicular traffic an ancient trade route which, had for millennia been used by traders of all nationalities. Now the road was closed to all but Chinese traffic. This road cut through the Aksai Chin peninsula, which the Chinese contended was part of Tibet rather than of Ladakh. Certainly the facts of the previous 150 years were that it had been either in British hands or part of the domain of the Sikh rulers of "the Punjab, Kashmir, and Beyond" (the official title of those rulers). The Aksai Chin issue was negotiable, however. Though the records showed it as part of India, it was not of particular value to India; any arrangements should, however, have kept it open to peaceful traders of all nationalities, as in the past. On the other hand, once the new Chinese government had selected Lop Nor for its nuclear tests and the neighborhood for important nuclear facilities, the Aksai Chin road—which ran through a remote Himalayan region that probably no Han Chinese had ever set foot upon at any time in history—assumed special significance because it greatly reduced the journey to Lop Nor. It should have been possible to divide Aksai Chin between India and China, and perhaps also to find another sector along the long Indo-Tibetan border where a sliver of compensatory territory could have been made over to India. None of this would have been easy. The Himalayan region has a very special "sacredness" for India. It figures very prominently in the ancient texts of the Vedas, in the great epics, the *Ramayana* and the *Mahabharata,* and in much of the mythology of the country. Also, these high mountains are dotted with Hindu or Hindu-Buddhist shrines and places of pilgrimage.

Although there were four meetings between Nehru and Chou En-lai, three in Delhi and one in Peking, this issue was not resolved. Meanwhile the Indian newspapers, largely conservative and right-wing, became increasingly strident in describing China as the aggressive wave of Communist power in Asia and not to be appeased, just as the Western world had decided not to appease the wave of Communist power in Europe. All this had a strong emotional appeal, but it was not a way of resolving conflict.

In short, for various reasons, negotiations on the issues between India and China in regard to their long common border were side-tracked. Meanwhile, the Chinese seemed unable to take into account the many acts of friendliness displayed by India in regard to China, and instead they focused their vision entirely on what they disliked, such as the matter of the Dalai Lama. For example, at the Bandung Conference of 1955, Nehru went out of his way to present Chou favorably to the other leaders on the ground that China had been so long isolated that all that was reasonably possible should be done to acquaint others with its leaders. Again, for many years, India led the movement in the United Nations to give the government of Peking the Chinese seat. It was clear that only that government could represent China. At five successive sessions of the UN General Assembly I personally wrote the explanatory memorandum arguing Peking's case in this matter. These and other efforts in behalf of Peking were known to the Chinese, but they decided other considerations were more important.

One of those considerations was the state of friendly relations between the Soviet Union and India. This was paradoxical. We, in India, assumed that these good relations would be regarded by the Chinese as an additional reason for good relations between them and ourselves. The first country that Khrushchev and Bulganin visited on their journeys outside the Soviet Union was India, where they were warmly received in 1955. After that, Indo-Soviet relations continued to improve, and in 1959, when the China-India border dispute came to the fore, Khrushchev made a statement to the effect that both parties should resolve the issue peacefully. The Chinese were incensed, taking this statement to herald a serious departure from the rule of international Communist solidarity, and they chose to give vent to their wrath by becoming more unfriendly toward India. In 1963, in the prolonged polemical exchanges between the Central Committee of the Communist party of the Soviet Union and its counterpart in China, the Chinese gave vent to bitter resentment at the attitude of the Soviet Union in regard to the dispute between themselves and India, citing it as one of the issues which had spoiled relations between the two Communist countries.

The deteriorating relationship between China and India need not have led to war had it not been for a difference in the styles of the two countries. I have mentioned the Indian style of righteous indignation over the Chinese claims, and the loud outcry in the Indian press against China. The Chinese style was to make large claims to territory, which apparently were not to be taken at face value in the final analysis. The tactic used was to make these grandiose claims, and later to be willing to let the other side keep much of the territory concerned so that China might appear magnanimous. What was needed was a forum for serious negotiations. But for reasons of prestige, neither country was willing to take definitive steps to provide such a forum. However, in the summer of 1962, it appeared that such a forum had fortuitously been found, at least for initial exchanges, on the occasion of the signing of the agreements on Laos at the end of the Geneva conference on Laos in July 1962. Marshal Chen Yi, not only foreign minister but also deputy prime minister and a member of the Politburo of the Communist party of China, and altogether a very important Chinese functionary, was present to sign the accords, as was Krishna Menon, defense minister of India and an informal deputy of Nehru in matters pertaining to foreign affairs. In Geneva, a series of three very important meetings took place between Chen Yi, Chang Han-fu, and Ch'iao Kuan-hua (until recently foreign minister of China) and, on the other side, Krishna Menon and me. At these meetings there was both cordiality and a serious exploration of the border dispute. It was relevant that all of us knew each other well. With Chang Han-fu, first deputy foreign minister of China, and my counterpart at the Laos conference, I had

had excellent relations for over a year. Ch'iao was always with Chang, and I had also gotten to know the Marshal well. Both of us were writers and enjoyed tallking about literature and the arts. Krishna Memon had been to Peking and knew the Chinese team quite well.

The Chinese soon made it clear to us that they were not thinking of disturbing the McMahon Line (though their large paper claims were in this area). What was important to them was to gain clear title to the territory through which they had modernized the road to Sinkiang. For Krishna Menon and myself the issue was a most delicate one. The Indian government and the Indian public were strongly opposed to the surrender of any territory. But in the Aksai Chin region, where the road was, some deal had to be worked out. The Chinese had already strengthened their position by setting up posts to the west of the road, thereby extending the area in their possession. In the discussions our strategy was to negotiate with the Chinese an agreement providing that both sides could set up posts in this area as long as they observed the rule that where one side had set up a post the other side would not attempt to set up a post on the same mountain feature. After each meeting we sent a telegram to Nehru to be sure we were not putting ourselves out on a limb. At the third meeting Chen Yi informed us that the proposal for intertwining posts was acceptable to them, provided restraint was exercised by each side. This implied that both sides would claim possession of some of the Aksai Chin, and that the territory would have to be divided, leaving the road on the Chinese side. But this would not sit well with Delhi, unless we could show some counteroffer for the territory which would have to be ceded by India. We raised the question of some small adjustment elsewhere along the border, in favor of India. Chen Yi did not reject this suggestion, but no specifics were mentioned.

At the end of the final meeting, Chen Yi surprised us with his proposal that a communique be issued to the press. He suggested the following language: "Two senior Ministers of the Governments of the Peoples Republic of China and the Republic of India have met and discussed the border situation between the two countries. These discussions have been constructive and fruitful, and it is the intention of the two governments that they should lead to further talks in the near future." On the face of it, this brief communique was not only acceptable but to be welcomed. However, in view of the delicacies involved we had to seek instructions from Nehru. We told Chen Yi that we would seek urgent instructions. He understood our position, and the parting was both cordial and hopeful. Alas, sometimes fortune does not favor peace. We were unaware that Nehru was not in Delhi, but somewhere in south India. Our telegram seeking instructions was delayed in reaching him, although the situation was desperately urgent. After our last morning meeting with him, Chen Yi was to be in Geneva only that day and the next, and Krishna Menon was due to leave for an important political meeting in Bombay even earlier. He was sure a reply from Nehru would come before Chen Yi was due to leave. "As soon as it comes, tell Chen Yi and issue the communique with their consent," he said to me. But there was no reply from Nehru before the departures. The day following these departures, a brief reply came from Nehru: "I agree. Issue communique." I tried to contact the Chinese, but it was too late; the constructive proposal in the draft communique, for the continuance of negotiations, was left hanging in the air.

Still, the situation might have been saved, but on Krishna Menon's return to Delhi there was an outcry in the Indian Parliament against his negotiations with Chen Yi. The fact of our meetings with the Chinese had been leaked to the press (perhaps by Krishna Menon himself!), but not their substance. Some members of Parliament were highly suspicious of Krishna Menon as a negotiator with the Chinese. At that point Nehru, already a sick man, denied that there had been any negotiations at all, which was far from the truth. He explained away the Geneva meetings by telling Parliament that when people are in the same town for the same official business (the signing of the Laos accords), some talk between them is inevitable, and this is all that happened. After this interpretation of the very important talks in Geneva, Nehru could not go ahead and follow up with further negotiations, which was the urgent need of the moment.

The Chinese naturally took Nehru's remarks to be a repudiation of the process of negotiation between the two countries. He did not mean to go that far, and after a few weeks he would have come around to a more sensible position; but as we have seen, he was his own foreign minister. If only the parliamentary furor had been handled by another minister, and then, if Nehru, as the head of the government, had assessed the effects of the exchange in Parliament, he might have realized, sick man though he was, the urgent need to be conciliatory and to resume negotiations with the Chinese. Unfortunately, negr tiations were never resumed, and the groundwork which had been so carefully laid by Krishna Menon and myself at Geneva was washed away.

I am confident that, if there had been another round of discussions with Marshal Chen Yi, armed conflict between India and China could have been averted. He was a person of quality who was, for a time, frequently mentioned as a possible successor to Mao Tse-tung. His senior deputy, Chang Han-fu, possessed the useful qualification of a sound working knowledge of English, which facilitated negotiations. The difficult member of the Chinese team was Ch'iao Kuanhua, later foreign minister until he was dismissed with "the gang of four." He was intelligent, but his blustering, emotional, and hot-tempered demeanor was hardly the temperament for diplomacy. I vividly remember his pounding his chest with clenched fist while he said hotly: "Ambassador Lall, we know the Americans much better than you do. We defeated them in Korea." This was his follow-up to a proposal for a compromise on part of one of the texts of the Laos accords which I had just made, and in regard to which I had expressed the view that the Americans might be able to consider it favorably.

In the absence of negotiations, relations between India and China were drifting toward war over the border in the second half of 1962. There is some evidence that by about the middle of August the Chinese decided that the Indians did not mean to negotiate, and that they would have to resort to arms to press their point of view. (As we have again seen in the four-week war with Vietnam in 1979, there seems to be a tendency for present-day China to see itself in the role of a punitive power, a rather archaic concept and one that, it is to be hoped, will soon be shed.) From the middle of August onward the Chinese deployed their forces on the border of India, whereas India did nothing of the kind. The "forward line" of India consisted of posts manned by three men each, certainly not a war formation; the next group of some twenty men was usually several miles behind. On September 8, 1962, apparently to provoke incidents which could lead to the Chinese "punitive action," the Chinese crossed the watershed at the Thagla Ridge and took a hamlet. The Indians were not militarily placed so as to react there at once, but they decided that they had to confront the Chinese and, true to style, Nehru announced publicly in mid-October that he had given orders to the Indian army to throw out the Chinese! He thought it was quite apparent that all he meant was a local push and shove at Thagla Ridge. But the Chinese took this as a clear indication that the Indians were planning to move on a wide front and they were not about to let the initiative pass over to the other side. Thus a week after Nehru's announcement, the Chinese attacked massively across a wide sector of the northeastern Indian frontier as well as in Aksai Chin, the location of the real prize they were after. On the northeast sector the Chinese cut through the sparse Indian posts with ease and maintained a momentum toward the plains of India. This shook the Indian government to its foundations. Nehru appealed to all countries for assistance but, abruptly, the war ended. Late in November 1962, the Chinese declared a cease-fire and withdrawal, and withdraw they did, to the line they had held on September 8, 1962—making the point that they would remain on the Indian side of the watershed at one place as a demonstration of their case.

After the Chinese withdrawal, six Asian and African countries sent representatives to Colombo, Sri Lanka, to form a mediating group. This was the idea of Prime Minister Sirimavo Bandaranaike of Sri Lanka. She worked hard and nobly, visiting both Nehru and Chou En-lai. Eventually her group produced a basis for negotiation between India and China. India accepted it without qualification; China accepted it in a broad sense but raised objections to two points in the plan. India felt it could not negotiate on the proposed basis until it had been fully accepted by China. This was reasonable enough because the plan stood as a whole. To remove one or two of its building blocks, which was what the Chinese qualified acceptance amounted to, meant the demolition of the structure.

The two countries did not break diplomatic relations, but reduced representation to the level of senior chargés d'affaires. In 1976 Indira Gandhi's government and the Chinese leaders agreed that each side should again send an ambassador to the other's capital. Still, there were no negotiations. The Janata government took matters a step further. In response to an invitation from the genial new Chinese foreign minister, Huang Hua, Atal Vajpayee, the Indian foreign minister, visted China in February 1979 and had useful discussions with all the top Chinese leaders, but there were, understandably, no negotiations specifically about the border. However, there were expressions of willingness and determination to find a peaceful solution. Unfortunately, during the visit of the Indian foreign minister, the Chinese forces launched their war against Vietnam, and the government of India decided that Vajpayee should cut short his trip to make it quite clear that India did not approve of the Chinese action. This unambiguous demonstration and adherence to its basic principles by India has not been without value in the situation. Together with the other objections raised to the Chinese course of action, it has given Peking something to think about in regard to its completely out-of-date attitude toward resort to arms in international affairs.

Meanwhile, as any reader of such Chinese periodicals as the *Beijing* [Peking] *Review* might have observed, the Chinese have ceased such abusive reference to India as "the running dog of the imperialists" and, in more recent years, "the lackey of the social imperialists." There is no evidence that China has forsaken this style altogether in its international relations, but perhaps there is a move in that direction as Peking becomes more acquainted with international norms and law. At any rate, so far as India and China are concerned, the media signals on both sides are benign now, and are in conformity with a full normalizing of relations.

In concluding this chapter on relations between India and China, I might be forgiven for adding a personal postscript about the effect the war between the two countries had on me. Shortly before the war broke out I had been selected by Nehru and Krishna Menon for appointment as defense secretary to the government of India, and I was to take up this new position at the beginning of 1963. However, as a result of the war Krishna Menon was forced out, and with this went my appointment. I had accepted on the basis that I would hold it for only two years and then run for election to the Indian Parliament. The first step was to lead to the next. Neither was taken. Such are the effects of world events on individuals!

Chapter Fifteen

SUMMING UP THE NEHRU ERA

During a time in which many governments were, or were becoming, autocratic, Nehru remained at the helm of India affairs for seventeen and a half years. From September 1946 until his death at the end of May 1964, he was the choice of the Congress party, and the elected head of government. Both he and his party survived three general elections, those of 1952, 1957, and 1962, in by far the biggest exercises in free elections that the world had ever known. Progressively, the percentage of the electorate—all persons aged 21 years and over—that went to the polls increased. In 1962, 55.42 percent of the 220 million voters cast ballots.

Nehru's greatest achievement was to consolidate the democratic tradition in India at a time when so many countries were choosing other, less popularly responsive, systems of government. This achievement alone makes Nehru unique in the contemporary annals of the developing world, and he must be reckoned a giant among men for having totally rejected all tendencies toward the pleas for arbitrary rule in India. There were voices, in India and elsewhere, which proclaimed that the problems of developing countries could be solved only by authoritarian governments. Nehru brushed them aside. Throughout his tenure, he remained sceptical of stories of the success of totalitarianism and facts which have come to light much later have shown that such scepticism was well founded. It is not an accident that certain societies are closed, and allow visitors to look only at what the governments wish them to see. They provide dressed showcases for visitors—in the form of communes, industrial units, or cultural enterprises. In India there was no window dressing. Visitors were allowed to see the stark poverty as well as the grandeur of Indian sculpture, the magnificence of its temples, and other specimens of architecture; and they saw also the factories, dams, and irrigation canals if they so wished—although they rarely did. They saw democracy at work, and democracy failing to achieve as much as the people would have liked it to achieve. As we have seen, the economic gains of the Nehru period were not spectacular, but they were, nevertheless, pretty well spread over the whole country. They were not simply a few projects in selected locations to show off to the outside world. A great effort was made to ensure that the whole country shared in the process of national development.

Nehru's second great achievement was that he personally set an example of complete uprightness and probity in governmental affairs. There was never any smell of corruption in regard to Nehru. At times, standards did deteriorate quite close to him, but he was never involved. His outstanding example was not to be duplicated in too many countries.

A third achievement of Nehru's, though it cramped his own capacity to develop certain much-needed policies for India, was that he kept the administration going smoothly. Early in the Nehru era, Dr. Paul Appleby, an American expert on administrative matters, recorded the view that the Indian administration was among the ten best in the world. This meant that it was better than some European administrations, and much better than administrations in most parts of the world. Nehru must be given a large part of the credit for this achievement, for he set an example of fantastically hard work, day after day, month after month, year after year. He set a personal example for the body of administrators in India: the example that governmental service was a dedication, and that the administrator owed a duty to the people to keep at his task and work as hard as he possibly could. There was nothing slipshod about Nehru, in his style of work or life, and in his own devotion to duty. He never took the easy path simply because it would relieve him of work. Nothing was too onerous for him to attempt, to struggle with, and generally to get the better of. This was a great and inspiring example, even if it was far too little followed in the country.

Every fortnight Nehru wrote a letter to the chief ministers (the heads of government) of all the states of the federation, which was also circulated to the members of his cabinet and to the secretaries to the government of India. In Delhi I was one of those who received these letters, and I continued to do so later, as head of a diplomatic mission until, in Nehru's later years, he gradually ceased writing them. The letters were marked "Top Secret," and were never published. This is a great pity, for they were extraordinarily sensitive and penetrating pieces of writing about India's problems, the needs of the people, the duties of the administration, and the whole political and social scene. I once proposed to Nehru that they be declassified and made available to all the people in the 570,000 villages and the scores of towns of India, over a facsimile of his signature. I said, "Panditji, think of what it would do for the tone of the country if the people could tune in to your intimate thoughts on matters of moment, on civic problems, the relationships of the people to the administration, and the feeling you have for the betterment of the lot of the people!" Pressed down by an enormous load of work, the idea had never occurred to him. Surprise changed to a spark of enthusiasm, and he said: "When I came to Delhi as Prime Minister I intended to be in close touch with the people. I planned to go on the air much more frequently than I do, but this job has bogged me down." He looked sad. I said to him: "Panditji, let me arrange this for you. The letters will get to every single village. I will do it." He was overburdened. "I want you to do other things at present." I was to go represent his government abroad. I did not press the point, as there were reasons why it seemed right for me then to go abroad. I hoped that he would talk to others about my idea; perhaps he did, and they told him of all the difficulties that would be encountered, and there the matter rested.

It was unfortunate that the impact of the greatness and the fine quality of this man did not reach its full potential even in his own country. He was held in the highest esteem and regard, and he was loved; but the impact should have been sustained by a continuous outflow to the people. Unfortunately his pedestal, although not because he so chose, became too high, and the real man, his thoughts, and his efforts became more remote from the people than they could have been. As the years passed, he became more and more a lonely figure. In part this stemmed from his consciousness of the inability of any individual to control the flow of the great stream of human life. The stream goes on, and one can only be there, perhaps at its crest, sensing its direction, occasionally doing something which gives it a forward impetus or slightly deflects its course. In a reflective mood, Nehru once talked to me in these terms about India and himself.

Though he had this perspective, still night and day he tended the stream, and when he slept he must have heard it thunder through dark caverns.

Nehru was not a person given to hearty sociability. There was an essential shyness, an introversion, in his nature. He could nevertheless be very warm, even passionate, and there was in him a deep inner flame of friendly emotions. An endearing characteristic was a certain absence of inhibition, which enabled him to pass swiftly from one shade of mood, say calm consideration, to another, for example an outburst against some inefficiency, some ineffectiveness, some falling away from honorable standards, some manifestation of greed; but never was there hatred. And quickly he would be back in his normal cast, poised and reflective.

This was the essential Nehru, in a sense remote from the people, and yet striving in their behalf. Even if he had been in closer contact with the people, as he would have been if those beautiful letters of his had been sent to all of them, he would still have remained remote. Yet he drew strength from the people, and consequently thought of himself as part of them. This was a myth he had invented for himself and it was fostered by the enormous responsiveness of the people. Wherever he went, hundreds of thousands (or even a million or more) people would turn out to see and hear him. He thrilled at this—not ostentatiously, but quietly, almost reverently. It gave him vigor, it gave him power of the right kind, the power of the people in him, a trust, not to be abused by him.

Nehru was not close to his immediate associates either, except that he maintained easy access to—but not from—several of them, such as Rafi Ahmed Kidwai, Lal Bahadur Shastri, Abul Kalam Azad, Krishna Menon, and Govind Vallabh Pant, who was the Congress party chief in Uttar Pradesh, the most populous state in the Union. But with none of them did the closeness lead to a full sharing of confidences. The only person in the world who was truly close to him was his daughter, Indira. With her his shyness was not a barrier, but almost part of their mutual communication. As to the members of his cabinet, Nehru felt they were giving their best, for the most part, but what a pity there was not more fine quality in them; what a pity that they were unable to see farther ahead than they did. He did not express this criticism, realizing that it would not help. However, those letters of his should have made any sensitive cabinet minister strive to do more for the country in every possible way.

Krishna Menon was close to Nehru, but not as close as he was reputed to be. Krishna Menon told that he never made direct suggestions to Nehru because he knew that they would have no chance of being accepted. He said to me: "People think I'm very close to Panditji, and that I tell him what to do. If they only knew! The best I can do with him is to bring up something as though we had discussed it before and say: 'Panditji, you remember when we discussed this matter you thought that such-and-such might be feasible? I think perhaps we should go ahead with it now.' " Nehru would ask Krishna to remind him more fully as to what he had previously said and, eventually, Nehru might (or might not) say: "All right, perhaps we had better do so-and-so." Abul Kalam Azad and Pant were freer to express their views, as was Rafi Ahmed Kidwai (a highly effective cabinet minister who died young), but there is little evidence that he acted as they suggested. Nehru's increasing remoteness as the years went by became a dangerous characteristic in one who had to carry as great a burden as he did. He could have been more effective both in regard to domestic problems of development and foreign affairs—such as India's relations with China—if he had been able to share his thoughts with at least a small group, an inner cabinet.

The shadow of Gandhi fell across the Nehru era and affected important decisions. Nehru could not but be gripped by the memory of his long experience of working with Gandhi, and by Gandhi's extraordinary feat of having steered India to freedom by launching a nonviolent mass movement which distinguished the Indian revolution for independence from other revolutions and gave it a uniquely humane and ethical flavor. But what was Nehru to do about the defense of India? Should he disband the army and adopt a truly Gandhian posture? Nehru realized that he could not do so because he would not be able to inculcate Gandhism into the people, and much less into India's neighbors. This realization should have led him to conclude that defense matters were to be looked at objectively, and that rational decisions would have to be taken. If he did, in the recesses of his mind, reach this conclusion, he did not act on it. It was only after the rude shock of the massive Chinese invasion that Nehru said in Parliament:

Honorable Members referred to my remark soon after the Chinese invasion took place, that we had been living in a world of unreality . . . what I meant was that this world is cruel. We had thought in terms of carrying the banner of peace everywhere, and we were betrayed. China has betrayed us; the world has betrayed us. Our efforts to follow the path of peace have been knocked on the head. We are forced to prepare for a defensive war, much against our will.[1]

Some months earlier, he had this to say, in Parliament, about the state of readiness of the Indian forces for combat: "They did not have semi-automatic rifles because our army does not possess them. . . . For about four years now we have been considering and discussing this matter. Various difficulties arose."[2] I wish I could record that the delay in taking a decision on semi-automatic and automatic weapons for the army was exceptional. Tragically, the facts were that for years on end—three, four, five, or more—the most pressing matters were bandied about the corridors of the government of India without decisions being taken. That was so under Nehru, and it continued to be so under the Janata government which became famous among cartoonists, humorists, and serious commentators for its excellence in nonperformance. One of the powerful underlying causes of this inability to act has been the absence of a consensus on the directions in which Indian society should move. On the one hand, there was the great appeal of the Gandhian world of quietness, the simplest fare and clothing, cottage industries, nonviolence, and no weapons at all. On the other hand there was the reality that "this world is cruel," which, however, Nehru learned only at the very end of his life. And there was the obvious need to modernize certain fields, such as the building of fertilizer plants, better agricultural machinery, so as to be able to feed the people; the construction of equipment required for elementary sanitation and health, and all the varieties of equipment required for an educational system for the whole country; transportation, communications, and so many other adjuncts of a healthy and sane society today (avoiding the synthetics and pollutants of other modern societies). India under Nehru fell between two poles: the Gandhian and the rationalistically modern. In a sense the shadow of Gandhi fell so heavily across the land that the people, including Nehru, lost their way under it.

Even though there was this floundering, there were some achievements on the economic side which we have looked at. In addition, Nehru, a Brahmin by birth, was able to subdue opposition to some

1. *Jawaharlal Nehru's Speeches* (New Delhi: Government of India, Publications Division Ministry of Information and Broadcasting, 1968), 5:198–99.
2. *Ibid.* (1964), 4:241–42.

modernization of Hindu customs. During his era, legislation was adopted to permit Hindus to marry outside their caste. Also, Hindu women were given the right to divorce, and a whole divorce code was established. Under another act of the Indian Parliament, girls were given equal rights with boys in the inheritance of family property. All disabilities relating to "untouchability" were made illegal. In Nehru's cabinet there were always persons from those strata of society that had previously been regarded as "untouchable," and there were considerable numbers of members of Parliament from these strata. There was also generally a higher proportion of women in the Indian Parliament than in most elected legislatures in the world.

Nehru died a saddened man who had not accomplished his mission in life, either domestically or internationally. The war with China had particularly shaken him, and it sent India into a deep decline internationally. Before the war India had become an important country in many world forums, and it had been largely instrumental in gaining for nonalignment international respect and recognition. After the war, even nonaligned friendly countries fell under the newly prevailing spell of regarding India as a weak and, consequently, unimportant country. It was an interesting experience for Indian representatives in other countries, at the UN and other international bodies, to find an overnight change from respect for India and its diplomats to relegation to the position of simply one of the inconsequential "small" countries. It was sobering to view on the international scene so blatant an exhibition of values based on power in the crudest sense. A country which has demonstrated some military power is acclaimed as a "great state," or even a "great power." In point of fact, a superior capacity to kill one's fellow beings is often accompanied by expressions of tendencies to domineer, to browbeat, and to seek control over the destinies of other countries and peoples, but these noxious characteristics are either condoned or overlooked, and by some even looked upon as the rightful perquisites of "greatness." Thoughts such as these disturbed the aging Nehru, and they troubled India.

An actual incident illustrates Nehru's anguish at the end of his era. When the Chinese were advancing in northeast India, Nehru appealed to all countries to help India with equipment to meet the aggression. The Indian ambassador in Washington took Nehru's letter to President Kennedy who, looking at the ambassador in puzzlement, said: "You couldn't hold them at bay for two weeks? Even that you couldn't do?" What was the ambassador to say? Nehru was informed, his face contorted sadly, and his sensitive eyes cloudy over as he slowly lowered them.

Given India's population, its resources, and the speed with which it developed various forms of technical competence, it could easily have become a military power of consequence under Nehru. It could have built nuclear weapons before China did. Nehru rejected these prospects, choosing instead "to carry the banner of peace everywhere." For doing so the world responded by putting him down, and it hurt.

Chapter Sixteen

DEVELOPMENT, VICTORY, AND THE PAINS OF POLITICAL GROWTH

1965–1975

If Mahatma Gandhi is the Father of the Nation, and he is so revered in India, then Nehru was his especially beloved son who came to power under the wing of the father, and then, as the years went by, himself acquired a father image. After two successive fathers, to be left fatherless was bound to be a very uncomfortable experience, but this was inevitable because Nehru made no clear nomination of a successor. As a result, since his death Indian politics have been more volatile than before. The years 1965 through 1975 were a period of uneasy growth during which some features thrived more than others, so that by the end of the eleven years it was difficult to hold all the strands together. The leaders lost their nerve, excesses followed, and there was a floundering, but this is the subject of the next chapter. Here we are concerned with the first exciting attempts at the maturation of modern India which will place in perspective the faltering that succeeded them.

For a year and a half after Nehru's death, Lal Bahadur Shastri was the elected Prime Minister. He was a remarkably unassuming man whose great strength was a compound of humility and firm principles based on the Gandhian mode of life. It was the type of strength which made him widely acceptable, and this was of prime importance after the departure of an outstanding leader. Shastri's era would probably have been unpretentious, with a steady drift to more traditional Indian styles, including decentralization of authority, had there not been a brief period of crisis. That crisis was thrust upon Shastri, a modest man who wanted only peace and quiet. It began in the mind of Field Marshal Ayub Khan, then military dictator of Pakistan, where it had been nurtured for so long that he could hardly wait until Nehru was dead.

Early in the 1960s, a friend of mine, a distinguished European who had become acquainted with Ayub Khan asked him for his views on the issue of Kashmir. Ayub smiled and replied: "I'm not worried about Kashmir. After Nehru's death we will have no difficulty in taking Kashmir and whatever else we want to take." Thus, in the summer of 1965, the Pakistani forces attacked Indian positions in Kashmir, and a full-scale war developed. Ayub soon realized, however, that he was not going to achieve his objective. Although his troops were using much more modern equipment than the Indians (mostly American materiel), and although the Indians did not even have a gun that could stop a Patton tank, the Indian defenders made a decidedly better showing than the attackers, and Ayub Khan was glad to call off the war at the behest of the UN Security Council. During this turbulent period, the new Indian Prime Minister was a firm and inspiring leader. He was able to rouse the spirit of the people without resort to the rhetoric of warmongering. He and Ayub Khan accepted an invitation from Prime Minister Kosygin of the USSR to meet together at Tashkent, and with his help they reached an accord which they signed early in January 1966. The same night, before leaving Tashkent, Shastri died of a heart attack, and again the succession to power became an urgent issue.

Shastri's democratic election was—whatever the outside world might have thought—no happenstance. After his death, Morarji Desai felt he had the best claim to the pinnacle of power, but the Congress party members in the Indian Parliament elected not him but Indira Gandhi, Jawaharlal Nehru's only child. The reasons for preferring her to Desai were significant. One was that Desai was already seventy, and two leaders had died in quick succession who were of Desai's generation. It seemed wise to elect a younger person, and Indira Gandhi was still in her forties. In addition, the country had had an inkling of where Shastri's more traditional outlook would take it after the relative dynamism of Nehru, and it seemed to prefer a quicker pace. Desai was clearly a traditionalist. Moreover, Indira Gandhi had received much instruction in statecraft from her father, and had experienced governmental affairs at the highest level almost first hand. Finally, the senior regional leaders, among whom Kamraj of the southern state of Tamil Nadu was prominent, preferred her because they thought she would be more amenable to their advice and perhaps direction than would be Desai, who was known for his rigidness.

The view that Indira Gandhi would be pliable was sheer male chauvinism. Its main basis was that she was a woman and, moreover, she was shy and reserved and would, obviously, need guidance about the large world from which she held herself aloof. True, she was shy and reserved. Her father had been remote, and she was even more so. It was not easy for her to communicate with anyone except a few close friends, and those were not political people. When she joined Tagore's university, Visva Bharati, at the age of sixteen, she described herself as "painfully shy with strangers." [1] Soon thereafter, this painfully shy young woman lost her mother, and felt more isolated than ever, especially as her father was frequently sent to jail for his role in the peaceful movement for the independence of India.

Another unsettling element had entered Indira Gandhi's perspective. The Nehru family had been affluent, and she had been brought up with a fair amount of luxury, but the breadwinners in the family had deliberately forsaken luxury for devotion to national politics. Her grandfather, Motilal Nehru, had given the Congress party his mansion, and built the family a smaller house—though still a mansion. He gave up his very lucrative law practice, and her father, Jawaharlal, though a qualified barrister, had not had the time or inclination for making money. In short, the family fortunes were rapidly shrinking, while the family members were all used to a high standard of living. The young Indira found herself faced with economic uncertainty. This bred in her a certain sense of economic insecurity and, by extension, a degree of insecurity about things in general.

What, then, drew this very reserved, shy, and rather insecure person into the maelstrom of politics? The reason is partly circumstantial—politics had become a family tradition—and partly that she was and is a woman of great courage and determination with which she overcomes the disadvantages of her reserve. Reserve, it should be observed, is not a disadvantage in all circumstances. It often amounts to keeping one's own counsel, which gives a leader a certain aura of strength.

Nehru's personality inducted her into politics in a somewhat oblique way. We have observed how he grew increasingly remote not

1. Indira Gandhi, *Speeches and Writings* (New York: Harper and Row, 1975), p. 15.

only from the people in general, but even from his cabinet and party colleagues. This latter group sorely needed a channel of communication with Nehru. What better channel than his daughter, who was at his side constantly from 1951 onward? With this in view, the Congress leaders thrust Indira into politics. From being an unknown figure in the political life of the country, she was straightaway made a member of the Congress Working Committee—the politiburo of Indian politics, and the policy-making body of the ruling party. It has to be admitted, without denigrating her in any respect, that she was placed in this select group mainly because she was able to provide a good channel of communication between the political elements in the country and her remote father. After she had served on that body for a few years it became time to look for a new president of the Congress party. Her father had already held that dignified position six times—the tenure is one year—which was unprecedented, and he was extremely busy as Prime Minister. Someone else had to be found for the leadership of the party. Most of the other leading members had been elevated to the presidency at least once, and the problem of communication with Nehru still remained an acute one. Well, why not elect Indira Gandhi, thereby increasing her stature? Maybe this would ensure that she would be listened to more attentively by her father, which would be to the advantage of those who had advanced her fortunes. Would it not also please Nehru that the other leaders were coming to recognize the merits of his daughter? All these considerations led the top leaders in the party, including the retiring president, to urge her to accept the presidency for 1959. She was somewhat taken aback, but the pressure on her came from all sides; she agreed to comply and become president of the Congress party. Now father and daughter held the two most important political positions in the country.

Having achieved this position, she had to be regarded as one of the important figures in the party, and in the country, in her own right. She held no governmental office, but in a way her position was more important than that of any office holder: she was her father's hostess, his constant companion, and a great deal of political and other information came to him through her. Moreover, he trusted her, and her own qualities of courage, sensitivity, good sense, and objectivity about issues and problems were such that Nehru was inclined to pay heed to what she said. When he died she could not be politically ignored, and Shastri immediately raised her to cabinet rank, giving her the portfolio of Information and Broadcasting, admittedly not one of the most important, but a sensitive ministry all the same.

Such was the person who was waiting in the wings during Shastri's brief term as prime minister. I have mentioned how well he steered the country through Ayub Khan's brief adventure in warfare against India. I was not surprised at Ayub's miscalculation, though I was nervous because his army was better armed than India's. When we were both young I had known Ayub well. Before World War II, his unit, the First-Fourteenth Punjab Regiment, was stationed at Jhelum, now in Pakistan, where I was assistant commissioner for the district. I frequently ate lunch and dinner at the officers' mess of Ayub's regiment. He was a captain, a large, handsome, and pleasant man with a homespun sense of humor; but I never heard a view from him which was not either commonplace or quite trivial. However, he seemed to me precisely the sort of military officer who might well aspire to rise to the rank of colonel. As it happened, he did not do too well in advancing to that rank. Toward the end of the war, in spite of the phenomenal increase in the number of colonels and generals, Ayub was still only a major in the Indian army. At that time we met again in Delhi. He was extremely disgruntled and woebegone. Bitterly he said to me: "I'm going to chuck this up. I've had enough. I'm not getting anywhere. They've kept me down. I'm only a major." But the war ended, and political events moved rapidly. Once Pakistan was created, I lost touch with Ayub. About fifteen years later, to my amazement, he emerged as the dictator of Pakistan.

When Indira Gandhi was elected to lead the government of India at the beginning of 1966, Ayub was still in power in Pakistan. He said to a mutual friend of ours, "That girl is much tougher than her father." Indeed, the new Prime Minister soon acquired the reputation of running a tight ship. It was said widely that her only disadvantage was that she had so many old men in her cabinet who were out of tune with the needs of the country, and thus acted as a brake on India's progress. Ironically, in this connection the name of Morarji Desai was often mentioned. She was magnanimous to her rival. She appointed Desai to the important portfolio of finance and designated him Deputy Prime Minister. But her early years as Prime Minister were years of hardship for the country. There had been a succession of poor harvests and food was scarce.

The United States was the only country from which grain could be obtained, but India was short of foreign exchange and could import only against credits. In 1966 she visited Washington in response to an invitation from President Johnson. Indira Gandhi was, and remains, a proud woman. She was not going to beg Johnson for favors, but the President took from his inner pocket a sheet of paper; he handed it to her saying, "Madame Prime Minister, here is a list of shipments of wheat which I'm sending you. I hope this will help." She told me this herself. She was naturally very pleased, and thanked the President warmly. The sheet she had been handed set out the dates of sailing of a score or so of vessels. Famine in India would be averted.

She returned to India and, both before she left the U.S. and on her return, she leaned over backwards—again to quote her—to avoid making critical remarks about American actions in Vietnam, though they were not in the least to her liking or in consonance with her foreign policy, a continuation, philosophically, of her father's. However, in spite of this restraint, the dates for the shipments came and went without any wheat from the United States; according to her, those shipments just never arrived. Of course, she did not protest. It was not her style to do so in the circumstances, and besides she had not asked for the food grains and was not in a position to offer to pay for them. She told me, in the presence of my American wife, that she was much embarrassed by the withholding of the shipments; this made her look absurd in the eyes of her colleagues, all of whom had been informed of President Johnson's magnificent gesture! I have never been able to fathom what went wrong, and why the shipments, promised in writing and on his own initiative by President Johnson, were withheld. There was no shortage of grain in the United States. The only reason can have been that the U.S., already running large deficits in its foreign transactions, decided to sell the grain to countries that could pay for it and thereby relieve the foreign exchange position of Washington. After all, as a previous President had said: "The business of America is business." In any event, the government of India was never informed why the proffered shipments had not materialized.

With the economic situation poor, the Prime Minister had to face nationwide general elections in 1967. The Indian constitution mandates such elections every five years, unless the government is upset earlier by a no-confidence vote, or chooses to resign and call for an election. In the 1967 elections, the fourth since the country had become a republic in 1950, the Congress party did worse than it had in the three previous elections, but still secured a working majority in the Indian Parliament. The lack of food had been an important factor and there was the feeling that Indira Gandhi had not been able to assert herself and get the country moving forward economically.

Indira Gandhi has never been a doctrinaire socialist, but in India it had long been obvious to almost all serious politicians, as well as to others interested in the wellbeing of the country, that governmental injections into the economic life of the community have to be more numerous and frequent than in, say, the United States or Canada. This is because there is not sufficient expertise, capital formation, and administrative capacity in the private sector for it to undertake the whole task of economic development. Even the British government in India had recognized this and it had—though not on ideological grounds—nationalized the extensive railway system of the country, most power generation with a decision to nationalize the rest and some of the large-scale industries such as the production of fertilizer. In independent India it was widely agreed that this process would have to be extended and accelerated. Mrs. Gandhi was, and is, a socialist simply in the sense that she feels that a fair amount of governmental activity must be undertaken in order to counteract existing grave inequities in Indian society that would be further aggravated if more wealth and more power came to be vested in the already rich and the large industrial corporations. In India this danger is far greater than it is in North America. Indian labor is much less well remunerated than is American labor, and the gap between management and labor is extremely great. If the country were to be allowed to develop solely through private enterprise, many fear that the rich would come to control the political apparatus, and run the country in their own interests while the lumpenproletariat would be relegated to the status of a perpetual lower caste. In India, where the caste system has been a dominant factor, the hierarchical pattern strongly tends to permeate all structures of society unless it is checked. It is widely agreed that the government must play a corrective role. K. Santanam, the editor of the well-known magazine *Swaraja*, wrote on May 21, 1977: "Socialism is generally professed by all political parties."[2] Santanam, once a senior member of the Congress party, now supports the Janata party.

Santanam called Morarji Desai a socialist, and although he would

2. *Swaraja*, 22, no. 47, May 21, 1977.

in general terms agree with this view, his socialism does not go quite as far as Prime Minister Gandhi's. In 1967 he joined her government as Deputy Prime Minister and finance minister, but his policies reflected his essentially conservative and traditionalist bent of mind. Proposals to pump money into urgently required industrial ventures such as steel production, fertilizer production, and machine tool plants would invariably meet with opposition from him. It became difficult for the two of them to work together. The final confrontation came over the nationalization of the banks. There was ample evidence that the leading commercial banks, most of them controlled by the large business houses of the country, were stifling rather than promoting the development of new industries and other productive units by technocrats and new entrepreneurs. They frequently refused even to consider requests for financing from new entrepreneurs, no matter how sound the projects. The funds available in the banks were regarded as the preserve of the big industrial houses, to serve their plans of expansion. Mrs. Gandhi was insistent that the banks be rescued from the stranglehold of the existing powerful financial and industrial interests so that finance could flow into new channels. Morarji Desai stoutly opposed such a move; the prevailing situation in the banking world was not one he found objectionable, though he talked somewhat vaguely about social control of the banks. Indira Gandhi dropped Desai from the cabinet and proceeded immediately to nationalize the fourteen leading private commercial banks.

The effect of this bold measure was as anticipated. Younger entrepreneurs were able to get financing from the banks, and industry began to move more rapidly into the hinterland soon after the nationalization in 1969. Economic enthusiasm began to surge forward in India. In the succeeding years a number of smaller Indian entrepreneurs spoke to me optimistically about the nationalization of the banks, and I visited some of the small-scale industrial enterprises they had been able to create with the help of finance that had been previously unavailable. Paradoxically, a step which appeared to be socialistic—the nationalization of the banks—was priming the pump for private enterprise on a much broader scale than previously. The measure was clearly in the best interests of the people of India. It is significant that Desai, who was adamantly opposed to it and split the Congress party over the issue, did nothing to move toward denationalizing the banks while he was Prime Minister in the late 1970s.

When he was dropped from the Gandhi cabinet in 1969, Desai responded by joining with others in splitting the Congress party. About 65 members of the Indian Parliament followed Desai onto the opposition benches but 200 remained with Indira Gandhi. Moreover, there were massive demonstrations in favor of nationalization of the banks. Again it seemed clear that India wanted Indira Gandhi and what she stood for rather than Desai's brand of society. However, the parliamentary situation was no longer stable; Mrs. Gandhi's followers were in a minority in the Lok Sabha. Taking advantage of a slight improvement in the economy, she dissolved Parliament and called for fresh elections early in 1971, a year before her mandate would have expired.

The elections turned out to be a striking endorsement of Indira Gandhi. She herself and her party were returned with massive majorities, while Desai's splinter section of the Congress party did extremely poorly. In a house of more than 500 members, his party returned barely a score of legislators. Desai himself just managed to retain his seat. Indira Gandhi's party ran on the platform *Gharibi Hatao* ("Remove Poverty") while Desai's candidates chose the slogan *Indira Hatao* ("Remove Indira"). The latter slogan was decisively rejected by the electorate of almost 300 million persons.

This victory gained, Indira Gandhi's power seemed practically unchallengeable. There seemed no reason now for lingering insecurities which had haunted her from her childhood. Moreover, though poverty was still rampant in most parts of the country, islands of prosperity were appearing and the future promised to be decidedly better for the people than anything they had known.

Taking their cue from the Prime Minister, some of the state governments created conditions, by making available basic services such as electricity, roads, sewage systems, and police protection, that stimulated the growth of industry. Particularly in the northern states of the Punjab and Hariyana, the governments built industrial parks and offered land in them on easy terms. The result has been thriving industrial estates such as Faridabad, about 25 miles from Delhi. Another such estate is growing a few miles from Chandigarh in the Punjab. In addition, a highly industrialized area has arisen in and around Ludhiana in the Punjab.

Agricultural yields were also on the upswing. During the Raj, the average yield per acre for wheat in the Punjab was a mere six to seven quintals (600 to 700 lbs.) Now the farmers were growing new high-yielding varieties developed in Mexico with American help. Other factors helped—fertilizers and deeper plowing—and the yields in the Punjab and Hariyana and in a few other areas for wheat shot up to a respectable 40 quintals (4000 lbs.) per acre. Soon, the Punjab became unrecognizable from what it had been before India's independence.

There were other indications, too, that the decade in which Indira Gandhi first ruled was a period of striking economic development. For example, the generation of electric power increased from 36.8 billion KWH to over 70 billion KWH. Investment in the Fifth Development Plan (for a five-year period) was about $63.5 billion as compared with an investment of $21.8 billion in the plan for 1961–66. Fertilizer production increased from 344,000 tons in 1965–66 to 1.6 million tons in 1974–75—still not anywhere near the needs of the country. Food grain production increased from 82 million tons a year at the beginning of the period to over 104 million tons in 1974–75. Irrigated agricultural lands increased from 75 million acres to 180 million acres during the decade. Trade expanded exponentially. Exports were valued at $1.7 billion in 1965, while in 1974–75 they rose to $4.33 billion in value. In the British era, as we have noted, India was reduced to the level of an exporter of raw materials, some cotton textiles and tea, but now there was a striking increase in the export of engineering goods, from about $50 million in 1965 to ten times as much by 1974–75.

Education made impressive gains, and a special effort was made in regard to family planning. In the third five-year plan (1961–66) the relevant financial provision was $52.21 million, while in the plan commencing in 1974 something of the order of $700 million was allocated. Earlier, under Nehru, India had been the first country in the world to initiate a governmental family planning program.

These economic and social developments began to have tangible sociological effects on Indian society. For example, until recently it had been unthinkable for a person who had acquired a university degree or who had been to college for a few years to seek manual occupation. He would accept only white collar work or remain unemployed. But by 1975 attitudes had changed. Young persons with strong educational backgrounds were taking factory and other manual jobs. Some of them could be found waiting tables in restaurants or hotels. A well-educated young man, whose whole family were professional people, was waiting on our table at a hotel dining room in south India in 1975. On questioning him over the course of a couple of days, I found that he had decided to learn the work "from the ground up," so that he would be equipped to seek employment as an assistant purser on a ship; and after working for some years on the high seas, he planned to explore his prospects for a shore job in a large hotel. This kind of mobility and enterprise had been virtually unknown previously.

In 1975 the average wages for workers in certain engineering workshops outside Bombay were as high as 1375 rupees a month. In terms of real purchasing power, this remuneration was worth about $500 a month, especially when one takes into account the fact that many of the workers were in heavily subsidized housing for which they paid a rent that would be ridiculously low by American standards. Wages at this level were a very recent, but by no means isolated, phenomenon in India. A doorman's wages had gone up thirtyfold since British times. For those who were able to find jobs in the first Indira Gandhi era, things were far better than they used to be.

By 1975, the problem of slums in some of the major cities was being attacked through education, job creation, and financial help. In the city of Hyderabad in Andhra Pradesh, for example, my wife and I got a close look at some excellent work which had created pleasant homes, clean lanes, and happy faces in previously derelict areas.

I have mentioned briefly the transformation of the Punjab: the farmers were being transformed from peasants into agricultural industrialists. They were living much as do people in small towns in much of the developed world, served by radio, even television; sometimes they own a scooter or motorcycle or a tractor with a hauling cart that can be used as an open-air bus for transporting families. Electricity, and a good deep well complete the scene. They dress in westernized clothes, and are generally much more "fashion-conscious" than they used to be. All the children are at school.

At the end of an extensive tour of the country, which was made for the most part by fourteen air journeys—six of them in Indian-built civil aircraft—we met with Indira Gandhi in March 1975. I told her that economic conditions were very much better than I had suspected from newspaper reports in the United States. There were real and numerous signs of prosperity, the beginnings, at last, of an exciting breakthrough. Her face lit up, but the smile that followed was wispy as she said: "I wish I could say the same about the political situation." There were ominous signs of trouble, stemming largely from student discontent in Gujarat and Bihar, two large and important states, the former being the home base of Morarji Desai, and the latter being Jayaprakash Narayan's state. We will turn to the Prime Minister's further remarks on this matter below.

India is more modernized than perhaps generally known. The country has a considerable aircraft industry and even exports planes. Nor is it widely known, even among the well-informed, that in the field of radar India has developed certain systems of such sophistication that the U.S. and Japan are the only other countries known to build them. In the atomic field India's scope and level of development place it among the first eight or ten countries in the world. Apart from a growing number of research and power reactors, India has its own plutonium separation plant, a uranium metal plant, a fuel fabrication plant, and a number of other important items of equipment. The Trombay complex has a staff of more than 2000 scientists and engineers and more than 3000 trained technicians. The facility is named for Homi Bhabha, the extremely creative genius who led India's efforts in this field. He was in addition a man of outstanding artistic and cultural talents and also had a passion for creating handsome buildings. One of the features at Trombay is an Indian-designed and Indian-built zero-energy fast breeder reactor. Work on fast breeders has commenced at the Reactor Research Center at Kalpakkam in south India. India's fast reactors will be geared to thorium, of which India possesses vast resources of fine quality. Though it appears likely that the country will soon be able to pump all the oil it needs for its own use, it does need to develop alternative energy sources, and thorium cycle reactors are regarded as a promising prospect. As early as November 1971, Dr. Sigvad Eklund, director general of the International Atomic Energy Agency, described India as "a very developed country in the field of nuclear research."[3] The country has made great strides since then.

As was typical of India, after years and years of weighing the pros and cons—and in a sense after having missed the boat—on May 18, 1974, the Atomic Energy Commission of India carried out a peaceful underground nuclear explosion, at a depth of more than a hundred meters below the surface of the Rajasthan desert. There was no radioactive release into the atmosphere. Did India make a mistake in eventually carrying out this experiment? In India, public opinion would say overwhelmingly: "Not at all; it was no mistake. In fact, we should have done it ten years ago, even earlier than that. Its im-

3. News item quoting Sigvad Eklund in *Indian and Foreign Review*, December 15, 1971, p. 9.

pact would have been greater then on the nuclear weapon states whom we sought to restrain by our action." Around 1960, Vasily Emelyanov, who was the head of the Soviet Atomic Energy Authority, told me that India was ahead of China in the nuclear field, and Homi Bhabha repeatedly said that we were about eighteen months from an atomic explosion if we decided to go that route. But India did not. A few years later, after the first Chinese explosion, Homi Bhabha wrote to me as follows:

While our Government has quite rightly decided to continue our peaceful policy, you are probably not aware of the strength of feeling in this country for producing a bomb, and if China sets off some more explosions, even this Government may be pushed into going ahead with a bomb programme. I hope this will not happen. A lot however depends on the Great Powers. They must take important steps towards disarmament if they are going to take a strong line against countries like China.

These words perfectly encapsulate mature Indian thinking on the subject. A year after Homi Bhabha wrote these words to me he was killed in an air accident, and so did not live to see that for years to come the Great Powers unfortunately would do nothing substantive in the field of disarmament and that China, too, would go on merrily exploding nuclear weapons, and that, in fact, some of the Great Powers, including the United States, would be pleased at this development because it would strengthen the "China Card" in the awesome power game which would continue to be played, even though it increased the risks of world conflagration.

In regard to the bomb-making prospects in some other countries, Bhabha, who was extremely well informed, wrote to me as follows:

While Japan is technically capable of making the bomb, she would have to set up plutonium producing reactors and a plutonium plant on her own. Even with her technical capacity, or for that matter Germany's, this would take in any case three years. Having a plutonium plant in operation we are definitely two to three years ahead of anyone else, not excluding Germany, Japan, or Sweden.[4]

Homi had an international standing and influence that might have had some effect on the behavior of the leading states in the nuclear field. He had been the president of the first UN Conference on the

4. This and the previous quotation are from a letter addressed to the author by Homi Bhabha, dated December 15, 1964.

Peaceful Uses of Atomic Energy, held in 1955, at which I was his principal political adviser as well as a delegate to the conference.

There were shrill cries in the media in many parts of the world that India had become a nuclear-weapon state. It was widely assumed that the explosion of May 1974 was clear evidence of a secret program. This view persists in many quarters, but the fact is that several years have passed since the explosion and there is simply not one shred of evidence that India has a nuclear weapons program. Indeed, there is no such program, and it is now clear that Desai was able to convince President Carter that this was the case. Thus, India is the only country that has voluntarily restricted itself to purely peaceful explosions of atomic devices—a uniqueness which some countries still look at with suspicion. Among the military dictatorships around the world, appetites for nuclear weapons have, if anything, been whetted by the Indian explosion. Since I was frequently asked by very senior officials of such regimes for assistance from India—or for a joint program with India—for building bombs, I am well aware what they are up to, despite their categorical denials. They apparently feel that if India could issue a denial about the production of weapons—in its case an honest denial—they can do likewise and thereby gain the advantage of concealing for some time the true nature of their activities.

On April 19, 1975, the first Indian scientific satellite (named for Aryabhata, a great Indian mathematician and astronomer of the fifth century), was launched from a Soviet rocket. It was fairly large and complex, considerably more so than several of the first satellites launched by the few other states which had preceded India in this exalted venture. It weighed 360 kilograms and was equipped to perform a number of experiments in space. India has plans to launch a satellite using its own four-stage rocket fueled with a solid propellant.[5] Again, India's developments in space will be for peaceful purposes alone, and again they will probably be misconstrued by many other countries.

India's foreign relations were made complicated by a dramatic development on the Indian subcontinent. Relations between the two wings of Pakistan (separated by a thousand miles of Indian territory) had been deteriorating for some years. East Pakistan, the eastern portion of partitioned Bengal, was the more populous of the two. How-

5. This was achieved in mid-1980, when India became one of a select group of seven countries that so far have placed their own satellites in orbit.

ever, West Pakistan had very early acquired the position of the leading partner, and by the 1960s it had become dominant to such an extent that the eastern portion came to feel subordinate. For much of its existence, Pakistan had been a military dictatorship, largely because of the British-inculcated tradition that the men of the Punjab, the North-West Frontier Province, and Baluchistan, were fighting men *par excellence*. The continuance of that tradition in West Pakistan tended to give the military an ascendancy in society. This was an unfortunate legacy of British times, in which East Bengal had no part. Consequently, the army of Pakistan, a very large one for a country with limited resources, was drawn almost exclusively from the west. The higher echelons of the civil service were also largely western, because the army set the pattern for the rest of the administration.

Naturally enough, this state of affairs was not acceptable in the east. The movement for autonomy gained ground, while the west grudgingly made paltry concessions. Finally, by the end of 1970, the east was in full revolt, and the west moved in about a quarter of its 400,000-man army to quell the rebellion. A reign of terror followed. The eastern Bengalis estimated that 3 million of their number had been slaughtered by the Pakistani army. At the same time, millions of refugees fled across the borders with India. The camps in which they were housed were visited by persons from all over the world, including Senator Edward Kennedy and André Malraux. Eventually 10 million refugees entered India. But this did not lead to any action to restrain the Pakistani army in its spree of killing and driving out people.

There was a complication. Pakistan had become a close friend of China, which publicly supported Pakistan's action to "maintain order" in East Pakistan. Meanwhile, the U.S. was angling for relations with Peking now that the rift between the Soviet Union and China was as wide as an ocean. Henry Kissinger was making signals to Peking through his friend, the military dictator of Pakistan, General Yahya Khan. Therefore, Kissinger and President Nixon closed their eyes to the massive carnage and witchhunting in East Bengal. Indeed, Nixon decided to continue aid to Pakistan and stated at a press conference: "We are not going to engage in public pressure on the Government of West Pakistan." There is no shred of evidence that any behind-the-scenes efforts were made to restrain Yahya Khan. On the contrary, the U.S. and China were prominent among those states which claimed that the whole matter was the "internal affair" of Pakistan—an internal affair when 10 million human beings in desperate circumstances had landed in a neighboring country. This was truly an amazing view to take, and a highly cynical one.

Meanwhile, it became clear to the Indian Embassy in Washington that, in the event of war between India and China—and the Chinese were resorting to threats over India's clear denunciation of what Pakistan was perpetrating in East Bengal—no help could be expected from Washington. From Delhi, it looked as if an anti-Indian axis were being formed, consisting of the U.S., China, and West Pakistan. In this very ominous situation, on August 9, 1971, Mrs. Gandhi's government signed a twenty-year treaty of peace, friendship, and cooperation with the Soviet Union. India sorely needed this modicum of insurance in a situation of diplomatic maneuvering which appeared to be aimed at isolating India. The treaty with the Soviet Union was no military alliance. It provided for no exchange of military commands, no joint exercises of forces, no military bases, and no granting of military facilities of any kind whatsoever, and there was no automatic military reaction clause. But one of the articles of the treaty stated that if either country were attacked or threatened, the two countries would "immediately start mutual consultations with a view to eliminating the threat, and taking appropriate effective measures to ensure peace and security for their countries."[6]

The strain on Indian resources caused by its assistance to 10 million refugees was beyond the capacity of the country, and yet the people and the government rose to the occasion. Meanwhile, the poorly armed people of Bengal were harrying their tormentors, the West Pakistan army. Eventually, presumably to warn India against military action to help the people of East Bengal, who had now declared independence as the state of Bangladesh, the Pakistan air force bombed targets in the Indian Punjab, just over the border from West Pakistan. India immediately manned its defenses against West Pakistan, and its forces entered Bangladesh on request from the people's movement there. In two weeks the Indian army took 93,000 prisoners from the West Pakistan army, and the military action was over. What made this possible was the fact that the whole of the pop-

6. Treaty of Peace, Friendship and Cooperation between the USSR and India, article 9. For text see *Survival* International Institute for Strategic Studies, London, October 1971, pp. 351–53.

ulation of East Bengal was on the side of the freedom fighters and the Indian army.

Sure that India would act as most other conquerors, China and other countries and sundry individuals asserted that the Indian army would never be withdrawn from Bangladesh, and that, with one excuse or another, India would take it over! These assertions were totally unfounded. As soon as all the prisoners were rounded up, and all elements of the Pakistan army had been disarmed, the Indian army withdrew fully, leaving the Bangladesh authorities in complete control of their own country.

Therefore, when 1972 dawned, the situation in India, both for the country and for the recently reelected government, was highly favorable. There had been significant scientific, technological, and fiscal developments (all pointing in the direction of a speedy economic "take-off"), political stability on the basis of a stunning electoral victory for Indira Gandhi's Congress party at the polls, and the setting free of a neighboring state on the Indian subcontinent. In spite of this impressive array of favorable factors, however, the political winds turned strongly and swiftly against Mrs. Gandhi.

Let us return to our conversation with the Prime Minister in March 1975: after her observation that the political situation was not developing satisfactorily, we discussed the matter. Indira Gandhi said that there had been a tremendous rise in the expectations of the large and growing student body leaving the universities each year, and it simply had not been possible for economic opportunities, though growing, to keep pace with the demands of the young people. Besides, the students—instead of finding how they could fit into the large programs of development in the country—chose the course of disorderly conduct; they seemed to want to be presented with jobs on a silver platter, without any effort on their part, and without a spirit of innovation. At the same time, Mrs. Gandhi regretted that it had not been possible to do enough for the large numbers of young people who were being turned out by the schools and universities. The restlessness of this vast group made her visibly uneasy, and I had the feeling that she was uncertain as to how it would all turn out, whether it would subside or erupt.

These rising discontents were not directed, in the main, against Indira Gandhi and her government, but rather at the state governments, which more directly affected the course of the lives of the people. Without work, frustrated and casting about for a villain, the students and their sympathizers turned their wrath on the state governments, particularly those of Bihar and Gujarat, which they assailed for corruption. It galled them that those in power in these states should be feathering their own nests, indulging in nepotism and blatant favoritism, while there were not even crumbs left for those without influence and connections. Their mass demonstrations and protests made it practically impossible for the government of Bihar to function. The chief minister—equivalent to an American governor—swore fealty to Indira Gandhi, and she responded by calling for restraint on the part of the discontented elements while she promised to look into the affairs of the state and to take steps to improve the administration. But the deterioration continued in Bihar and soon Jayaprakash Narayan, the prestigious follower of Mahatma Gandhi, became involved. He called for the resignation of the Bihar government. Mrs. Gandhi responded indignantly. How, she asked, was that possible? The state government had very recently been placed in power by the votes of the people and should be given a chance to run the affairs of the state; indeed this was its right under the Constitution. Legally she was absolutely right, but this was no answer to the grievances of the people, and it did not alter the fact that corruption was widespread in the state administration.

In 1972 the Gandhi government pushed legislation that ended the pensions of the former rulers of the princely states—about 500 of them. This was largely a public relations action designed to win the support of the broad masses who were assumed to have no sympathy for the ex-rulers. This was true, but the discontinuance of the payments to the nobles brought no financial relief whatsoever to the masses. The amount involved was small relative to the needs of the country and the calls on the federal exchequer were already myriad and pressing. The abolition of the princes' privy purses, as their allowances were called, did little to rehabilitate the government in the eyes of people. In general the economy was not showing the results it had achieved in earlier years. In 1973–74 industrial production was 7 percent less than in 1972–73, and the inflation rate was rising. Both these ills were largely the result of the steep climb in oil prices. The economic situation was especially bad in Bihar and Gujarat, which were seething with discontent anyway, and in 1974 inflation in the country was galloping at the rate of 30.1 percent.

Worst of all, during these very crucial years Mrs. Gandhi was falling deeper into the Nehruvian tendency to remoteness. The result was far worse than in the case of her father who, by enormous dedication and sheer hard work, had managed to accomplish a great deal. In this period she came to rely heavily on her second son, Sanjay, who clearly had developed a large appetite for political power which he was voraciously satisfying. Though he held neither elected nor appointed office, he had nevertheless succeeded in installing himself as the main channel of communication with his mother. There was, however, no parallel with her own case under Nehru. In Nehru's later years she had been politically advanced through the Congress party and had made herself acceptable to the High Command and other members of the party. Most important of all, she had not usurped any governmental functions. Her son, on the other hand, did little to win over the party leaders, and seemed to expect them to kowtow to him. Some of them did just this, which encouraged him to persevere. Moreover, by 1974, Sanjay was said to be virtually dominating the Delhi administration. He would have orders sent to the chief commissioner of Delhi who, assuming these to be the orders of the Prime Minister, would carry them out.

One important functionary, P. N. Haksar, Indira Gandhi's chief of cabinet, had raised questions about the activities of Sanjay. Haksar was one of the Prime Minister's greatest assets—extremely able, knowledgeable, liked by the party, and trusted by all who came in contact with him because he was not advancing any personal cause. Apparently unaware of his great value to her, she relieved him of his appointment. Her well-wishers were staggered, but there were those among them who thought that her action was perhaps all to the good because it could mean that she had decided to assert herself and run the country aided by her cabinet. However, the hopes of a more active role by her were quickly dashed; her informal advisors became increasingly assertive, with a corresponding demoralization among the elected heads of state governments and the senior members of the state and central administrations.

Jayaprakash Narayan sought to arrest this drift in his own way. Visionary though he was, he met with Mrs. Gandhi twice in 1973 and sought to reach agreement on measures to clean up the administration. From her point of view he asked too high a price—the dismissal of certain state governments and the holding of fresh elections. Negotiations broke down, and Narayan now made no secret of his view that the Prime Minister was a bad influence in the country and that her government had to be toppled. She sneered back, "Look at the majority I have in Parliament. How can I be toppled?" "Indira must go!" proclaimed Narayan. The country was divided. There were those, not a few, who held Narayan in great respect, regarding him as the spiritual successor to the great Mahatma, and who were willing to follow all his injunctions. On the other side there were those who regarded Narayan as a man who refused to see the realities of the situation and who wanted to scrap the constitution and set up a system with no political parties, very little power in the central government, and with a base of village democracies which would practically run the affairs of the country. What about external dangers? What about the need for steel, oil, chemical industries, watch-making, automobiles, ballpoint pens, and a hundred other items? It was true that Narayan had not worked all this out, but he was generally open-minded, and his ideas were obviously not self-serving, a point that gave them tremendous appeal among the Indian public. The conclusion of this one man that Mrs. Gandhi was not the right ruler for India gradually undermined her vast power base.

During periods of comparative economic well-being, Indian society is able to absorb or condone corruption and inefficiency, regarding them as rather low-priority social maladjustments to be attended to later. But when there is an economic pinch, inefficiency and corruption become intolerable. The 1973–74 economic downturn was more severe than a mere pinch; it was caused largely by the worldwide oil crisis which resulted in greatly increased prices, beyond India's economic capacity. Many units of production, large and small, that were dependent on oil simply had to stop work. Goods became scarce and employment shrank. In this situation, corruption among the functionaries of the various administrations, as well as among many of the politicians, became more onerous than society could tolerate. Young engineers and others who wished to set up units of production found that they would have to grease a number of palms, and once in production would have to pay off the income tax department, whose assessors promoted corrupt practices by demanding a rake-off from profits. "Show low profits but give us a big rake-off," was their slogan in dealing with businessmen. Profits were shrinking anyway, but still the demand for large rake-offs was unyielding. Imagine the effects on society of these ubiquitous depredations.

Bureaucratic inefficiency also became intolerable. Why should there be so many forms to fill out, so many permits to gain before anything could be done in the economic sphere? These questions were on the lips not only of business people, but of their wives and friends as well. The bureaucracy merely looked on stonily, many of them hoping to take their own profit in these endlessly lengthy processes.

Apart from the outcry of the students, there were the discontents of the growing middle classes in the urban areas. In the rural areas, too, a middle class was growing up, the farmers who had struck it rich as a result of the new farming—better varieties of seed, fertilizer, irrigation, better equipment. For example, the industrious and innovative Sikh farmers of the Punjab explained their plight to me, just before my 1975 meeting with Indira Gandhi. The government was ruining them with its regulations about land ceilings. How did it expect efficient farming when the ceiling on the size of a farm was to be no more than 15 or 18 acres? How was the country to be fed within these constraints? They were doing their best to get around the regulations, but it was not easy, and officials would have to be paid off, which would decrease profits substantially and take away the incentive to farm. "We'll sell our lands and go somewhere else, Australia if we can. We're fed up with the government. Who do they think they are, ruining us? We'll elect you. Go to Delhi and fight our battles!" They were all worked up, and this was the mood too in other prosperous farming communities.

Little wonder then that Indira Gandhi, who was informed by her intelligence people about the state of the country, said she was unhappy about the political situation. And little wonder too that the editors of *Seminar,* an independent journal, wrote a few months later: "The Indian capacity for making a jungle of administrative procedures to establish a secure feeling of non-responsibility is now well-known in this unhappy land and has given us a reputation of notorious non-performers throughout the world."[7]

A decade of development, triumph, and hope was going out in a clamor of growing discontent and bitter disillusion.

7. *Seminar,* New Delhi, August 1975, 192:10.

Chapter Seventeen

THE POLITICAL STORM BREAKS

Jayaprakash Narayan, the aging titan, had, over a period of almost forty years, acquired a unique aura as an unassuming saint-politician-philosopher, a combination the Indian people find irresistible. Gandhi, who combined these qualities, showed that the people of India could be so moved by them that no authority, even that of the then redoubtable British Empire, would not fall before them. In 1975 Narayan's ambivalent early years had been reinterpreted in his favor. He had begun his political life as a marxist, which could be viewed as a sign of an early ardent interest in change for the betterment of the masses of the people. Then he joined the Congress party but, tiring of its slow methods, he developed the "Forward Bloc," which espoused a more vigorously socialistic platform. He seemed disillusioned with Gandhism.

When India regained its independence, Nehru wanted Jayaprakash to join the government as a cabinet minister, but he was unable to persuade Narayan to accept. Narayan's decision was widely read to be an indication that he was not interested in holding a political office, even the prime ministership—which he might have risen to because he was always well-liked in the country and was also respected by Nehru. Increasing the distance between himself and practical politics, he eventually became, in his writings, an out-and-out Gandhian believing in complete nonviolence and decentralization of power. He gave great strength to the land gift movement started by another leading Gandhian, Vinoba Bhave. Vinoba and Narayan and others walked the countryside, mostly in central India, and persuaded the more substantial landowners to give up part of their land, which was then made over to landless peasants. In this way, without any governmental action and without monetary compensation, more than 2 million acres of land were transferred to landless agriculturists. This said a great deal about Bhave and Narayan, and it also said a great deal about India.

In the sixties, another "miracle" was wrought by Narayan. In the rugged hills and dense forests of central India have flourished for centuries bands of lawless men ("dacoits") who live by raiding the villages that surround their hideouts, from which they take away grain, clothing, arms if they can find any, jewelry, money, and the most comely young women. All through the Middle Ages these daredevils prospered, and, indeed, by the time the British made their appearance, the freebooters had set up something of an empire. The British won the formal battles, disarmed the countryside, but did not completely subdue their foe. The hard core of the bands retreated to the most remote mountain fastnesses, from which they occasionally sallied forth. After the departure of the British, the raids became more frequent and the area they covered larger. In scores of villages life became extremely hazardous. Special police forces were called in, but the men of the mountains held their own. Jayaprakash visited the area, learned of the misery of the villagers, and then appealed to the dacoits, urging them to give up their centuries-long habits, to become law-abiding farmers and workers, and to surrender their arms. After a few months, the most renowned of the leaders of the lawless bands sent word to Narayan that they had decided to heed his appeal because of their respect for him, but they would surrender not to the police, but directly to him. Jayaprakash Narayan accepted this condition, but told them that they would have to be tried under the law and suffer the consequences of what they had done. More than 150 of the leading dacoits came, laid their arms at Narayan's feet, and allowed the police to take them into custody. Some of them were subsequently jailed, but to this too they submitted, and the old tradition of armed dacoity was given up.

Narayan was also most active in Bihar in devising and arranging for the implementation of projects to improve agriculture, education, and social habits. His concern was for the lowest orders of rural society, and his work led to real accomplishments. In the early 1970s he arranged, at our request, for my wife and me to meet with his workers and to visit some of the sites at which they were engaged. The sincerity and devotion to work, without any funds to speak of, were most moving. Meanwhile, Jayaprakash continued to write in advocacy of a partyless system of government—he believed that the party system led to corruption, confrontation, and waste and that the best way of getting things done was consensus and decentralization of power.

In 1971 he came to the United States to urge the U.S. authorities and people to take a serious view of the terrible inhumanities being perpetrated by the Pakistan army in East Bengal; he felt the U.S. had a special responsibility because the Pakistan army was armed with U.S. weaponry that had been supplied for use against aggression by communist states and not to decimate its own people for demanding their rights. During this mission, we had about twenty-five or thirty prominent American citizens meet him at our home for dinner. In his usual calm, low-pitched informal way he made a presentation and I believe created an impression on the gathering, but he was unable to shake the Nixon administration into any action against its friends in Islamabad.

This is the man who, as we have already seen, had decided by 1974 that Mrs. Gandhi was not the right person to rule the country, and his word carried weight among some strata of Indian society. When early in 1975 he counseled the bureaucracy, the police, and the army to decide on the basis of their own conscience whether they should carry out the instructions of the administration, his word was regarded as the harbinger of a possible revolution in India. He rejected the view that governments were inevitably to retain power for their full term. Each day a government and administration had to prove itself by its actions, and if it was corrupt, inefficient, and careless of the interests of the people, it should be removed. Thus, he had demanded that the state government in Bihar should be dismissed, and fresh elections held. Mrs. Gandhi rejected this demand, and Narayan came to the conclusion that no more truck with her was possible.

He did not leave matters simply at the level of an interrupted dialogue. He called upon the people of Bihar to set up village committees and to proceed to run the affairs of the village by open discussion and eventual consensus. Similarly, for each larger administrative unit a council was to be created, consisting of representatives of the villages or groups of villages. In this way he intended to displace the discredited—in his view—state and local administrations in Bihar. All this made Mrs. Gandhi even more adamant, and her people talked indignantly of Jayaprakash's being a subverter of the constitution and a man who had no sense of the realities of administration;

by all means let him decry corruption and work to end it, but he must understand that he was not authorized by the people or the law to set up an alternative system of government. This was no mere academic crossing of swords. The situation in Bihar was deteriorating steadily, and in certain parts of the state, and for certain purposes, no one knew who was in charge.

Meanwhile, in 1974–75, contemporaneously with the events in Bihar, a crisis of equal severity was brewing in the western state of Gujarat. There two years of drought had compounded the problems of the government, which was unable to deal effectively with economic hardship. Morarji Desai, the most senior Gujarati leader and, at the same time, in some political need to refurbish his own image, decided that the ineffectual corrupt government of Gujarat had to be brought down. He resorted to the time-honored Gandhian tactic of going on a fast, which he announced to be a fast unto death, until the state government were dismissed by the federal government. Mrs. Gandhi complied with this demand, and the administration of the state was temporarily taken over by the central government. But Desai undertook a second fast, demanding fresh elections so that a popularly elected government could be placed in power.

Meanwhile, at long last, the small noncommunist opposition parties in the Indian Parliament had managed to work out arrangements for mutual cooperation, and they decided that when elections were eventually held in Gujarat, they would present a united slate to the electorate. People were sceptical that the alliance would hold, because opposition to the ruling Congress had always been badly splintered. Most of the political wizards, including those who were soon to be important members of the Janata party, expected Indira Gandhi to come up with a grand political maneuver which would again split her opponents and leave her victorious. Events were to put these speculations to the test, for the Prime Minister announced elections in Gujarat for early 1975.

Meanwhile Jayaprakash Narayan, inspired by the enthusiasm of the people, called for "total revolution." His first major pronouncement toward this end, was, according to him, greeted with "thunderous applause," although he offered no details about it.[1] By now Jayaprakash was being encouraged by Indira Gandhi's other opponents to hold meetings, lead processions, and otherwise rouse the

1. Jayaprakash Narayan, *Prison Diary, 1975* (Pune, India: Abhay Prakashan, Jan. 1977), p. 34.

people against the Gandhi government. Morarji Desai did not go along with such notions as "total revolution," but they were useful in stimulating the growing ferment against the government. In this sense, the others were using Jayaprakash, but he, always somewhat starry-eyed, was unaware that this was the case.

In February 1975 he came to Delhi and decided to address a meeting just outside the main complex of the office buildings of the government of India. The audience consisted largely of civil and military functionaries of the government. The local press reported his remarks as follows:

Jayaprakash Narayan said today the police, magistracy, and other functionaries should not hesitate to revolt against those official directives which are "unethical and immoral" in character. "Your loyalty is to the national flag and the Constitution, not to the Prime Minister or the Government of the day. If an order appears to your conscience as something against the popular will and the national interest, then it is your duty not to obey such an order."[2]

The notion that each functionary should, whenever presented with an order, ask himself or herself, "Is this against the popular will and national interest?" is not administratively practicable. No administration anywhere in the world could function on that basis. It would have made more sense if Jayaprakash had said that he had come to the conclusion that Indira Gandhi's government no longer represented the will of the people, and that those members of the bureaucracy and other officials who agreed with him should tender their resignations. Over and above this, was it necessary or desirable for Narayan to make a speech of this kind to public servants in a country with a sound democratic constitution which provided that within a year's time there would be another general election, as a result of which Gandhi could be thrown out? But Narayan had no faith in the normal democratic processes. He favored a nonparty system and consensus making—excellent objectives to work toward, but not relevant to the existing situation. However, the net effect of his exhortations to the bureaucracy and others was to undermine in some degree the disciplined functioning of the administration. Besides, his words had a welcome romantic ring in the mood of growing frustration.

Whether because she was ill-advised, or because she felt confident

2. *Hindusthan Times,* Delhi, February 16, 1975.

of her position in the country, Mrs. Gandhi did not adopt the measures which might still have deflected the mounting unrest. Those
measures would have had to have been essentially conciliatory, such
as, for example, suggesting to Jayaprakash that they should each des-
ignate a person, with a third being agreed to by the first two, and
that the three should jointly enquire into the state of affairs in Bihar
and Gujarat, make recommendations as to these two states, and also
generally draw up strong measures against corruption and inefficiency in the country. But she made no such proposals, and soon
time ran out for her. Speaking at a mammoth meeting on February
22, 1975, Narayan said that there could be no dialogue with Indira
Gandhi on Bihar because several efforts to resolve the issue had been
blocked by the Congress leaders.[3]

However, he gave the Prime Minister one more opening. On
March 6, 1975, he led a massive march in Delhi, in which perhaps
half a million people joined, with a view to presenting a petition to
the Indian Parliament setting out a number of demands against corruption, inefficiency, and the remoteness from the people of the administration and the leaders of the government. The petition was presented peacefully and the marchers dispersed, but Indira Gandhi
refused to see Jayaprakash Narayan, and he complained that nothing
was done about the petition. Had the two opponents met, he with
the popular leadership into which he had grown, and she with all the
endowments of her high office, a new path might have been worked
out, in which Narayan could have helped fight corruption, inefficiency, and other ills. He and others would have had access to
Indira Gandhi, and the whole tone of the government would have
become one of greater attentiveness to the needs of the people. On
this basis Narayan could have agreed to restrain the people, and the
students in particular, for a while, so that elections, such as the up-
coming ones in Gujarat, might proceed peacefully. Unfortunately, the
Prime Minister's coterie of advisers, persons for the most part too
self-interested to think in these terms, were bent on confrontation.
They were not disposed to negotiate with the "enemy." How ill-
advised this point of view was the near future would show.

The massive support given Jayaprakash needs to be analyzed. Certainly there was corruption and inefficiency in many of the state governments, and the federal government was not untainted. Moreover,

3. *The Sunday Standard,* New Delhi, February 23, 1975.

the weight of regulations administered by the bureaucracy was great enough to sap the spirit of any citizenry; the bureaucracy should have been greatly simplified and much of it simply scrapped. But because these phenomena had existed since long before Indira Gandhi came to power, and since the general state of the economy had improved during her tenure, some other forces were also at work. It would seem that among them would have to be included the support which Narayan was getting for his view that one had the right to subject the orders and regulations of the administration to the scrutiny of one's conscience and to refuse to carry them out if thus judged immoral or opposed to the national interest. This was held to be high politics in the tradition of the great Mahatma Gandhi.

If this was so, it would seem to follow that there was a considerable section of Indian society that would have preferred a system based on the sovereign jurisdiction of the individual instead of one based on popular majority. In Narayan's view one of the most pressing needs was a drastic rewriting of the constitution so as to devolve nearly all power back to the individual and the villages. The overall Indian polity was to become a loosely structured directorate handing down moral precepts. In this view the considerable trappings of power at Delhi were automatically suspect and without moral sanction.

What is more, as a result of a long period of foreign rule the people had largely lost respect for governmental authority, treating it as an incubus to be thrown off as soon as possible. By and large a ruler was to exist only in an idealized sense, as the upholder of the *dharma,* the divine law, while the institution of the village panchayat, in one form or another would continue. Regulating the affairs of such a microcommunity is like running the business of a large family; the injunctions of the ruler must be carried out, because the ruler possesses superior force. If the ruler becomes too authoritarian, however, revolts will spring up and eventually he will be thrown out.

It is in this historical pattern that we must look at the response to Jayaprakash's campaign against the administration. The government of India, whether headed by Mrs. Gandhi or the leaders of the Janata or any other party, would have had to adopt a very different position from Jayaprakash's. That would be the position of a constitutionally elected government which would claim that it must maintain the rule of law and the sovereignty of the constitutional process rather than the sovereignty of the individual citizen. And this is why any constitutionally elected government in the world would look askance at its Jayaprakash Narayans.

The four parties that were trying to weld a common front against Mrs. Gandhi were the Jan Sangh, with a background of communal militancy. Its leaders now included the well-balanced Atal B. Vajpayee and L. K. Advani; the Bharatiya Lok Dal (BLD), a largely peasant and farmers party led by Charan Singh of Uttar Pradesh who, as a member of a splinter group of the Congress party, had served as chief minister of his mammoth state; the Socialist party— social democrats—with George Fernandes, a well-known labor leader, as its main spokesman; and, finally, the Organization Congress—the rump Congress in which Morarji Desai was the foremost personality but which contained a number of seasoned if rather old-fashioned Congress politicians. Of course, not included in this incipient coalition were the two communist parties, which were also part of the parliamentary opposition. Each of them had a slightly larger membership in Parliament than any of the other opposition parties. The original Communist Party of India (CPI) was to some extent supportive of Mrs. Gandhi's government, whereas the other Communist Party of India (Marxist) was vociferous in its total opposition to the government. These two left-wing groups were at each other's throats, and in a parliamentary sense they cancelled each other out.

The special general election in Gujarat, for which Morarji Desai staged his second fast of the season, was to take place at the beginning of June 1975. The four noncommunist opposition parties ran as a united front against Congress. Realizing the great significance of this election to her party and herself, the Prime Minister campaigned vigorously in Gujarat. During the campaign she complained that her meetings were broken up by rowdyism, that there was stone-throwing, shouting, and other kinds of interruption, including the use of force (in spite of the claim of Jayaprakash and Desai that their followers were nonviolent). There is little doubt that it was often an ugly and lawless election campaign.

As the second week of June 1975 ended, two massive blows were struck against Mrs. Gandhi. The first concerned her in a very personal sense. Her defeated opponent in the general election of 1971, Raj Narain, had presented an election petition against her, with more than thirty grounds for declaring her election void. The proceedings had dragged on before a judge of the Uttar Pradesh High Court. Finally, Mrs. Gandhi had to appear personally, and at the appearance she was so remote that some observers in the courtroom felt that she unwittingly gave offense to the judge. This could well have been the cause of the judgment going the way it did. At any rate, the judge's verdict, delivered on June 12, 1975, was to acquit Mrs. Gandhi on all the major charges, and to sustain only two very minor counts. One was that a man on her personal staff had begun to campaign for her before his resignation from office was formally announced. The second was that the officials of the district had made arrangements for her protection and had lent, in this sense, official support to her candidacy. Mrs. Gandhi's lawyers filed an appeal to the Supreme Court. However, there were immediate vociferous calls from the opposition parties, particularly from Jayaprakash and Morarji Desai and their followers, that she resign forthwith.

On the same day, the election results for Gujarat came in. Mrs. Gandhi's party had been defeated; she had only 75 of the 182 seats. The opposition coalition had not obtained a clear majority, but with some support from splinter groups and independents, it was able to form a new government for the state. The opposition leaders renewed their cries for the ouster of Mrs. Gandhi from the position of Prime Minister on the ground that she was losing support in the country.

Indira Gandhi wavered. She was on the point of resigning but Sanjay, together with Defense Minister Bansi Lal and a few others, counseled her to remain in office. She did not accept their advice, but decided instead to put the matter to the Congress party which, on June 18, 1975, affirmed its "fullest faith" in her and termed her continued leadership to be "indispensable."

The judge who had convicted her had suspended judgment against her until the appeal. After a preliminary hearing, the appellate judge stated that several months would be required to complete a review and that in the meanwhile, although she could remain Prime Minister, she could not vote in Parliament. This interesting decision left Indira Gandhi as a hobbled Prime Minister, an impossible position for the head of a government. It gave the opposition another argument for her immediate resignation.

The opposition parties formed a national coordinating committee, under the chairmanship of Jayaprakash Narayan, which decided to incite action in many parts of India aimed at unseating the Prime

Minister. In order to launch the national movement, a mass meeting was held in Delhi on June 25, 1975. Narayan and Desai were the main speakers. They announced a program, to begin four days later, for a national civil disobedience movement and a no-tax campaign. They called on their followers, as part of this campaign, to surround the homes of Indira Gandhi and her ministers so as to lock them in and prevent them from functioning. In this way, the government would be paralyzed and forced to resign. These actions were regarded as permissible under the heading of "nonviolent civil disobedience." Apart from this over-liberal interpretation of nonviolence, judging from events in Bihar, Gujarat, and elsewhere, it was to be expected that the more radical proponents of change would resort to sabotage of a more vigorous character, including the use of force in several forms, but not extending to the use of firearms. What was clear was that under Narayan's leadership a tremendous surge of emotion and conviction had blended together to create an immense force in the country.

The type of leader who is able to appeal most effectively to the people of India is not the great orator who resorts to tub-thumping, rhetorical flourishes and other dramatic gestures. Mahatma Gandhi, Jawaharlal Nehru, Jayaprakash Narayan, Vinoba Bhave, have all spoken in a quiet, gentle voice to the people. They have struggled to share their inmost thoughts with the people who, instead of being thundered at, have felt themselves being lifted to the level of their leaders. It was in this manner that Narayan talked to the people. He knew that while some of his followers might well overstep the rules of nonviolence, most of them would not; and since the current frustrations over the lack of employment opportunities, and the rising anger about maladministration and corruption, were in any case bound to express themselves in a mighty movement, he felt he was doing his best to keep it within the bounds of nonviolence. He demanded much of his audiences; though his voice was gentle, his injunctions were daring and far-reaching. His call was for total revolution. It was bound to rouse the people to action of a radical character far more so than he foresaw.

It was impossible to say to what extent the people were on Narayan's side. The audiences were large, but that is an Indian tradition. Narayan was the kind of leader for whom the people would turn out, but for many who listened he was a man given to idealistic dreams, a man who shunned the day-to-day drudgeries of political and administrative life. They supported him as someone who could stir up the government and improve its performance, but by no means were they all for total revolution. By the same token, the people were not for excessive measures against him or, indeed, for a total counterrevolution. The pragmatic Indian people are for results: a good administration that promotes an orderly society, does not interfere in the daily pursuits of the people, and yet makes certain that people are able to engage in their daily pursuits. So, the Indian people, not unlike civilized people elsewhere, want government at once to do as little as possible, and yet to provide jobs, education, medical treatment, and stable prices! They saw Narayan as an effective spur to the Gandhi government, and they saw better days in store for themselves as a result of his efforts.

But what if the government were to be unable to respond to the lash being cracked over it by Narayan, the modern-day Krishna? This was the question that troubled Indira Gandhi. In early March 1975, when we talked to her, she had no prescription for quick results in the directions that the people were pointing to. She saw the problems and her answer was restraint on the part of the people, particularly the students who were clamoring for jobs and who were not, as she said, putting their energies into the many constructive channels of work which existed in the villages and the small towns; they all wanted easy jobs in the metropolises. Since she had no startlingly effective answers, the obvious political wisdom would have been to seek a dialogue with Narayan; but she had lost her chance to do so. She was too proud to humble herself before him, whereas a Mahatma Gandhi in power would have done just that. The best possible answers would have evolved, and the people would have been satisfied. The country would thus have been spared the excesses of the ensuing confrontation.

What made the situation desperate was that by the beginning of 1975, the inflation rate in the country reached 30 percent, which virtually put existence itself out of the reach of the poorest strata. By instituting some controls, the Gandhi government was able to bring down the rate fractionally by April 1975, but the overall situation still remained extremely serious. Fortunately, the harvest prospects were bright, and conceivably the downward trend in prices could be maintained, particularly in food grains which were, and remain, basic to the Indian economy. The reduction would help to hold down industrial labor costs and thereby stop the operation of the cost-push factor. That, in its turn, could stimulate industrial production and increase utilization of existing capacity in the country's factories. These indicators encouraged the government economists to take the view that if the government could hold on for a few months, the general situation would begin to look better. These technicians had, of course, not taken into account the sudden events of June 12, 1975, which pushed the country into the most severe crisis since the reattainment of independence in 1947. But on the facts before them, their optimism was not ill-founded. In spite of inflation, there was still an economic buoyancy in the country: small entrepreneurs were busy applying to the banks for loans to set up new industries, and there was an increasing flow of goods from the varied handicraft industries.

Moreover, there was something of a renaissance in the local dance, drama, and painting ateliers spread over the country from the extreme south through Rajasthan to the Himalayan hills and valleys. This surge of artistic activity showed that the people were not allowing the cries of Narayan or the inequities of the administrations to dampen their spirits. However, their sympathies generally lay with all efforts to give India a cleaner and more responsive governmental system, and many of them were more radical than either Indira Gandhi or Jayaprakash Narayan.

Chapter Eighteen

INDIRA GANDHI AND THE EMERGENCY

JUNE 26, 1975 TO MARCH 1977

From 1972 through 1974, Indira Gandhi's position seemed unassailable. "The downtrodden people of India gave her such affection and support, which they bestowed on no one except Mahatma Gandhi, and a *carte blanche* which they gave no one, not even Gandhi," wrote a fervent supporter of the opposition parties in 1975.[1] What, then, made it possible for Narayan to develop an opposition movement of such magnitude that by the spring of 1975 she had arrived at the brink of disaster? It was her very strength that undid her. She was overconfident of the strength of her position as the chosen leader of the country; she felt herself so secure that the minions around her, a brash son, sycophantic officials, and the "downtrodden people of India" could not undermine her. She failed to realize, at this crucial phase of her career, that popular leaders cannot rest on their laurels. They depend upon the continuing support of the people, and such support will inevitably take into account the manner in which governmental polices are implemented. Because of the great trust the people had reposed in her, the more closely did many of them watch her. The pinnacle of power to which she had risen was extremely exalted and for this very reason it was very precarious.

After 1972, though scattered favorable developments took place—several of them were spectacular—Mrs. Gandhi seemed to have become remote from a whole array of affairs that touched the lives of the people. She seemed unaware that some of the state governments were conducting themselves ineptly and in an atmosphere of

1. J. D. Sethi, *India in Crisis* (New Delhi: Vikas Publishing House, 1975), p. 224.

growing corruption, and she was unable to give the younger generation the guidance or words of encouragement that would have helped it face a difficult future. All over the country, people said to each other in despair: "I can't believe that Mrs. Gandhi really knows what's going on. I don't believe she knows how corrupt this administration is, or how frustrating and difficult it is to stand in line and wait for permits, or for one's rations, and what a burden it is becoming to live our daily lives with prices going sky-high." Again, people would turn and say: "Maybe the government doesn't really represent us. It seems to follow concepts it has inherited from the outside, not from India. It applies to India rules and regulations it has learned from the British, and which are not applicable to us. We don't want to be governed by concepts that we thought we had got rid of. What good is this? And the administrators are the same elite who were in charge under the British." Such statements could be heard all over the country—I heard them myself, during a journey through the country in February–March 1975.

Reasonable people did not attribute the corruption personally to the Prime Minister. They realized that it had long preceded her rule, but was growing. The deterioration was cumulative and had come to a head in her time. People were giving notice not just to her, but to the whole system. They were beginning to say that the fruits of independence as offered to them were inadequate; the people wanted something sweeter and fuller.

The discontent was not merely psychological. So powerful had the manipulators of wealth in the country become that each year some 4 billion rupees entered the black market, and by 1974–75 a parallel black-market economy was so prevalent that it distorted the price structure and made it virtually impossible for honest persons to subsist. Therefore, many perceived that the Congress party, which they had so long supported as an alternative to Marxism on the one hand and to pure capitalism on the other, was failing to provide for the development of the country. Furthermore, a large number of members of Parliament and members of the state legislatures were virtually in the pay of prominent businesses or wealthy individuals. In addition, there was now the strong suspicion of a political analogue to the black market: a cabal of behind-the-scenes political intrigue.

A problem was also being created by Mrs. Gandhi's relationship with the states of the federal union. Under her father, the center tried to strengthen the hands of proven popular leaders in the states. However, as the years passed, it became increasingly Indira Gandhi's policy not to encourage the states to run their own affairs. On the contrary, they were to carry out the will of Delhi, particularly in respect to important questions of leadership. Perhaps this was the result of Mrs. Gandhi's assessment that some of the state leaders were inept, but to try to run state affairs from Delhi was to raise ineptness to Himalayan heights.

These events, which were fast reaching the explosion point, led a student of governmental affairs to write: "As of now, the Congress is a deadlock, and needs to be broken up if a new, rational party system is to emerge." [2]

On top of this deadlocked situation fell Narayan's movement for a total change. By now the Congress party had become so permissive regarding the economic and administrative evils which were strangling the people that it had lost the respect of the country. It was quite unable to stand up to the blow Narayan delivered. The only person who could have saved the situation was Mrs. Gandhi herself, but she, by remaining remote, not only from the people but from the essential strengths of the party (such as the popular leaders in the states), could no longer offer an acceptable alternative. She chose to depend mainly on a narrow group of supporters instead of on those who were popular with the people. A democratic system must stand on a broad base, but the Indian political system had seemingly turned on its head. No stable political system can function that way.

The June 18, 1975, Congress party meeting in Delhi, which endorsed Mrs. Gandhi as leader, was hardly an expression of widespread support. A general party convention might well have sounded warnings, and these would have been of more value to Mrs. Gandhi and to the country than the overwhelming endorsement given by the narrowly based Delhi meeting. As it was, Mrs. Gandhi believed that the meeting of June 18 was a reendorsement of her landslide election of 1971. This encouraged the Prime Minister to impose a stringent Emergency on the country. It was imposed on the night of June 25, in response to a mass meeting held by the opposition leaders earlier that day, at which they had, undeniably, charted a very drastic program of popular action against Indira Gandhi herself and her ministers and other functionaries. The program included measures of constraint of a "nonviolent" character, such as capturing the Cabinet

2. *Ibid.,* p. 115.

and holding it by force. Strong action against such a program was clearly necessary.

Emergencies had been declared before, but only in response to external aggression. This time, however, the government invoked the powers which authorize the President of India—acting on the advice of the Council of Ministers (article 74 of the Indian Constitution)—to make a proclamation that a "grave emergency exists whereby the security of India is threatened . . . by . . . internal disturbance" (article 352[1] of the Constitution). This action may be taken before the actual occurrence of any disturbance (article 352[3] of the Constitution). The President complied with the request made to him by the Prime Minister in the very early hours of June 26, 1975.

The declaration of an emergency was not especially reprehensible in itself. It suspended no constitutional or judicial processes, but it gave Parliament the authority to make laws in areas that normally would be within the purview of the state legislatures. Besides, any proclamation of emergency is conceived as a relatively short-term measure, to last not more than two months unless extended by a resolution of both houses of Parliament.

What was extraordinary was the swiftness and severity with which the administration acted. In the dead of night, minutes after the President had signed the proclamation, its police officers were taking into custody Jayaprakash Narayan, Morarji Desai, and scores of other leading opponents of her regime. It took this action because it was convinced that the measures they had urged were highly irresponsible and tended to incite people to violence and general lawlessness that would plunge the country into near-chaos. Besides, there can be little doubt that Mrs. Gandhi was acting under stress. Moreover, Sanjay and her inner group of advisers were urging her to take strong action to crush the nation-destroying moves of the opposition. Perhaps it would have been wiser to wait and see whether the protest movement of her opponents did in fact develop in ugly ways. Then she could have used legitimate police measures while simultaneously asking the opposition to parley with her and offering them some inducement such as cllling for elections in Bihar. Meanwhile the Supreme Court would have taken up her case again, and it was highly likely that within a couple of months she would have been fully acquited, and that thereby a major charge against her by the opposition would have been totally deflated. This line of development would have been far better for India. The political situation would have remained somewhat tense, but the next general election for the country would have been held only a few months later, thus constituting a steadying factor for the country.

The early wave of arrests and the introduction of censorship of the press shook the country. At the same time there were benefits of the kind people appreciated. Government offices were manned punctually, there was a sharp decline in corruption and crime, goods were more easily available, and prices stopped skyrocketing. Besides, there was the widespread expectancy that the Emergency would be lifted after six months at most. Had not Mrs. Gandhi herself virtually promised this in her address to the nation on June 26, 1975 on the promulgation of the Emergency? She had said: "I am sure that internal conditions will speedily improve to enable us to dispense with this proclamation as soon as possible."

With notable exceptions, the people were, therefore, willing to wait and see. And for the first few months they certainly saw encouraging signs. The country made impressive social and economic gains which Mrs. Gandhi probably expected to offset the adverse effects of her harshness to her political foes. For example, the GNP for 1975–76 rose 8.5 percent over the figure for the previous year. Under a twenty-point program which had been announced immediately after the commencement of the Emergency, fair-price shops had been opened which brought essential goods to the people at reasonable prices. It was claimed that country-wide there was a 12 percent drop in prices in 1975 compared with the previous year, so that India had a minus inflation rate, whereas most of the rest of the world was experincing high rates of inflation. Easy credit facilities were made available for landless rural labor, rural indebtedness was liquidated, and strict measures were taken against tax evasion and smuggling. The practice of bonded labor was abolished and this measure was strictly enforced. The speed of electrification of the villages was accelerated, and measures were taken to promote small-scale industry by easy credit terms and special steps to improve the availability of raw materials. It was a broad program that touched village life where it was weakest and city life where the abuses were the most glaring, and on the whole its results were salutary.

Outsiders came to recognize the change for the better. On January 4, 1977, the *Christian Science Monitor* published an article based largely on the findings of Jeremiah Novak, who had represented

Physon Inc. in South Asia. The article pointed out that India's output of goods and services was up by 10.6 percent in the fiscal year ending June 30, 1976. In the same year exports were up by 10 percent, though world trade in general had declined by 6 percent in the same year. As a result, India had accumulated the largest balance of payments surplus that it had ever had. Mr. Novak cited another American businessman who had said: "It is India, not China, that represents the great market of the future, and my company is putting its best men to work on capitalizing on the new environment." [3] The same *Monitor* article mentioned that the previous very high income tax rates had been reduced by over a third, and the wealth tax had also been substantially pruned. The complex industrial licensing rules had been withdrawn or greatly simplified. In government-owned enterprises output grew 16 percent in fiscal 1976, and for the first time handsome profits were made. In 1975–76, irrigation had been extended to an additional 2.9 million hectares of agricultural land and, aided by a good monsoon, agricultural output had climbed by 18 percent, enabling India to start building a food reserve. The *Monitor* article concluded with the following observation: "What the Silent Revolution means for the world is that India is once more back in the economic horse race with China."

During the Emergency India became a net exporter of steel products, and there was a sizable spurt in her exports of manufactured and semimanufactured goods. Also, India became a major supplier of goods and services to neighboring parts of the world. In the years 1975–76 the government of India broke the link between the rupee and the British pound, and in that period the rupee was revalued upward on nine occasions, showing the strength of the Indian currency on the world money markets.

The Emergency achieved a major success in crushing both the black market and smuggling. The government announced that those who had not paid taxes on their concealed holdings would be given an amnesty if they would make a disclosure and pay a reasonable rate of tax on the money. The equivalent of nearly $2 billion, which was estimated to be about half the total unaccounted wealth, was disclosed in a three-month amnesty period. This had the effect of virtually eliminating the black market with its heavy inflationary pressure. As to smuggling, more than 2000 persons were summarily de-

3. *Christian Science Monitor,* article by Jeremiah Novak, Jan. 4, 1977.

tained, the property of absconders was confiscated, and 4500 other smugglers were prosecuted for various customs offenses. All the major smuggling networks were smashed.

Since all this was improving the general situation, the expectation that any morning the end of the Emergency would be announced grew stronger day by day. The disappointment was profound when Mrs. Gandhi confirmed, early in 1976—after her son had spoken disparagingly of elections in general—that the general elections due in February 1976 would be postponed. The conviction deepended that the country had entered a new phase in which autocracy would continue indefinitely. My own feelings were less pessimistic. I remained convinced that Indira Gandhi was using what she considered to be a necessary tactic, although a harsh one, but that autocratic rule was something that she could not live with for long. I recall a meeting with my old friend, A. M. (Abe) Rosenthal, then managing editor of the *New York Times* (he is now that paper's executive editor). Abe Rosenthal knew India well, having represented the *Times* in Delhi for about four years. He said to me: "She's just a damned dictator. She'll never give up power. They never do. I've seen how this works—in Poland, and elsewhere. Indian democracy has had it."

I replied, "I don't agree. As soon as she feels she can, she'll call a general election. She's not a dictator." Abe laughed and used unparliamentary language. "You wait and see," I said, pretty sure that Abe and many others who felt as he did would turn out to be wrong.

Things, however, looked very bleak. The indefinite postponement of the elections was a signal to the police and other officials. They interpreted the postponement the way Abe did—dictatorship was going to be the new order for the foreseeable future. There would be no public discussion, no free press, no criticism of the officials. On this basis, the police and other officials increased their harassment of the people in the hinterland, an area that had been relatively immune from the ill effects of the Emergency. The house of any person of substance could be raided and the officials could take what they wished. The police could offer the better-off a choice of imprisonment or payoff. The only difference from earlier times was that the rates for the payoffs of the police and others went up; they explained quite cogently that they had to raise their prices because the risks of bribe taking were very great; if they were caught Indira would act sternly against them. And it should be mentioned that on the rare occasions when someone was able to complain to the right quarters the guilty police officer was very severely punished. Perhaps Mrs. Gandhi did not realize how widespread official misbehavior had become.

The powers of arbitrary arrest and confinement, moreover, were not directly connected to the proclamation of the Emergency. The government already possessed them under the Maintenance of Internal Security Act (MISA) of 1971—the reason at the time for this act had been the war with Pakistan. It was under MISA that the waves of arrest and detention were made. But the government decided that these powers were too restrictive; under the 1971 act a person could not be imprisoned for more than a year without formal charges and due process of law. In January 1976 Mrs. Gandhi's government got a submissive Parliament to pass legislation under which persons whose period of detention under the 1971 act had expired could be immediately rearrested, thus continuing the period of detention indefinitely—a horrifying prospect and one which brought nothing but anger and disgust among the people.

The powers of confinement were frequently used for petty personal reasons such as paying off old scores. The widely respected cousin of a close friend of mine was jailed simply because a rival wanted to harass him. It was such a glaring case of abuse of power that the jailer could not bring himself to treat the prisoner as prescribed by law. He permitted the jailed man all sorts of privileges, including weekly visits to his family!

Then there was the case of an American-educated niece of mine who was highly motivated to create a better India, particularly for the poor. A few days after the commencement of the Emergency she was arrested at the Delhi airport, on her return from England, and whisked away from her six-year-old son who was traveling with her. The boy was left stranded at the airport after he saw the police take his mother. Moreover, for weeks none in the family knew where she was interned. Finally contact was established, by which time her parents were near breakdowns. Later I was able to obtain a copy of the police report on her as a result of the efforts of my wife, who spoke to T. N. Kaul, an old friend of ours and India's ambassador in Washington at the time. There were no specific charges in the police report of offenses committed. The young woman was said to have contacts with "a foreign power." Of course she had contacts with foreigners; her husband happened to be English! The whole thing was pure fantasy, and though appeals were planned behind the scenes by distinguished women in England who had known Indira Gandhi at Oxford, my niece was not released until the Janata government came to power. I happen to know that her main accuser was a person whose understanding of my niece's activities was scant. However, Mrs. Gandhi was convinced that my niece was converting an area on the outskirts of Delhi into an extreme left-wing commune—"Naxalite territory," as Indira Gandhi herself dubbed it about a year later in another talk with me.

Meanwhile, the person who really seemed to enjoy the Emergency was Sanjay Gandhi. He had become a leader of the Youth Congress, a wing of the Congress party. A few years previously, he had been given a license to establish a factory for the manufacture of a "people's car," but the venture had been a dismal failure. Politics attracted him, and the Emergency gave him a virgin field for activities that would not be opposed, and were certain to win plaudits from those who were seeking the favors of the authorities. Sanjay decided that he had the answers to India's problems. These were: a vigorous program of family planning, the planting of trees, abolition of dowry at marriage, and the extermination of all vestiges of the caste system. All were laudable objectives, but required time for implementation. Sanjay was in a hurry, however, and he saw no reason why his objectives could not all be adopted immediately, by fiat. So, though he had no official position, either elected or appointed, he apparently caused orders to be sent to the chief ministers of the states to fix monthly targets for vasectomies and report progress, and he made it clear that these targets should be substantial. Some states vied with each other to see who could fix the largest targets and then they proceeded, backed by the police, to give vasectomies in the cities and the rural areas, no matter how uninformed the people were. In some areas the countryside was terrorized and, in order to achieve—or over-achieve—targets, there were sometimes glaring abuses. There were charges that old men in their seventies, young men who had not yet raised families, and those who had already been through the operation, were not spared. However necessary it is for India to control its population, and the need does certainly exist, these methods were counterproductive.

In pursuance of Sanjay's program, the same kind of peremptory orders were issued in regard to tree planting. Trees were, without exception, to be planted at regular intervals of, say, 25 feet on both sides of all roads. As a result, a tree might well be planted in a driveway entrance! Such cases actually occurred and it required an appeal to Sanjay himself before the saplings could be removed.

These methods were also applied to Sanjay's determination that slums be removed. There was at times scant regard for those who were displaced, and this too contributed to reducing the administration's acceptability close to zero. The net result was that with each passing week more and more people were antagonized by the regime which had allowed things to come to this pass.

Several other points relating to the Emergency are noteworthy. One is the extraordinary fact that Mrs. Gandhi, with her intimate knowledge of pre-independence politics in India, was seemingly insensitive to the traumatic effect of a large-scale use of preventive detention without trial on a population that still related this form of governmental repression to the alien rule of the British. As the arrests continued and increased—by the end of the Emergency at least 100,000 people had been interned in this manner—people asked all over the country: "What is this? Are we under alien rule again?" The politically alert in the country, who were asking these questions and making these remarks, were numerous, more numerous than a 30 percent literacy rate would indicate. The electoral turnout has been about double the literacy rate, and this is because interest in politics has always been strong in India. It has been nurtured in the villages for millennia, through the political participation of adults in the panchayats. Therefore the means chosen by the administration to buttress the proclamation of the Emergency were particularly distasteful to the Indian people and could not fail to rouse antagonism.

Another point to be noted is the submissiveness of Indira Gandhi's own colleagues in the government and the party. Many of them were respected and important political figures in the country. Why didn't they stand up to her and oppose some of her actions during the Emergency? An answer was given by one of her most senior colleagues, Jagjivan Ram, who had been a member of the cabinet for about twenty-five years, after he had defected from her party following the end of the Emergency. He then said that if he had spoken out earlier he would not have been heard from again, because she would have put him in jail. Actually, I seriously contest his judgment. What was nearer the truth was that all through the Emergency, in spite of the harshness of the regime, most people in India took it for granted that Mrs. Gandhi herself was invulnerable politically and that therefore it was wise to cling to her. In other words, the silence of those around her is to be attributed to their assessment that silence best served the interests of their own political fortunes.

A third point worthy of note is that Indira Gandhi was apparently unaware of the plain fact that authority, concentrated in one person who is insulated from the views of the people by the inhibiting decrees he or she has issued, inevitably becomes very precarious. This is all the more true when a leader is surrounded by a self-serving clique which distorts whatever intimations from the populace manage to pierce the barrier it has created. Finally, the whole point is further magnified in India, where one is dealing with a population of over 650 million, a large proportion of which is politically sensitive. Her isolation made her position even more precarious than that of the ruler of a totalitarian state. In such a state there is a large and not quiescent political party which sends up floods of information about the country and, besides, at the apex of power is not one person but generally a politburo of a dozen or more. When the leader of the politburo takes too great a share of power into his own hands he becomes vulnerable. This is what happened to Khrushchev. I learned in the Soviet Union, from an important functionary whose father had been a prominent member of the politburo, that after having observed the rules of their system for seven years or so, Khrushchev became too sure of himself and began to act without consulting the politburo, which caused his downfall. During the Emergency, and indeed on occasion before it, Mrs. Gandhi had acted without prior consultation with her cabinet. Indeed, she decided on the proclamation of Emergency without such consultation. Had she consulted, it is likely that there would have either been no declaration or its less drastic implementation and Mrs. Gandhi might have been spared the political crash she suffered in 1977.

The whole atmosphere of the Emergency had a psychologically disturbing effect on most people who had any connection with the Indian political scene, and though Mrs. Gandhi generally gave the impression of poise and calm, perhaps no one was as seriously affected as she. This alone can explain the fact that she permitted the Indian Parliament to address itself to introducing legislation which would place the election of the Prime Minister above judicial review. As might have been anticipated, this discriminatory piece of legislation was totally unnecessary because two months later the Supreme Court set aside the judgment which had found Indira Gandhi guilty of two very minor electoral infractions.

Though some people paid a heavy price for the continuing Emergency, the very fact that it ran on with a momentum of accelerating injustices for over a year and a half ensured that it became an experience they were not likely to forget. If anything, this harsh experience revitalized the democratic tradition in India.

Once police corruption reemerged, and with greater virulence than before, the original justifications for the Emergency began to sound hollow. No explanation that the regime was interested only in the people's welfare could counteract the exactions, tyranny, and brutality of the police and other officials, to which was added the indiscriminate vasectomy program, particularly in northern India.

Toward the end of 1976 the country was hoping that Mrs. Gandhi would announce that the general elections would not be postponed again but would be held in February 1977. However, before the year ended an official spokesman stated that the government was considering another postponement. Again Sanjay stated that, after all, elections were of no great importance and that there were other ways of ascertaining the wishes of the people. Simultaneously it became known that no instructions had been given to the elections commissioner to prepare electoral rolls for elections in February 1977. It seemed as if Sanjay had been authorized to sound the death knell of democracy in India. Profound despair was everywhere: There was restiveness among labor, and a wave of strikes occurred in spite of the strict prohibition of such action under the "laws" of the Emergency.

The situation seemed hopeless, but reverberations from the unrest in the country at last reached Mrs. Gandhi. The state of affairs was not as glowing as she had thought it was. Besides, she became apprehensive about a basic economic determinant: agricultural outputs. For two years these had been sustained by successive excellent monsoons which had enabled her to start building up food stocks and had freed the country from P.L. 480 assistance and other imports of food grains. But how long could she expect the monsoons to remain favorable? The next monsoon was very likely to be below average, and food grain production would fall, perhaps steeply. After much silent thought, and this time brushing aside the pleadings of her advisers, she went on All India Radio and surprised her listeners by telling them that early in March 1977, the postponed general elections would be held.

In justification for this immense step forward she said: "The

Twenty-Point and Five-Point Programs have shown tangible results." The first-named program was a governmental one, but the latter was her son's formula. By mentioning it in this key announcement, she was raising Sanjay's program to the level of governmental policy. She seemed to be recommending his good deeds to the nation. This led the people to believe that her son would play a significant role in the elections. She warned that it was not permissible to mar the election campaign by preaching hatred, practicing violence, encouraging subversive activities, or lowering the standards of public life. As the statement drew to a close she uttered words which hinted that she was unsure of the way the election would go. She said: "Every election is an act of faith. It is an opportunity to cleanse public life of confusion. So let us go to the polls with a resolve to reaffirm the power of the people, and to uphold the fair name of India as a land committed to the path of reconciliation, peace, and progress."[4] These sentences, redolent with high purpose, signified clearly that the Prime Minister was a very different kind of person from the Hitlers, Stalins, Amins, and a host of other dictators. It was not expediency that took her to the polls; she told a few people privately before the election that she doubted that she could win, but she had to "reaffirm the power of the people."

It is much to the credit of Mrs. Gandhi that, following the announcement of January 18, 1977, the press was freed from its shackles, those political leaders who were still in jail or under other restraints were released, except for a handful against whom there were criminal charges (many of them had been released before she made her statement), and political campaigning was to go forward in an atmosphere of complete freedom. There was only one condition: violence was to be abjured; and this injunction had been accepted by all the principal parties in the field. Thus, instead of continuing the politics of repression, or of permitting the situation to degenerate to the level of street politics, (to which alternative Jayaprakash Narayan had felt driven in the first half of 1975) Indira Gandhi, by calling for general elections, brought back orderly democracy to India and for this act of good sense she deserves the credit which many of the world's "shrewd observers" were positive she would never earn. By her wise action the people of India were spared much suffering and a bitter factional struggle that could have plunged the country into violence.

4. *India News,* Jan. 28, 1977 (published by the Embassy of India, Washington, D.C.). Mrs. Gandhi's radio broadcast was made on January 18, 1977.

Chapter Nineteen

THE 1977 GENERAL ELECTION AND ITS RESULTS

Even before the statement of January 18, 1977, representatives of the four major non-Communist parties in opposition to Mrs. Gandhi—the Bharatiya Lok Dal (BLD), the Socialists, the small group of the Congress party that had not joined her when the party split in 1969, and the Jan Sangh—had started discussions about a common front. Immediately after the call for general elections, these four parties decided to present a joint list of candidates against the Congress party. This was an ominous sign for Mrs. Gandhi because the statistics of previous elections showed that though the Congress party had secured a majority of seats in the Indian Parliament, it had never secured a majority of the total votes cast. It had the largest share by far, always gaining 40 to 45 percent of the vote, while the opposition parties and independents won 55 to 60 percent. But because a plurality can win an election in an Indian constituency, the number of opposition members elected has always been much smaller than the number of successful Congress party candidates. Though the new united front against her boded ill, and she had tasted defeat in Gujarat in 1975 against just such a front, Mrs. Gandhi campaigned vigorously and everyone predicted a hard struggle.

On February 2, 1977, her most senior cabinet colleague, Jagjivan Ram, the generally acclaimed national leader of the former untouchables, and a man who was said to control about eighty members of Parliament, defected and announced that he would collaborate with the opposition. This was not only a major defection but a prognostication on the part of a shrewd politician that Mrs. Gandhi was not going to win. Indeed, after this event Mrs. Gandhi was fighting with her back to the wall.

She decided that she still had a chance if she could explain to the people the real purpose of the Emergency and apologize for the suffering it had caused against her own wishes. She made a major speech two days after Jagjivan Ram's defection, but although her speech was impassioned, she was unable to sound convincing on either count. She spoke of the "inconvenience and hardships" caused. "Inconvenience" particularly irked the people, for it showed that she thought the vexations some had suffered amounted to no more than, say, keeping a visitor waiting for twenty minutes instead of seeing him at the appointed hour. This formulation added fuel to the feeling against her. In the main her speech dwelt on the achievements of the Congress party over a span of 90 years, and more particularly during the 11 years of her stewardship. But, more than listening to her words, the large audience gaped at the stage from which she addressed them. It was decorated not only with her portraits but also with huge 12-foot-tall color portraits of Sanjay. Her supporters were so politically unwise as to offer not the leadership of Indira Gandhi, for which she would have been able to rouse great enthusiasm, but virtually a duumvirate of Sanjay and herself.

Did she not know that ever since Sanjay had ventured into politics his name had raised questions? Sanjay Gandhi began to claim political importance in the counsels of his mother long before the Emergency. It was after his mother's great election victory in 1971 that he seemed to decide that he had achieved a degree of political good sense and was entitled to share in that victory. In 1973 a very close relative of Mrs. Gandhi's, and an important official in her government, said to me: "That young fellow is going to destroy his mother." I asked: "Why don't you tell her so?" Upon which he shrugged his shoulders and replied: "Who can tell her this?"

Mrs. Gandhi was cool even to her close relatives—(except when they were talking, say, about babies and furnishings) including those who were in prominent positions. In general, she was far more remote than her father, who was certainly not gregarious. Under Jawaharlal Nehru's regime, I would visit him whenever I went to Delhi for consultations or otherwise, and invariably I would be invited to the house for lunch or dinner, followed or preceded by a tête-à-tête. However, I once had the occasion to ask the senior official, who also happened to be a close relation of Mrs. Gandhi's, whether he had met her on his most recent visit to Delhi.

"Of course I met her," he replied. When I asked if Sanjay were there he explained, "I didn't go to the house. I met her in her office."

"But didn't she ask you to the house for a meal or something?"
"No."

Mrs. Gandhi's small menage had become a sanctuary from which all others were excluded—yet another example of how effectively she was shielded from the people, from her cabinet, from senior officials, and from others who would have kept her up to date with what was going on.

As the election campaign progressed, and particularly after the defection of Jagjivan Ram, the opposition party sometimes drew mammoth crowds and received the rousing enthusiasm of the public. Certain symbols of the new mood were emerging. The Congress party, as the vanguard of the fight for independence and because of its connection with Mahatma Gandhi and Nehru, had been the foremost political symbol for decades but, largely because of ill-considered activities during the Emergency, the Congress symbol had been smirched. The people were eager for new ones. The four parties which were opposing the old tarnished symbol hit upon a name that at once became a powerful symbol. The name was "Janata," and Janata is "the people." Overnight, the people came to feel that they had been given a party of their own, a party that was not subservient to those in power and could carry the banner of the people's demands, wants, and hopes.

The leaders, too, were symbols. On the Congress side the only leader who could draw crowds was Indira Gandhi herself. On the other side there were more than a handful who had become symbols: Jayaprakash Narayan, Morarji Desai, Jagjivan Ram, Acharya Kripalani, and (in a fairly substantial region), Charan Singh. Among them younger names too were rising, such as Chandra Shekhar. Though not able to campaign because he was still in jail, there was George Fernandes, who had also risen rapidly to become a symbol of defiance and concern for the workers.

A telling phrase was coined by Jagjivan Ram about Indira and Sanjay. He quipped that the so-called Congress government was not the government of the party, or of the cabinet, but a dictatorship of one and a half (the "half," of course was Sanjay). Some people took this up with fervor, and they also related it to the symbol of the Congress party at the polling booths. That symbol was a cow and its calf.

Though united and led by political stalwarts, the opposition did not dare to hope that it could defeat Mrs. Gandhi. This made it all the more determined to try hard. It was frequently stated by the

friends of Jagjivan Ram that he saw himself and his group of followers as holding the balance in the new Parliament. He felt that the
Congress might emerge with a few more seats than the Janata party,
but not with a majority. He anticipated that it would be the party
behind which he threw his weight that would rule the country. At
this stage it was not certain which way he would go. His attitude
reflected that of a considerable segment of leaders and voters: "Let us
bring out the vote so that we ensure the creation of a strong opposition party to Indira in Parliament." Running scared and taking the
the fullest advantage of the return of complete freedom for elec-
tioneering, the Janata voters and candidates surprised themselves by
capturing the government.

The country-wide elections, held from March 16 to March 18,
1977, were a magnificent display of unfettered democracy at work
on a scale unattained in any other part of the world. In a population
of over 625 million, there were more than 380 million voters. More
than 375,000 polling stations were set up, and about 194 million
voters cast ballots, (60.54 percent of the total electorate). This was
the second highest percentage in the history of India's six general
elections. It had been topped only in 1967, when 61.33 percent of
the voters cast ballots. I witnessed the polling in two states (Maharashtra and Gujarat), visiting a large number of polling stations.
There was enormous enthusiasm but no disorder. The representatives
of the parties were grouped at the prescribed distance from the polling booths while long lines of voters were formed at the booths
themselves. When the results of the polling came through, in many
places there was dancing in the streets. My wife and I witnessed this
exuberance at Sanchi in Madhya Pradesh, where sweets were distrib-
uted to all and sundry. It was reminiscent of August 15, 1947; as if the
country was experiencing a rebirth.

The percentage of voting was highest in the most highly educated
and the most prosperous states. Kerala, which has the highest percentage of literacy among the major states, saw 79.21 percent go to
the polls. The figure in the prosperous Punjab was 73.38 percent,
while in neighboring Haryana, it was 73.26 percent. In a few of the
mini-states the percentage of votes cast was even higher than these
figures.

For Indira Gandhi herself the election was a stunning reversal from
power and prestige to the humiliation of rejection. Not only did her
party, which had won every one of the previous five general elec-

tions, suffer decisive defeat, securing only 153 seats out of a total of 542, but both she, and her son who had swaggered around the country until a few weeks before, were roundly defeated by individuals who were far less well known than they. The electorate had not been swayed by the claim that Mrs. Gandhi's family had served the country with distinction for generations; and other great names of the past—such as Pant and Malaviya—fared no better in Uttar Pradesh, the erstwhile major stronghold of the Congress party. What the voters clearly demanded was people whom they could recognize as their own, not people who had come to feel that they had an inherited or prescriptive right to power. In this sense, the 1977 election was a people's revolution, and the revolution was reflected in the types of members of Parliament returned in 1977. Members of both major parties, the Janata and the Congress, informed me that by and large, the persons returned to Parliament were closer to the masses of India; there were more small farmers and struggling professionals than in previous houses. Statistics support this view. In the 1977–79 Indian Parliament, over 40 percent of the members were farmers, compared with 14 percent ten years earlier.[1] This was a welcome development, and one which appeared to give the new Parliament greater potential stability than that enjoyed by previously elected legislatures. For almost two and a half years the Janata party, though an amalgam of five groups, remained at least superficially cohesive. There were anxious times, however. For example, in late 1978 Charan Singh, the powerful leader of the BLD section of the party was dismissed from the cabinet and many thought that his large group would pull out of the party. However, within a couple of months he was back in the government, and now as deputy prime minister. Moreover, the previous wide rift between him and Jagjivan Ram seemingly narrowed. Both agreed to serve as deputy prime ministers, with the question of seniority between them pushed aside. However, all this turned out to be precarious.

Why did the Indira Gandhi regime crumble and fall so decisively? Was it that she was pushing India too hard in a modernization program? This was so in the eyes of a few, but they could not have brought about her downfall. What undid her was the use of methods which were alien to a much larger segment of the Indian people, and these methods were being directed not only toward modernization

1. Marcus Franda, "Farmer Power and Charan Singh," *ASIA,* September/October 1979 (published by the Asia Society Inc., New York City), pp. 33–36.

but also apparently toward the dominance of a small group. Non-violence and *ahimsa* are more deeply embedded and pervasive in Indian society than probably in any other society in the world. In India the prescription for the removal of ills cannot be the excessive use of force, or even authority. Such a course rouses too many deep-rooted sentiments in the country, and the net result is to disempower those who set it in motion. When power receded from the people and became high-handed and arbitrary, as it did from 1975 onward, then the authority of Mrs. Gandhi, in spite of her brilliant 1971 election victory and the many scientific and economic gains, became precarious.

The Janata government thoroughly detested Mrs. Gandhi, and yet its first annual economic survey of India paid tribute to the previous regime's achievements. Industrial production had risen 10 percent which, the survey noted, was something that had not happened for a decade. Exports that year rose 23 percent, a considerable jump, while imports fell by 7 percent. The result was a trade surplus and a very considerable balance of payments surplus. The survey pointed out that India's foreign exchange reserves reached a record level of $3.3 billion. The development of the steel industry during the Gandhi era was notable, and it illustrated the overall industrial expansion. The plant at Bokaro was being enlarged from a capacity of 1.7 million ingot tons to 4.7 million tons, while the Bhilai plant was going up from 2.5 million tons to 4 million tons. In addition, preliminary work on several other steel plants was in hand, and the Tata plant was also expanding. Looking ahead, the steel authorities were planning to raise steel-making capacity to 75 million tons a year over the next twenty-five years. When achieved, this level of productive capacity will place India among the foremost steel-making countries. The target is attainable because India has the resources, both mineral and human, required for it. Finally, a point which must not be missed, India's merchant marine was developing significantly, and by the end of the Gandhi era it had reached the sizable proportions of 5 million gross registered tons.

It bears repetition that Mrs. Gandhi, who was roundly accused abroad and in many Indian circles, too, of being a dictator and the person who killed Indian democracy, announced on January 18, 1977, that a fair general election would be held. This announcement was carried out to the letter, and by so doing Mrs. Gandhi regained respect as a political leader in India, which she had in some measure lost during the last year or so of the Emergency, when many in the administration had acted in disregard of the laws of the land. Tacitly she withdrew from the autocratic procedures she had permitted during the Emergency.

Chapter Twenty

THE JANATA GOVERNMENT

On March 24, 1977, at the age of 81, Morarji Desai, a veteran congressman who had served in the cabinets of both Jawaharlal Nehru and Indira Gandhi, was designated Janata party leader, and thus Prime Minister, in the newly elected government. He finally had achieved the position that had eluded him in 1964 and 1966, at the deaths of Nehru and Shastri. In making the decision to name Desai Prime Minister, Narayan, widely acknowledged by the Janata party as the architect of the successful national movement against the Gandhi government, recognized the delicacy of the situation by associating himself with the nonagenerian J. B. Kripalani, the doyen of the Indian political scene. Kripalani had been for many years Secretary General of the Congress party under Nehru, and later came to be recognized as a national leader in his own right. However, he never achieved high office, perhaps because of his acerbic nature. Unlike Krishna Menon (whom, indeed, he had once defeated for a seat in Parliament), this negative quality was not balanced by extreme brilliance.

The transformation from a Congress government to the Janata was at first sight not much more than a change in name. Including himself, Desai's cabinet numbered twenty, of whom as many as fourteen had been at some time or other congressmen in good standing. Only six came from other parties: two from the Jan Sangh group which had followed a somewhat militant "Hindu culture for India" policy and in this respect was quite different from the Congress; two from the Socialist party, the social democratic group; one from the defunct Swatantra party, a right-wing group, and one from the Akali party of the Punjab, a Sikh group.

The new government quickly adjusted itself to some of the classic lessons of parliamentary democracy, which include accommodation to many of the policies of the previous government, particularly those in economic and foreign policy. For example, Morarji Desai had strenuously opposed the nationalization of the banks, an issue that brought to a head his differences with Indira Gandhi and led to her relieving him of the post of Deputy Prime Minister. However, as Prime Minister he did nothing to undo the new order in the banking world. Similarly, though widely regarded as being somewhat to the right of Nehru and his daughter, Desai continued the foreign policy of nonalignment which Nehru originated in 1946 and which both Shastri and Indira Gandhi pursued. However, he stated that his government would be "genuinely" nonaligned, and this adverb was welcomed in Western circles as indicating that there would be a more evenhanded policy between the United States and the Soviet Union. Desai paid an early visit to Washington, President Carter went to Delhi early in his tenure, and there was evidence of a sincere desire of each to understand the other. Not that all problems were solved. India continued Indira Gandhi's refusal to adhere to the non-proliferation treaty unless all states, including the present nuclear weapons states, agreed to bring all their atomic industries under safeguards to ensure that they would be used only for peaceful purposes. This caused Washington some annoyance and it complicated practical relations between India and the United States. The latter made it clear that in spite of a contractual obligation to supply nuclear fuel for an electrical power-generating reactor north of Bombay, it would have to stop supplies unless India agreed to safeguards—that is, the placing of all its nuclear programs under controls run by the International Atomic Energy Agency. Desai categorically rejected this condition, which is still being pressed by the United States.

Meanwhile, the Desai government reaffirmed its adherence to the treaty of peace, friendship, and cooperation with the Soviet Union negotiated by Mrs. Gandhi in 1971. That treaty was interpreted in the West as evidence that India was closer to the Soviets than to the Atlantic Powers. Indeed, Soviet dignitaries were in at least as close touch with the Desai government as they had been with its predecessors. Almost immediately after the formation of the Janata government, Soviet Foreign Minister Andrei Gromyko, a full member of the Soviet politburo, came to Delhi and was warmly received. Other high-level Soviet visits included one by Kosygin in April 1979. As was expected, there were slightly different perspectives on the Vietnamese involvement in Cambodia (Kampuchia), but not enough to disrupt the constructive tone and results of Indo-Soviet interchanges. The Soviet Union continued to assist India with technology and equipment badly needed to develop India's mineral resources and not easily available from other sources. In addition, Desai reportedly asked the Soviets to assist in drawing up the final plans for a most ambitious system of canals, known popularly as the Garland canals, which will capture, control, and link the water resources of the rivers of the north with those of the south. The scheme could well entail the construction of some 6000 or 7000 kilometers of canals, and the results for agriculture, flood contol, and power generation would be so great that they would do for many parts of India what good farming has done in the Punjab.

Relations with China still suffered because of the consequences of the war between the two countries in 1962. What was galling to India was that China had apparently adopted a policy of using its might swiftly and "punitively" whenever it thought fit to do so. When, early in 1979, China took such action against Vietnam, Indian Foreign Minister Vajpayee, who was in China as a guest of the Peking government—and the first high-level guest since the war of 1962—cut short his scheduled visit and returned to Delhi. Simultaneously, Desai called for the immediate and complete withdrawal of Chinese forces from Vietnam.

In spite of differences of outlook, and recognizing that they must not constitute a bar to good relations, the Janata government continued the effort started by Indira Gandhi, and Vajpayee's visit was a significant move in that direction, even if it had to be cut short. In an earlier era, Chou En-lai came to Delhi three times, whereas Nehru visited Peking only once. The Indian leaders have reiterated that China must vacate all Indian territory, but to this date there has not been any indication that China is going to return the territory it occupied in 1962. It is too early to say whether relations will become warm between the two countries.

Relations developed reasonably well with Pakistan, considering the background of irresponsibily stimulated hostility which goes back to the partition. Pakistan, on its creation, obtained less territory than it desired and has never become adjusted to this situation. Jinnah is on record as having stated categorically that he would accept the accession of Kashmir to India, under the terms of the agreement between the British, Indian, and Pakistani governments. But it would appear that Pakistan had no intention of accepting this accession, which it anticipated. Therefore, elements of its army invaded Kashmir, and at the cease fire Pakistan was left in possession of about a third of Kashmir—not a bad dividend for an invader but not enough to satisfy Pakistan's appetite. The result has been periodic wars between Pakistan and India. In mid-1980 another such bout does not seem imminent, and perhaps the two countries will eventually decide to live with what territories they have.

Meanwhile, another ominous cloud has appeared on the horizon. The United States, the European powers, and India have all acquired evidence that Pakistan is putting together the items which could go to the making of nuclear weapons, and this evidence has been acquired after Muammar al-Qadafi, the Libyan leader, and former Pakistani President Zulfikar Ali Bhutto spoke of the need to have an "Islamic bomb." Could it be that we are entering an era when the nuclear weapon is to be an adjunct of religion, and thus spiritual values and devilish capabilities of destruction are to be brought under one banner? If so, the end of the twentieth century will turn out to be the end of human civilization. Perhaps leaders will arise capable of arresting the plunge to this ominous state of affairs. At the moment I see no new star in the heavens that signals the return of the Prince of Peace.

In its relations with Bangladesh the Desai government had a positive record. It reached agreement in principle with Bangladesh on the division of the waters of the eastern rivers; this had been the major problem between the two states going back to the time when East Bengal was part of Pakistan. With its other neighbors, and indeed with all other countries except South Africa, India's relations were good, and they were conducted skillfully by Atal Bihari Vajpayee, the foreign minister. B. K. Nehru, until recently the most senior ambassador of India, told me in April 1979 that Vajpayee had not made a single blunder in two years as foreign minister, and this was an achievement.

On the domestic front, the Janata government did not depart significantly from the objectives of its predecessor. It declared that it would eradicate poverty and unemployment within a period of ten years, which was reminiscent of Mrs. Gandhi's return to power in 1971 on the slogan "Abolish Poverty!" The Janata program, had two objectives: The first was to encourage small-scale industries (this was by no means a new policy, but it was proclaimed with fanfare); unfortunately, the results achieved during the Janata rule were insignificant, though Desai repeatedly declared himself strongly in favor of economic decentralization. The second was related to its attitude toward big business and large-scale industry. In this connection, on April 4, 1977, in his first radio broadcast to the nation, Desai said: "To those concerned with business and industry I would commend the Gandhian principle of trusteeship of wealth, that they must contribute to the Nation out of full utilization of the productive capacity of their units and I call upon them to eschew temptation to exploit the people's need." This moral appeal to industrialists and businessmen was different from the approach of the previous government, which relied more heavily on the regulation of industry and the sense of patriotism of industrialists to keep production at high levels.

Although the minister for Industries, George Fernandes, had tilted with big business for years as a prominent labor leader, the Janata government looked more kindly on the businessman than did the Nehru and Gandhi governments. But business was unhappy with one aspect of Janata policy. As a reaction to the Gandhi emergency period, when strikes were prohibited, Janata reestablished labor's right to strike. This right was extensively exercised and businessmen found their plans disrupted. However, they were solaced by the fact that the Janata government moved further than Mrs. Gandhi had in removing and simplifying regulations and controls. For example, import licenses were no longer required for a wide range of goods connected with such manufacturing sectors as electronics, space, oil, and heavy industries.

The Janata government's five-year development plan for 1978–83 was to expend the equivalent of somewhat over $120 billion, and achieve an annual growth rate of 5 percent—a substantial step forward for a population of about 700 million. Forty million new jobs were to be created, even if this would still leave about 25 million unemployed. By the end of the plan 90 percent of children in the 6 to 14 year age group were to be in school and 60 million adults were to receive instruction. All of India's 570,000 villages were to receive good drinking water and 50 percent were to get electricity. There were also to be extensive health, housing, and nutrition programs. Besides all this, additional activities were to be encouraged in the private sector both in urban and rural areas. The prospects were bright.

However, when the Janata government fell in July 1979, very little had been done. Some areas, particularly the Punjab, Haryana, Tamil

Nadu, and Maharashtra made progress, but on the whole the economy of the country was increasingly sluggish, and there was widespread disillusion about the capacity of the Janata government to implement its policies. Registered unemployment actually jumped 31 percent.

The government did better in undoing the Emergency policies. The Janata government adopted a family planning policy which made it clear that force and coercion would not be used. Desai himself stated on April 28, 1977, barely a month after he took office, that "the government policy is to have family planning and population control as vigorously as possible on a voluntary basis but not on a coercive basis."[1] The name of the ministry concerned was changed from the Ministry for Family Planning to the Ministry for Family Welfare. The new government made a statement on family welfare which pledged special emphasis on the need to ensure the fullest utilization of all media of publicity, and on enhancing motivation through the "extension" approach. It also indicated that the government would give special attention to the promotion of research in the field of reproductive biology and contraception. It reiterated that "compulsion in the area of family welfare must be ruled out for all time to come."[2] However, these pronouncements were just rhetoric. The immediate result was a sharp fall in the number of vasectomies. The long-term solution is education, but since some groups in India are more resistant to education than others, particularly to the education of women, the uneven way education will progress is not to the liking of all groups. Some fear that it will result in sociological imbalances.

As was to be expected, the Janata government passed legislation to undo some of the legislative innovations of the previous regime. There was no difficulty in making one change: legislation was introduced and adopted to undo the measure taken during the Emergency to place the election of the Prime Minister above the normal election laws. But the pledges to undo the power to put people in preventive detention without trial, and to revoke the constitutional power to declare an emergency because of internal disturbances were not entirely fulfilled. Instead, the new legislation on preventive detention simply introduced the limitation that a person detained could ask for and be given the advantage of a review, to be conducted by a

1. *India News,* May 9, 1977 (published by the Embassy of India, Washington, D.C.).
2. *Ibid.*

panel headed by a High Court judge, and an internal emergency could be declared only in the event of an "armed rebellion," and not in conditions of internal disturbances but "armed rebellion" could be widely construed.

At the same time, the Janata government resorted to the extraordinary and quite unnecessary measure of setting up, by legislation, special courts to try Mrs. Gandhi and her associates for their acts during the emergency. The existing courts were the proper venue for such trials, if they were to take place at all. To create special courts was to resort to emergency measures at a time when there was not even the semblance of emergency conditions in the country. The judges for the special courts would be hand-picked, and this would still further vitiate the whole process of justice. Fortunately there were indications of wiser counsels from influential quarters. At the end of April 1979, the head of the RSS (the militant wing of the Jan Sangh party now merged in the Janata party) addressed a press conference at which he said that the Janata government should adopt an attitude of forgive and forget toward past rulers, including Mrs. Gandhi. He added: "Both sides should adopt an attitude of reconciliation." [3] However, the special courts were created, but they made no progress with the trials of Mrs. Gandhi, and little in regard to other trials, mainly because there was little evidence to support the charges made. The special courts and their proceedings became a laughing stock, and when the Janata government fell—followed by the fall of Charan Singh's effort to put together a government—they were soon terminated.

The Janata government collapsed in July 1979, brought down by internal dissension as well as by its consistent record of nonperformance. Of special concern to the people were the rising prices—at an annual rate of over 20 percent—increasing crime in the urban areas, a lack of firmness in dealing with inter-caste and inter-community feuds, administrative inefficiency because of a sharp decline in the morale of virtually all levels of officials, and the apparent acceptance as part of the system of such social ills as corruption, black market operations, and price fixing by hoarding of essential commodities. Many in the country began to look back nostalgically to the efficiency of the disciplined times of the emergency of 1975–77.

The factions in the Janata patchwork were so hopelessly at logger-

3. *News India*, May 4, 1979 (a weekly, published by Hiba Publishing, New York), p. 6.

heads that the President of India was quite right in denying to Jag-jivan Ram the opportunity to try to put together another divided and unworkable coalition to succeed Charan Singh, who had taken over from Desai in August 1979 but found himself at the head of a minor-ity government which was viable only provisionally while the country geared itself up for another general election. The Janata completely dissolved by the time of the election in January 1980. It thus became clear that the temporary coalition it had represented was not an al-ternative to the Congress party, even though the latter had been through inevitable restructurings.

Almost all the media and commentators expected the Janata and Charan Singh's Lok Dal party to emerge to the new elections as sub-stantial groups, together large enough to form a majority in the Lok Sabha and thus frustrate Mrs. Gandhi's attempt to return to power. The fact that Charan Singh was in power when the country went to the polls was expected to give his party an advantage. It did, indeed, so far the collection of campaign funds was concerned—particularly from the sugar industry. Except for two journalists no one predicted a clear majority for Mrs. Gandhi's Congress party.

However, the general election of January, 1980 ended in a re-sounding victory for the Congress (I) party, and Mrs. Gandhi was swept back to power with a better than two-thirds majority in Parlia-ment. She herself was elected by large majorities in two different con-stituencies, and Sanjay won handsomely in the same constituency which had rejected him in 1977. He ousted the sitting Janata mem-ber.

Why this dramatic turn around by an electorate of over 300 mil-lion? The answer is that the shrewd Indian voters had given the Janata party (a combination of all the political noncommunist forces opposed to the Congress) a two and one-half year period to prove its worth, and it failed dismally both in regard to basic economic neces-sities for the people and in the maintenance of law and order. Its can-didates had thus forfeited the right to return to power. At the same time, the electorate that had clearly expressed its displeasure over the excesses of the regime during 1975–77 decided that to continue to keep Mrs. Gandhi out would be to spite itself. It felt the need to replace the Janata and the Lok Dal by a strong stable government capable of controlling prices, ensuring country-wide distribution of necessities, and improving the law and order situation. The answer to its needs was seen to be Mrs. Gandhi's party. In the new Parliament the Janata and the Lok Dal were reduced to such small groups that neither of them qualified as the official opposition.

The 1980 general election was undoubtedly a personal triumph for Mrs. Gandhi. It was also a successful assertion by her party that it represented continuity with the main stream of the Indian National Congress, the party which had struggled for and achieved Indian independence and had brought the country stability and progress for thirty years, before it was displaced in 1977. This continuity is a powerful factor in a broadly conservative and largely traditional society such as India. The vote for the Congress (I) was also a vote for a strong federal center rather than greater devolution of powers to the constituent states, which had been much discussed but not acted upon during the Janata regime.

Chapter Twenty-One

1980: THE CONGRESS RETURNS
TO POWER

At the beginning of 1980, Mrs. Gandhi was swept back to power after a spectacular victory by her party in a mid-term general election. She was indisputably the chosen leader of the people. Why, then, does this chapter have the title "The *Congress* Returns to Power"? In reelecting her, the voters asked that Indira Gandhi lead them down the firmer and more acceptable paths of the traditional Congress party rather than in the chaotic and ill-defined ways of the Janata party. The Janata had claimed that it would be an improvement but it turned out to offer an unacceptable difference: more corruption, more inefficiency, more ineptness in economic affairs and far less capability to ensure domestic security and peace. In 1980 the voters wanted to remedy these vexing shortcomings.

Mrs. Gandhi understood clearly the nature of the failings of the Janata, and knew what she was expected to do. But the conditions in the country, as well as internationally, were extremely difficult. The upward thrust of oil prices had created numerous obstacles to economic betterment; price rises and shortages of essential commodities had rendered the situation grim in many parts of the country. All this Mrs. Gandhi well realized, as I learned on March 8, 1980, when we discussed the situation she had inherited.

There were special problems in northeast India. In Assam and Tripura there had been, over the past three decades, a steady influx of migrants from neighboring areas, particularly Bangladesh (and before 1971 from its predecessor, East Pakistan). People infiltrated across the international frontier without papers or permission and gradually grew to be a significant segment of the population. There was also a much smaller trickle of people from West Bengal and other parts of India. Being an easygoing people the Assamese said and did nothing until the immigrants were present in numbers large enough to be perceived as a threat to the local way of life. Now the young and the educated Assamese want all the outsiders to be sent back to where they came from. Mrs. Gandhi has given priority to this complex issue that came to a head shortly before she returned to power. The main body of popular agitation in Assam has been conducted nonviolently but toward mid-1980 there were some unfortunate outbreaks of violence.

In the northwest of the subcontinent the region in and around Afghanistan had become disturbed. In the early part of 1979 it became clear that the Afghan revolution of April 1978 had run into serious problems. Internecine rivalries resulted in the death of Taraki, the original leader of the revolution, and then of his successor, Amin. These events, as well as other developments such as outside aid to rebel elements, mostly though not exclusively in Pakistan, weakened the grip of the authorities in Kabul and before the end of December 1979, the Soviet Union sent in its troops to "assist" them. The United Nations responded by convening an emergency session of the General Assembly, which called for the full withdrawal of foreign forces from Afghanistan. Meanwhile, Iran too was seething and in the region in general there were ominous portents of possible conflict which could involve the superpowers and others.

Mrs. Gandhi's reactions to these grave events has been statesmanlike. She has not favored either the taking of American hostages by Iran or the presence of foreign forces in Afghanistan, and she has said so repeatedly. However, she does see the point of view of the Iranian authorities, and she recognizes that to some extent events and circumstances beyond the control of the Soviets have contributed to their military presence in Afghanistan. She has favored quiet diplomacy to resolve both these sets of problems, and for her diplomacy does not include raising the level of armaments and military preparedness in the region. To rush in arms and naval armadas could simply increase the chances of conflict either now or in the future while doing less than nothing to ensure peace and the resolving of conflict.

Mrs. Gandhi's policy of restraint but readiness to join in the search for solutions led General Zia, the military ruler of Pakistan, to say that he would welcome her assistance in efforts to persuade the Soviet Union to withdraw its forces from Afghanistan. Aware of the concerns of the countries involved, and with concerns of its own, India has probably been in a position to put together the elements of a solution. Such suggestions would require parallel restraints on the part of those involved rather than one-sided actions. Indian perceptions have been along these lines, and behind the scenes Mrs. Gandhi's government has worked to gain a hearing for them.

Domestically, Mrs. Gandhi's government has begun its attack on high prices, hoarding, and gangster-like lawless behavior. The country is in a mood to rally behind her government in its measures to grapple with these problems.

An interesting and welcome feature of the situation in 1980 was the large number of younger members of Parliament committed to action rather than interminable talk—the latter having been the bane of the government process in India as it also is in many other parts of the world. At least a hundred members of the Indian Parliament were "Sanjay's men," young or youngish men and women who want to help move the country forward to accomplish its basic goals. Some observers estimate that the group of Sanjay Gandhi's followers in Parliament had swollen to 160 or even 180 by the time of his death on June 23, 1980, in the crash of a small plane. Sanjay was still pressing the adoption of his five-point program first unveiled during the Emergency of 1975–77—the abolition of illiteracy, slum clearance, tree planting, abolition of dowries, and the complete ending of all vestiges of the caste system. Presumably his followers remain committed to these measures and will also press for a faster moving administration and bureaucracy, strong measures against hoarders, higher salaries for all public servants, ceilings on the prices of essential commodities, and so on. The badly needed influx of young political leaders and potential leaders was at least 10 years overdue. This legacy of Sanjay's is bound to have a reinvigorating effect on the country's political life.

The crucial strength of the Congress party under Indira Gandhi, as it was in her father's time, is that it steers India away from a right-left polarization which has been and is the harsh fate of many countries in our era, both developed and developing. This achievement has been fashioned by maintaining a wide political spectrum within the ruling party that extends from the moderate left through the center to the moderate right, and by pursuing policies that embrace elements of both socialism and regulated capitalism. Only the extremists on both sides oppose this kind of reasonable pragmatism, and even they are generally half-hearted in their opposition. Hence India's relative stability, and hence also the strong general consensus for continuing with democratic ways of governance based on universal suffrage, the secret ballot, and power vested in a party that enjoys a wide base of popular support.

The fact that in September 1980 the government again armed itself with certain powers to detain before—rather than without—formal charges and trial is in no sense a portent of a nation-wide political emergency. This is a procedure to deal with unruly elements who were given a long rope, particularly during the Janata period, and who are creating disorder among the various communities and are also indulging in economic malpractices such as hoarding, black market activities, and price gouging. There is provision in the legislation for immediate review by a quasi-judicial board, which can result in the detention orders being overturned; and there is provision also for recourse to the courts by writ petitions. Ever since 1950 the governments of India, not excluding the Janata government, have been armed with some powers of detention. In various ways somewhat analagous procedures exist in some western democracies. Their purpose is the protection of the citizen—and not repression. It is in this sense that the new powers in India are to be construed.

Until the world develops the wisdom to give itself a more effective system of international order, and until it embarks on massive steps of disarmament in all parts of the globe, no country can claim that its future is truly bright. However, in the inevitable interplay of light and shadow in India it can be fairly asserted that the brightness predominates.

Chapter Twenty-Two

THE CONTINUING PROCESS

Throughout the vast and populous regions which lie to the east of India, stretching through China to Japan and through Thailand and the southeastern peninsula of the Asian land mass to Indonesia, over a period which is to be reckoned in millennia, India has been a basic and pervasive humanistic influence in philosophy, religion, and art forms. To the west of India live practical people, full of spirit, as Aristotle observed, to whom India has been able to offer its arithmetic, its algebra, and its trade. Gibbon, in his *Decline and Fall of the Roman Empire,* mentions the importance of trade with India. The Arabs carried to the rest of the Western world the great Indian discoveries of the zero, the system of numerals now in use, and knowledge of advanced equations. In his writing on "The Spirit of the Age of Reconnaisance," Professor J. H. Parry of Harvard tells us the following: "Arithmetic, which freed men from dependence upon the abacus, was made practicable by Hindu numerals, first introduced into Europe by Leonardo of Pisa's book of arithmetic at the beginning of the thirteenth century." [1] He reminds us that this made it possible for sailors and explorers to seize on arithmetic as a tool in their great adventures.

In more modern times, interchanges among peoples have been profoundly influenced by the emergence of the nation-state and of the notion that each of these budding leviathans must seek to equip itself as a power center to safeguard its own specific geographical identity against its neighbors and other possible aggressors. Because for two hundred years or so it came under the dominance of the Brit-

1. *Renaissance, Reformation and Absolutism: 1450–1650,* 2d ed. Studies and Interpretations by Jacob Burckhardt, J. H. Parry, et al. (New York: Thomas Y. Crowell, 1972), p. 63.

ish, India has been a latecomer to this still relatively new system. Had it been left to itself it would probably have appeared on the world stage as a larger entity than it now is, but as a much looser one than the Western style of nation-state. That it intended to maintain some degree of cohesion is clear from the fact that the Mogul emperor in Delhi was being supported by a number of diverse states throughout the country in the eighteenth and the early part of the nineteenth centuries, long after the emperor could command any real authority. He served as the symbol of unity in the varied Indian world. The Rajput, the Maharatta, the Bengali, and other groups, each with its own language, addressed the court and the emperor in Persian, which continued as the official language of Delhi in the higher echelons. Of course Persian was a foreign language and sooner or later it would have had to be displaced by a native tongue, just as English is being displaced in Delhi these days by Hindi. The point, however, is that the use of a number of languages in India does not in itself negate the underlying sense of common identity among the people. Eventually a very sizable proportion of the population will become bilingual or trilingual and, indeed, this has been the tradition for centuries. For example, the native tongue of the Punjabi—whether a Hindu, a Muslim, or a Sikh—is Punjabi, but under the British the official languages in use were English and, at the local level, Urdu. Even when the Sikhs ruled the Punjab, Kashmir, and Beyond, they supplemented Punjabi with Persian for certain occasions and purposes. In brief, the Indian is accustomed to living and working in a two-language system. The fact that there are over a dozen official languages in India baffles many outsiders but does not appear to the Indian to be a sign of the absence of an all-pervading Indianness in the country. It is convenient at the state level to work in one language, and where necessary state boundaries have been redrawn on linguistic lines, but no language group demands independence on the ground that its language is different from that of another state. This matter of language shows that the yardsticks in use elsewhere to characterize a nation-state are not necessarily applicable universally.

From the very beginning of India's reemergence in independence, Jawaharlal Nehru began to advance an extraordinarily valuable idea as the basis of the modern world system. He made a unique enunciation of the Indian view of non-power—a derivative of the concept of *ahimsa*—as the appropriate posture for all states and of particular relevance to their relations with each other. He gave form to this concept by sketching out the tenets of a policy that came to be known as nonalignment. It was far-reaching and admittedly not easy to attain though, as he saw it, it was a policy which was increasingly a necessity in our world. He spelled out a system of dealings among sovereign states that rejected the dominant practice of relationships based on power, power alliances, and the notion that there would be or were vacuums of power which had to be filled by the development of military strength and the structuring of military alliances. His concept was so novel that "the Powers" simply shrugged incredulously. They saw it as an extension of Gandhism, too idealistic for them to consider seriously. For Nehru, however, Gandhian approaches were far from being impractical idealism; they were the reality with which he had worked and lived for thirty years.

That India should seek to advance itself on the world stage as a non-power was something that most politicians and statesmen were totally unable to understand. In 1978, Richard Nixon noted with some relish that in conversation with him the Chinese leaders had expressed their contempt for India because it lacked military power. To Mr. Nixon this seemed to establish India as contemptible and to give sanction for the contempt with which he himself had treated India in 1971. It also showed that the Chinese were advancing on the proper high road of power, and this was something Mr. Nixon understood and could respond to with respect. But of course, to a country that deliberately chose to be powerless he could not respond with respect. His statement corroborates the views of commentators from various parts of the world who have sneered at India as being a "soft state." This term was first used by Gunnar Myrdal, whose understanding of India was woefully slight, though he had looked at a lot of statistics. The term has been taken up by publicists and journalists and has become part of the current coinage of clichés about India and other states which are not strong militarily or economically. To this notion of strength India poses the opposite idea: that the building of military power is incompatible with humanity's true destiny, which can be fulfilled only by movement toward a nonviolent cooperative world system in which all peoples will share, without values being based on military might. This was, in essence, the meaning of the concept of nonalignment as Nehru enunciated it. In the course of time some of the major aspects of nonalignment were accepted by a large number of other countries, but Nehru's full meaning became blurred.

Nehru's concept of non-power could have become truly operative only if it had gained acceptance among the leading nations. Jointly, they could have made the world more benign, but in a largely non-benign world Nehru's notion broke down, and after the 1962 war with China, he had to reassess the situation. Reluctantly, he decided on a certain degree of armament for India. The measures he took were never wholehearted and, unlike the leaders of most great powers, he never urged them with much sense of purpose. As I pointed out earlier, around 1960 the Indian nuclear program was far enough advanced for it to proceed, had India chosen such a course, to a nuclear test by 1962. However, as I have shown, no effort whatsoever was made in that direction, basically because the policy of India was dictated by the notion of non-power.

Internally, too, India is likely to pursue policies that will probably have the effect of continuing the gap in living standards between its people and those of the materially highly advanced countries of the world. This will result from the fact that future governments—as have those in the past—will focus a great deal of their economic developmental effort on the stimulation of small-scale and medium-scale industries, mainly in the villages. These low-power units will never match, in quantity or in drabness, the output of large-scale mass production. If effectively implemented, the Indian formula will provide the citizenry with enough to eat and wear, education, and tolerable sanitary conditions. India will, moreover, preserve and develop a sense of beauty and creativity among millions of producers instead of following the designs turned out by a few. Is this a picture to scoff at, even if it is part of the "soft state" scenario which the "powers" brush aside? Let those who are comfortable with their alternative systems of state-craft and production cast the first stone!

Such an emphasis will not prevent significant increases in the production of steel, oil, coal, industrial chemicals, fertilizers, cement, power, and nonferrous metals. For example, by 1983 India will probably be able to produce 15 million tons of steel a year, and its oil production will about double, bringing the country close to self-sufficiency in this ever-more-precious commodity. Compared with other countries that are regarded as developed, the heavy-industry sector will be relatively small, but it will play a prominent socioeconomic role. Other countries will continue to produce automobiles that will be larger and travel faster than Indian automobiles, but what of that? Indian automobiles will continue to take one from Delhi to Chandigarh, and even to Bombay or elsewhere. They will continue to be small and not particularly comfortable; but they will be serviceable.

These approaches and schematics are deeply rooted in the traditions and ethos of India. No regime can close its eyes to them. Mrs. Gandhi, too, is well aware of them. On July 22, 1975, when she asked the Indian Parliament to approve the Emergency which had been declared a few weeks earlier, she said: "Nobody wants an emergency situation to continue forever. . . . This is what we want to do; we want to bring democracy back on the rails. We want to have greater decentralization. We want to have greater participation of the people in all areas, whether it is the industrial worker, whether it is the farmer, or whether it is a woman."[2]

In the rural areas, with their 500 million people, this sense of participation is increasingly a reality and it expresses itself in tangible terms in a much more vigorous agricultural industry than previously. A long-time American scholarly observer of the Indian scene has recently brought out a number of significant facts in this area. He finds that in the past fourteen years wheat production in India has tripled. In 1978 Indian rice production set an all-time record, and this American observer visited a farm in the Punjab on which the rice yield was nearly four tons per acre, "more on a per-acre basis than is grown in Kansas." He also stated that the "consumption of food grains, even among the poor segments of the population, has increased 22 percent in the last two years." The oil-rich Persian Gulf countries, the Soviet Union, Mauritius, Bangladesh, and others are importing food grains from India. The same American observer concluded his remarks thus: "Even more significant is the possibility that India could become the first developing nation in Asia, Africa, or Latin America where the wealth that has been the privilege of a small minority spreads to the great masses of the people."[3] And India is not just a typical developing country: it constitutes a sixth of the world's people.

It may well be the wider sociological aspects of the picture will develop in the most interesting way of all. Jayaprakash Narayan had a self-imposed mission to launch a total revolution to rid Indian society

2. *India News*, July 24, 1975 (published by the Consulate General of India, New York).

3. Marcus Franda, "Farmer Power and Charan Singh," *Asia*, September/October 1979.

of those centuries-old accretions that did not reflect its own best ideals. He said to the nation: "I should like to repeat my faith in what I have called total revolution, and pledge myself to work for it as soon as my health permits. In our heritage from the past there are some things that are noble and valuable. They have to be preserved and strengthened. But we have also inherited a great deal of superstition and wrong values and unjust human and social relations. The caste system among the Hindus is a glaring example of our evil inheritance. From the time of Lord Buddha [sixth century B.C.], and maybe from even earlier times, attempts have been made to destroy this hierarchical system of caste. But it still flourishes in every part of the country. It is time that we blotted out this black spot from Hindu society, and proclaim and practice equality and brotherhood of all men. Similarly, there are rotten customs and manners associated with such things as marriage, birth, death, etc. Purging of these evils also falls within the purview of a total revolution."[4] Narayan went on to deal with other urgently needed changes, such as a more rational educational system, improved conditions for workers, and other economic reforms. He closed his address with a ringing slogan: "Complete revolution; the future is in our hands!"[5]

Narayan never recovered his health and he died in October 1979. The total revolution he preached has eluded India, but most of his goals are, in fact, being striven toward by forces already at work in Indian society. Their time has come. This explains, at least in a measure, the fact that Sanjay Gandhi, while not using such terminology as total revolution and while approaching these matters from a very different perspective, advocated some of the very same revolutionary changes that Jayaprakash wanted: abolition of caste and illiteracy and the shedding of a host of socially regressive customs connected with birth, marriage, and death. It seems that from all sides Indian society is being stirred up, and it is not unlikely that the cumulative effect of change over the next two decades will indeed be revolutionary.

Other trends and intimations illustrate the continuing ferment in Indian society, bringing out its increasing Indianness, in the best sense. One of these trends relates to panchayats. In chapter 2, I drew attention to the surprise of a senior British administrator upon his discovery that, outside the official system, there existed panchayats

4. *India News,* April 25, 1977.
5. *Ibid.*

which were performing a variety of administrative functions. In the 1950s, some of the states adopted legislation to institutionalize these bodies, and Nehru, who was keen to see them develop, appointed a committee to inquire into their functioning. The committee, known as the Balwant Rai committee, after its chairman, reported in 1958, as a result of which there was a great revival or refurbishing of village panchayats all over the country. At that time Nehru spoke inspiringly about the panchayats: "Democracy is not merely Parliament at the top or in the states but something that excites every person and something which trains everyone to take his proper place and indeed any place in the country if the need arises. I have said, and I mean it, that all this Panchayati Raj, whatever things we are doing, are ultimately meant to train up every individual in India to be a potential Prime Minister of India." [6] By the time his daughter's first era ended, it was estimated that 90 percent of the rural population was being served by panchayats.

However, though the panchayats aroused a great wave of interest and enthusiasm in the 1960s, in the following decade they fell into disrepute in many parts of the country. The criticism was that the wealthy farmers had captured them, that they were faction-ridden, and accomplished only a few showpieces—such as an approach road to the village which was used mostly by the wealthier farmers—and very little to improve living conditions in the villages. There is no doubt that whereas Narayan wanted the panchayats kept outside party politics, they were in fact being used by the parties as their basic vote-getting machines in the rural areas. In a sense, there was nothing wrong with this; in fact, it was regarded by most people as a healthy part of the democratic processes that were burgeoning in the country after independence.

As was to be expected, the Janata government immediately turned its attention to the panchayats because they were truly traditional and potentially of great value in the revival of the vitality of village life. At the end of 1977 the government appointed a very prestigious committee consisting of some chief ministers of states, members of Parliament and previous cabinet ministers, under the chairmanship of Ashoka Mehta, an elder statesman, himself a previous Congress party cabinet minister in the central government and widely acceptable as a national figure. The committee was given a wide mandate

6. *Seminar,* New Delhi, Feb. 1979, 234:23.

to review and make suggestions for improvements. It reported in August 1978. In the review part of the report, while some short-comings such as factionalism and control by a small but wealthy section of the community were noted, the committee stated that there had been significant achievements, both socioculturally and in the political and administrative spheres. Its main recommendation was a practical and sensible one. Basing itself on the view that in prevailing conditions the village was no longer a viable unit for the purposes of most developmental projects—and this was a tacit admission that the old Gandhian ideal of self-contained village communities was unattainable—it recommended that the village panchayat virtually be displaced by a panchayat serving a cluster of villages with a population of 15,000 to 20,000 persons. A unit of this size can formulate and hope to implement a rational plan for development within its confines, whereas a village with a population of some five hundred could not hope to do so. However, the political opposition to the change is by no means negligible. It will mean taking away the authority of most of the village bodies, which are already objecting strenuously. The political consequences of falling afoul of the elite of so large a number of villages has led to a slowing down of panchayat reform. What will happen is that both the old and the new systems will exist side by side, which is not at all a bad temporary solution. In some areas cooperation among village panchayats will evolve in the struggle to keep the village bodies alive. All this is part of democracy at work at the village level, and the chances are that political involvement at that level will continue to increase, no matter what the prevailing system might be. This will be to the advantage of the political process in the country as a whole, and will help to strengthen the hold on Indian society of democratic processes, based on one vote per adult, from village institutions upward through state bodies to the central Parliament.

Another trend, at present still low-keyed but potentially of great significance, is to be found in the efforts to implement Mahatma Gandhi's notion that wealth is a trust, and that the big landowner and the industrialist must share their well-being with their workers. His own words on the subject included the following: "What I expect of you therefore is that you should hold all your riches as a trust to be used solely in the interest of those who sweat for you, and to whose industry and labour you owe all your position and prosperity.

I want you to make your labourers co-partners of your wealth." [7] He wanted the owners of factories to establish the spirit, if not the form, of co-ownership with the workers. In the same work he stated: "From the moment your men come to realize that the mills are theirs no less than yours, they will begin to feel toward you as blood-brothers. There would be no question of their acting against the common interest and the need for having a heavy supervisory establishment over them." [8]

Since Gandhi was against the use of any kind of force, he did not favor a system of economics based on increased power for the state, e.g., state ownership of the means of production. Toward the end of his life he said: "I look upon an increase of the power of the State with the greatest fear, because although while apparently doing good by minimizing exploitation, it does the greatest harm to mankind by destroying individuality, which lies at the root of all progress." [9]

Gandhi was not very explicit about how the trustee was to be remunerated, but in one of his later writings he said that "The State would regulate the rate of commission which they would get commensurate with service rendered and its value to society. Their children would inherit the stewardship only if they proved their fitness for it." [10]

Attempts have been made to interpret and put in practice the trusteeship system, but I doubt that Gandhi himself would have, on examination, declared that more than a few steps in the direction of trusteeship had been taken. One case, written up by the owner of a textile mill in Bombay as an experiment on the concept of trusteeship management, does not mention remuneration on a commission basis, or profit sharing or joint decision making. The experiment amounts to no more than enlightened and benign treatment of the workers. In his brief book, *An Anthology of Gandhiji's Thoughts on Trusteeship Management with An Experiment on the Concept,* Shri Vijay Merchant, the mill owner, cites instances of free medical care not only for the workers but also for members of their families, free legal advice, housing at a low rental of about 10 percent or less of emoluments, a

7. Shri Vijay Merchant, *Gandhiji on Trusteeship Management* (Bombay: Indian Centre for Encouraging Excellence, 1969), p. 3.
8. *Ibid.,* p. 4.
9. *Ibid.,* p. 21.
10. *Ibid.,* p. 18.

library for the workers' children and subsidized meals. Shri Merchant's report covers three years of the experiment. During this period there was one strike which lasted a half day! The issue was the amount of bonus for the workers. The strike ended when the owner invited the workers to examine all his account books, and they were apparently completely satisfied that the owner had given them all that he could spare after meeting running expenses and presumably "legitimate" profits. The finance minister of the government of India (in the mid-1960s), a Western-educated man, asked the owner, "Vijay, what is the return?" The owner's reply was interesting, and will give the reader some understanding of why it is that experiments such as his can be made in India: "Sir, I do not know and do not care to know . . . the day on which the type of service that we render to our workers and their families is calculated in terms of money, the grace and charm of what we do will be completely gone." [11] But some spiritual return Vijay Merchant does imagine will come to him. The closing words in his book are: "What comes back to us from our workers and their families may not be visible; it may not go into our account books but I am sure it will be credited to the Greatest Of All Banks—The Bank of Humanity—which no Government can ever nationalize." [12]

The main, though not the only, organization active in the cause of Gandhi's trusteeship idea is the Trusteeship Foundation, with its headquarters in Bombay. It has a membership that includes a number of India's industrialists, and is now trying to internationalize the trusteeship movement. The first international conference on trusteeship was held in October 1979 at Bangalore. Interested groups in England, the Federal Republic of Germany, France, Yugoslavia, and Spain were among those that attended. This conference increased the visibility of the movement in India itself. Influential governmental circles on New Delhi are also studying the trusteeship alternative to capitalism on the one hand and communism on the other. Early in 1979, Dr. Raj Krishna, a member of the government of India's Planning Commission, gave the annual Gandhi Memorial Lecture at the Gandhi Peace Foundation in Delhi. During his speech he formulated the following question: "How long should we wait for the main industrialists to transform themselves and their companies into Trusteeships before we invoke Gandhi's statement that 'If the

11. *Ibid.*, p. 46.
12. *Ibid.*, p. 47.

capitalists do not transform themselves into Trusteeships after a reasonable amount of time, then it will be necessary for the State to use
a minimum of violence to accomplish the purpose'? Isn't thirty years
a reasonable amount of time?" [13] Perhaps India will soon see more
definitive trusteeship arrangements than those that have been introduced Vijay Merchant's textile mill. The Gandhian idea is not
dead. In fact, the trusteeship ferment is gaining in strength.

Village democracy, wealth as a trust, the sun god being tamed to
give energy to the villages, and a renewed drive against caste privileges and certain marriage customs, as well as the polite declining of
the offer of the Soviet Union to build a very large atomic energy
power station in India, are all very Indian. The reason for turning
down the Russian offer was not that it had come from Communist
Moscow, but simply that it would have meant dependence on the Soviet Union for fuel and other equipment, and India has just seen what
such dependence means in the case of the atomic power reactor at
Tarapur, concerning which the United States has given notice that it
will probably not be able to fulfill its contract to supply fuel. India
feels it is much more practical to design plants that can be fueled and
maintained by Indian resources. As to solar energy, one of the early
prominent scientists of independent India, Shanti Sarup Bhatnagar,
designed solar cookers and other solar gadgets, but it was discovered
that the sun could do more than these simple tricks. Therefore the
government has now pledged a billion rupees—which in India will
support as much activity as half a billion dollars will in the United
States—for solar research and development, and India might soon be
thanking the sun god fervently for all he is doing for the country.

An Indian might develop the most economical photovoltaic process, but he would not grow rich because of his success; that would
be regarded as un-Indian, almost immoral. However, honors would
be heaped on him, and an institute might well be named after him.
Meanwhile, a variety of festivals, such as Durga Puja or Dussehra,
Holi, Basant, Diwali, Shivratri, the Buddha's birthday, Guru Nanak's
birthday, Muhammed's birthday, Id, Moharrum, Christmas, and
others will be celebrated because the Indian world embraces Hindus,
Muslims, Sikhs, Buddhists, Christians, and others. All of them demand recognition and attention, for all of them have the same rights

13. Quoted by Bob Swann of the Institute of Community Economics, Inc., Cambridge, MA, in a report titled "Reflections on the six-week trip to India and its personal significance," dated Feb. 5, 1979. The report is unpublished.

and privileges under the Constitution and the laws of the land. All this is colorful and much of it is easygoing; and the tradition has found room for all these continuities, adventures, and experiments. There is not much scope left for winning the race to "modernize," or for drawing even with the "developed world," or for paying much attention to the values of such eminent civilizations as, say, the French or the Spanish, nor, it must be said, is there much reason to take too much to heart the criticisms and epithets hurled at India in the media or by a host of writers who find the impact of certain aspects of India disturbing and even distressing—the poverty, the lack of services, the pernicious social hierarchy. Many Indians are acutely aware of these problems, and many are working on them. Most of those who have a hand in the struggle to effect changes have rejected the use of force, dictatorship, and the easy appeal to chauvinism to which many societes fall prey. The results therefore are not spectacular and consequently droves of admiring tourists do not flock to see them.

India has another aspect which, though by no means unique, is prominent in a degree and manner that is probably not found elsewhere. This is the search for the inner meanings of life, the focusing on the spiritual and a turning away from the material; a hankering for unity with the universal consciousness, a thirst for the bliss of the mystical experience, for the rending apart of the cloud of unknowing. Yoga, yogis, swamis, gurus, and acharyas have virtually become a major export from India. Of course, the nature of this field is such that some of the exports are spurious and some are not as valuable as they claim, but there are also among them the rarest gems in the flood. So that the reader is not left wondering what precisely I mean, let him read some of the works of Gopi Krishna, the extraordinary mystic and thinker whose books are published by the Kundalini Research Foundation in New Delhi, Zurich, and New York.[14] The appeal of Gopi Krishna's work is universal, nonsectarian, scientific, philosophical, spiritual, and religious in the sense that man today needs to enlarge his vision and reorient himself. Should a society be evaluated only on the basis of its material prosperity and the other tangible aspects of its achievements—those in the sciences and often too hastily applied technology? Perhaps it contributes to the admit-

14. The reader in the United States can obtain full information on Gopi Krishna's books and other writings from New Concepts Publishing, Inc., 10 East 39th Street, New York, N.Y. 10016.

tedly too great material poverty in the country that most Indians feel that material achievements of all kinds are of secondary significance compared with spiritual fulfillment.

India emphatically opposes expressions of regional hegemony, and much more strongly so than is the current fashion in many other parts of the world. At no time in recorded history has China exercised or claimed to exercise any kind of hegemony in the Indian subcontinent, and the notion that India should now bow to the military might of the superpowers or China is intolerable. In the Indian view, military might is not an accomplishment worthy of honor among nations; it is, rather, an unfortunate and unsavory manifestation of tendencies in some countries which deflect the world community from developing a rational and humane code of international conduct. The use of military might, and therefore its cultivation, should have been abandoned by states long ago, and now, with the appearance of nuclear weapons on the scene, such abandonment is necessary for survival.

As we have seen, over the course of the last several thousand years, the problem facing India has been to discover a prescription for maintaining the Indian entity in the face of the continued glorification of military might, and a readiness to use it to gain access to India by other major societies in the world. To the Indian mind, basically nurtured on the principle of *ahimsa*, this problem continues to be worrisome. If this had not been so, by 1962 India would have become a nuclear power. Meanwhile, other more militant societies around India have become, or are discernibly in the process of becoming, nuclear powers. Soon the enduring historical question will take the form of a categorical demand to Indian policymakers that they decide on submission to hostile, nuclear-armed forces or come up with a countervailing military response. It is an ugly predicament. Rational and effective rescue from it can only come when all countries do as Nehru demanded twenty-five years ago, and as Shastri, Indira Gandhi, and Desai too have demanded—i.e., give up nuclear weapons, their possession and manufacture; and for this purpose adopt, by agreement, all the necessary international safeguards to ensure compliance.

The medieval nature of standards of judgment about societies and states is starkly illustrated by the fact that after the Indian army assisted the Bangladeshi patriots to create an independent state, Washington decided that India was definitely the major "power" in

South Asia. As if the deeds of the Indian army had done anything to add to India's stature as the home of a society which has had a long commitment to humane values. The amazing fact about our world is that successful deployment of military power gains increased prestige for a country and gives it the right to claim more recognition in the world community. These are not values that India finds acceptable. They are part of the continuing dilemma facing the country.

The main hazard that will remain to haunt India is the one that militarily weaker societies face in our power-driven and power-worshipping world, in spite of the United Nations, itself a weak organization. Perhaps the hazard is worth the risk, even if the consequences in the past have been extremely painful. Though not a major military power, India will tenaciously defend its independence. The country has a population of almost 700 million, and can best play a role in the world community by adhering to and further developing its distinctive non-power stance which counterposes to the notion of power the notion that in the final analysis human well-being and peace can only be secured by abandoning the prevailing reliance on military might.

However, in order to play this role effectively, India must overcome the second hazard it faces. This is the more insidious hazard of being overwhelmed by the continuing morass of poverty, lack of education, paucity of health and sanitation programs, and general laxity of nationwide efforts to develop a healthy, vibrant society. The scrambles of the politicians for power and their tendency to grab for themselves whatever material advantages come their way absorb their energies. The general good suffers lamentable consequences. These internal cancers must be cured; otherwise there can be little, if any, impact of the great tradition of non-power and nonviolence on which the Indian approach to life is built. Besides, India must sweep away those social ills to which Jayaprakash Narayan and others drew attention. Unless these goals can be reached, the great tradition will remain lost in a sea of misery and the Indian example will be poorly regarded everywhere. The contradiction between spiritual sublimity and material and social degradation must be urgently resolved. Since independence, there have been only minimal gains for the Indian people. Their needs are known, and the leaders must rouse them to disciplined mass participation in meeting those needs.

With the Indian homeland thus truly regenerated and made the scene of good, if not model, conditions of life, its example of non-power and nonviolence could become effective. There might, in time, be some chance of these notions being accepted elsewhere. Events may well compel a more serious look at the Indian notions, and an important world constituency for them might be created. This would become a demonstration of the way other countries, too, must go —assuredly including the Great Powers—if human civilization is to be preserved and developed to a higher plane on this planet. Can the example of India eventually have this impact? Perhaps so, but who can say for sure?

APPENDIX

A Plan for the Settlement of the Question of India's Independence, prepared by the Author in March 1946, and Accepted by Jawaharlal Nehru and Abul Kalam Azad, President of the Indian National Congress Party, and by Sir Stafford Cripps, Member of the British Cabinet Mission

A. The following basis for a settlement is accepted:

1. Fully effective autonomy for the various areas of India is compatible with the association of the peoples of India for purposes which may be agreed to be of common concern. Accordingly, and so as to assist the various areas to decide how they should exercise the right of self-determination, it is agreed that the following points should be included in the Constitution to be framed for a free India:

(a) The boundaries of the Punjab, Bengal, and Assam may be realigned so as to constitute Muslim majority areas into separate Provinces. Muslim majority areas shall be defined as the contiguous districts in these Provinces in which the Muslims constitute a majority of the population.

(b) A positive programme for the social services and economic, including industrial, development will be pursued in each Province. The object of this policy will be to accelerate and equate the development of all Provinces, including the most backward.

(c) No area shall be developed to the detriment of other areas.

(d) The cultural and linguistic features of each area shall be fostered.

(e) There shall be complete religious freedom.

(f) All social disabilities shall be removed.

(g) A Central Government will be set up on an agreed basis to administer Defence, External Affairs, and other subjects which may be agreed upon such as Customs, Currency, Waterways, and Communications.

(h) A Bill of Fundamental Rights shall be drawn up by the representatives of all the parties which should include the above points, any other points which may be agreed upon, and guarantees for the protection of minorities in their religious, cultural, and social life.

2. If, notwithstanding the contents of clause 1 of this document, the Muslim majority areas wish to consider the formation of one or more States the following principles will apply:

(a) Muslim majority areas shall be defined as comprising the North-West Frontier Province, Sind, Baluchistan, and those contiguous Districts in the Punjab, Bengal, and Assam in which the Muslims constitute a majority of the population. The boundaries of the Punjab, Bengal, and Assam will be realigned so as to constitute Muslim and non-Muslim provinces on this basis.

(b) The Muslim majority areas voting Province by Province, may then decide, either by plebiscite or by majority vote of the elected members of the Provincial Legislative Assemblies, or by any other method which may be more acceptable to the major parties, to set up one or more States.

(c) Any other contiguous area similarly expressing a wish to do so, may join any State so formed.

(d) Should one or more areas vote themselves out as provided in clauses (b) and (c) above they will consider entering into joint arrangements with the rest of the country for Defence and connected matters, and any other matters which may be agreed upon.

3. Even if the Muslim majority areas decide to form States of their own, their representatives will join in drawing up a Bill of Fundamental Rights, on the lines indicated, for the whole of India.

B. The procedure for implementing the above:

Stage 1. The Central and Provincial Legislatures shall constitute electoral colleges in which the representatives of each community shall elect $1/20$ of their membership to a Central Body. Where the number of members from a community in the Central or in a Provincial Assembly is below 20 the members of that community in two or more Assemblies shall vote together. For this purpose members elected by non-communal constituencies and members of the smaller and more dispersed communities e.g., the Parsis and the Indian Christians may, if they so wish, join with any other community.

Stage 2. The Central Body so formed will draw up a Bill of Fundamental Rights on the lines indicated, and proceed to consider clause 1 of the basis of settlement.

Stage 3. If the decision in stage 2 above is for a Federal or other form of Constitution for all India, the Central Body shall become a Constituent Assembly to draw up the Indian Constitution.

Stage 4. If the decision is against one Constitution for all India, clause 2 (a), (b) and (c) of the basis of settlement shall become operative.

Stage 5. Representatives of the various States so formed shall then meet to consider joint arrangements for Defence, and connected matters, and for any other matters which may be agreed upon.

Stage 6. The free Indian State or States may enter into treaty relations with the United Kingdom.

INDEX